NIPPON

NIPPON
NEW SUPERPOWER
JAPAN · SINCE · 1945

WILLIAM HORSLEY & ROGER BUCKLEY

BBC BOOKS

TO

Angela Horsley

and

Luke Dai and Henry Tetsu Buckley

ISBN 0 563 20875 9

Published by BBC Books
a division of BBC Enterprises Limited
Woodlands, 80 Wood Lane, London W12 0TT

Set in Plantin by Butler & Tanner Ltd, Frome
Printed and bound in Great Britain by Butler & Tanner Ltd, Frome
Jacket printed by Belmont Press Ltd, Northampton

Contents

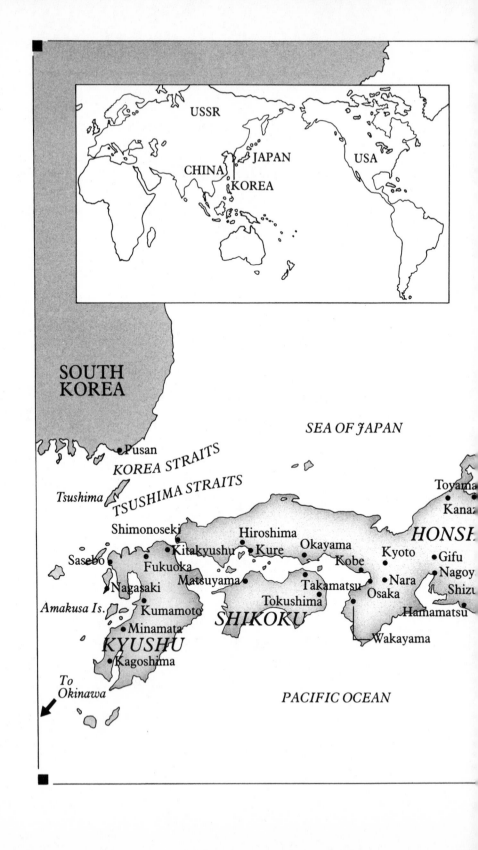

USSR

JAPAN

CHINA

KOREA

USA

SOUTH
KOREA

SEA OF JAPAN

Pusan

KOREA STRAITS

Tsushima

TSUSHIMA STRAITS

Toyama

Kanaz

HONSH

Shimonoseki

Hiroshima

Kitakyushu

Kure

Okayama

Kyoto

Gifu

Sasebo

Fukuoka

Kobe

Nagoy

Nagasaki

Matsuyama

Takamatsu

Nara

Shizu

Amakusa Is.

Kumamoto

Tokushima

Osaka

Hamamatsu

Minamata

SHIKOKU

Wakayama

KYUSHU

Kagoshima

To
Okinawa

PACIFIC OCEAN

SOYA STRAITS

•Wakkanai

•Asahikawa

•Sapporo

HOKKAIDO

Occupied by
USSR

*TSUGARU
STRAITS* ———— •Hakodate

•Aomori

•Akita

do

•Niigata   •Sendai

•Koriyama

ruizawa   •Iwaki
  •Utsunomiya
  —Yokohama
Tokyo
  •Narita

N

—Kawasaki
—Yokosuka
—Kamakura

JAPAN

0   100   200 miles
Scale
0   100   200   300 km

Picture Credits

Preface

This book was originally inspired by a television series about the extra-ordinary achievements of a nation. In February 1988 when Peter Pag-namenta, the executive producer of the BBC's *Nippon* series, began his research on the ground in Japan, the country was on the point of overtaking the UK as the wealthiest nation in human history in terms of worldwide assets. *Nippon* set out to re-create and tell the story of what Japan did, and how, through the eyes of the Japanese people themselves.

We are greatly indebted to Peter for suggesting that we write a book together to accompany the TV series. The collaboration, between a broad-casting journalist and a scholar, has been far freer of the inevitable jolts and tensions than we imagined when we started out.

We felt strongly that to do justice to our subject meant to write about Japan in all its principal dimensions: social, economic and political. We confirmed that Japan's particular way of ordering its affairs stems not simply from a desire for economic efficiency or social harmony. In principle, all nations presumably seek these things. It grows instead out of Japan's own sense of history and tradition, which like a genetic code has shaped its post-war society. The environment of the post-war world has determined the possibilities for the Japanese, too, and it has been overwhelmingly favourable.

Japan is a challenge to the minds of people in the West. It does not fit into the ordinary framework of world history taught in most Western schools. We have tried to describe, in all too brief a way, how the Japanese have preserved their essential identity in a world devised by others. We have investigated the crossroads that the Japanese have faced since the end of the Second World War – the Occupation, the struggle over the revision of the US–Japan Security Treaty around 1960, and lately the phenomenal world influence that it has gained, and that is only just starting to be acknowledged. We see it as a certainty that Japan's influence overseas will grow without let-up. We came to address the paradox that Japan is driven by the craving for more involvement in the world outside, yet the Japanese remain inarticulate about their purposes, reserved, shy. They feel happier with what is secret and implicit than with what is open and proclaimed.

We have been fortunate in being able to draw on many interviews done for the *Nippon* series over the past two years for a rich fund of first-hand testimony from Japanese people of all ages, ranks and political beliefs. These we have incorporated in the attempt to make our own portrait of the nation in action.

We are enormously grateful to Peter Pagnamenta for his continuous interest and support in the course of our writing: his integrity and good judgement helped to light the path. The production team, including especially Peter Grimsdale, Glynn Jones, Alan Bookbinder, Andy Stevenson, Colleen Toomey, Vivian Ducat, Simon Crow and Christine Whittaker, did everything humanly possible to provide answers to our impatient requests, and we were able to share in their discoveries. Yukiko Shimahara, the chief co-ordinator for the series, replied gracefully to our detailed queries; and others in Kensington House and in Tokyo kept the faxes flying on our behalf.

Our warm thanks go to those who gave generously of their time and knowledge in reviewing our manuscript: Hikaru Kerns, Hirokuni Sugahara, Michael Connors, Professor Masao Kunihiro, Toshi Marks and Dr Albert Novick. Many others gave valuable advice and provided information. Any errors of fact or judgement, of course, are ours alone.

In the text Japanese names are given in the Western order, that is, the given name first, followed by the surname.

We thank the editors of BBC News and Current Affairs for their understanding and patience in allowing William the necessary time away from his normal work. Our fulsome gratitude goes to Brenda Thomson and Martha Caute, the editors who worked with energy and professionalism; and to Sheila Ableman, whose enthusiastic commitment turned the whole project from an idea into reality.

Lastly, we thank our families for putting up with our moods, and with all the lost weeks and weekends. Noriko's research and her first opinion on the text were a lifeline for William throughout; and without Machiko's moral support, Roger would never have made the journey so many hundreds of times up the hill from Ichigaya station.

WH AND RB
TOKYO JULY 1990

1

After the Rain

DEFEAT AND OCCUPATION

Inside the hot, crowded underground bunker there was silence. It was shortly after noon on 14 August 1945, and the Cabinet ministers of Imperial Japan waited nervously for Emperor Hirohito to speak. Yet again they had failed to agree among themselves on how to respond to the Allied demand for the army's unconditional surrender. The War and Munitions Ministers and the Chief of the Army General Staff were still opposed to allowing the enemy to occupy the 'land of the gods'. They wanted to pursue the war whatever the cost, unless the Emperor's position as supreme ruler could be completely assured.

Emperor Hirohito was a frail figure, forty-four years old, wearing round spectacles. Now he made a historic and final decision to accept Japan's defeat. His voice breaking with emotion, he rose to address his ministers:

> I realise that there are those of you who distrust the intentions of the Allies. This is, of course, quite natural, but to my mind the Allied reply is evidence of the peaceful and friendly intentions of the enemy.... I cannot endure the thought of letting my people suffer any longer. A continuation of the war would bring death to tens, perhaps even hundreds, of thousands of people. The whole nation would be reduced to ashes. How then could I carry on the wishes of my Imperial ancestors?

In his speech he praised the bravery and loyalty of Japan's armed forces, adding:

> I appreciate how difficult it will be for the officers and men of the Army and Navy to surrender their arms to the enemy and see their homeland occupied. Indeed, it is difficult for me to issue the order making this

1

necessary, and to delivery so many of my trusted servants into the hands of the Allied authorities by whom they will be accused of being war criminals.

Hirohito solemnly recalled an earlier humiliation for Japan at the hands of the West when in 1895 Russia, France and Germany had colluded to make Japan give up territory on the Asian mainland won in the Sino-Japanese War. His grandfather had been on the throne then, and now Hirohito declared: 'The decision I have reached is akin to the one forced upon my grandfather, the Emperor Meiji, at the time of the Triple Intervention. As he endured the unendurable, so shall I, and so must you.'

Then Hirohito instructed the Cabinet to draw up at once an Imperial Rescript announcing Japan's acceptance of the surrender terms of the Potsdam Declaration. He said he would broadcast it in his own voice to the whole nation. The war was over.

When the slight, uniformed figure left the room the ministers began to weep aloud. The Emperor stood at the heart of the myth of Japan's invincibility, supposedly the direct descendant of the Sun Goddess. Throughout the years of war his authority had been used, often cynically, by his generals to justify the attempt to conquer Asia. Only a few senior people in public life had dared to speak out against the war. Now Japan lay devastated and at the mercy of foreign powers. It was the first defeat in the country's history, and a catastrophic end to the first century of modern Japan's contacts with the West.

For more than a year it had been obvious to Japan's military planners that the war could not be won, yet even after the atom bombs were dropped on Hiroshima on 6 August and on Nagasaki three days later, the die-hards in the Imperial Cabinet still wanted to fight on. On the night of 9 August the Cabinet convened for the first time in the Emperor's presence to consider surrender, but its members had been bitterly split. The main sticking-point had been the fear that Japan's distinctive national identity and pride – embodied in what was known as the *kokutai*, or 'national structure', with the Emperor at its centre – might be ended, or even that Hirohito would be held responsible for the war and executed. On that occasion the Cabinet had made the rare move of turning to the Emperor himself to resolve the question, and Hirohito had made it unmistakably clear that he favoured ending the war at once.

The Pacific War began with the surprise attack on Pearl Harbor on 7 December 1941, followed by a string of swift Japanese victories over the Allies across South-east Asia. It was an extraordinary military feat, and there was euphoria in Japan over each of the early successes, especially over Britain's humiliating surrender in Singapore on 15 February 1942. The assault on Singapore was achieved by rushing troops and supplies down the Malay peninsula, mainly by bicycle, while Singapore's defences faced the wrong way, out to sea. The victories reinforced the national belief that, despite the material advantages of the West, Japan was far superior in spirit. In Asia the Japanese conquests overturned the long-held assumption of European moral and military superiority. But soon the Imperial Army and Navy were overstretched, defending a vast empire extending from Manchuria to New Guinea and from the mid-Pacific islands to the borders of India. Japan's armed forces had been unable to withstand the collective might and manpower of the Allies.

After the battle of Midway in June 1942 the tide turned. US forces leapfrogged their way across the great expanse of the Pacific, while British and Commonwealth troops under General William Slim doggedly fought their 'forgotten war' in the jungles of Burma. General Hideki Tojo, who led Japan to war, resigned in 1944 after the disastrous loss to the Americans of Saipan and the Mariana Islands. Eventually, in June 1945, the island of Okinawa, 1000 miles south of Tokyo, fell. That battle had lasted more than three months and had been the bloodiest of the Pacific War, resulting in the deaths of over 150 000 men. As the Allies closed the ring, even the desperate use of *kamikaze* suicide attacks on American warships could not delay for long the invasion of Japan itself.

The defeat of Nazi Germany in May was followed on 26 July by the Potsdam Declaration, in which the Western Allies offered Japan a last chance to surrender its forces or face their 'inevitable and complete destruction' as well as 'the utter devastation of the Japanese homeland'. American B-29 bombers were flying at will up 'Hirohito Alley' from the Mariana Islands to bomb Tokyo and other cities with only token resistance from Japanese anti-aircraft guns. Japan's leaders knew the USA was well on the way to developing the atom bomb, but they had no idea of its real destructive power. In any case, the code of the warrior did not permit even the thought of surrender, and some young officers openly threatened to kill their superiors who broached the possibility. In this climate the government, under a compromise leader, Kantaro Suzuki, failed to respond clearly to the West's ultimatum.

Suzuki let it be known, on 28 July, that the Cabinet was 'ignoring' the Potsdam Declaration. Nine days later the Americans, after consulting Britain, dropped the A-bomb on Hiroshima. The Japanese authorities suppressed news of the horror and loss of life both there,

3

where about 100 000 people were killed by blast, burns and radiation, and in Nagasaki, where the immediate death toll was about 60 000. To the government the Soviet declaration of war on 8 August was as serious a setback as these nuclear attacks. Japan's supposedly first-rate Kwangtung Army crumbled, leaving Manchuria and northern Korea to Stalin's Red Army.

The ideology for which Japan had ostensibly gone to war was at best simplistic. Many scholars doubt that it can properly be called a system of belief; it was rather a ruling structure, the *tennosei*, or Emperor system, which was bolstered by an authoritarian government and police system, and by the state-supported Shinto religion. The wartime *tennosei* held that the Emperor was the father of the country, and that the state could not exist without him. He alone could conclude foreign treaties, and Imperial decrees overruled the work of the Diet, Japan's parliament. In the 1930s a prominent scholar, Tatsukichi Minobe, led an intellectual movement to establish that the Emperor's powers must be legally constrained by the other organs of government, but he was hounded out of public life in a counter-movement to 'clarify the national structure'.

The ministers of the 1945 Cabinet were steeped in the ideology of the Imperial state, which had been gradually made into a national creed by the late nineteenth century, as Japan was obliged to break out of more than 200 years of seclusion. Before then, from the time of the first historical Emperor in the fifth century, the dynastic line of the *tenno*, or 'Heavenly Sovereigns', had continued – with only very brief exceptions – as symbols of authority with little or no actual role in governing the country. They had fulfilled the part of high priests of the Shinto religion, while various regents, influential families and *shogun* (military commanders) had ruled in their name. In 1868, however, the paramount status of the Emperor was used by an energetic group of lower-ranking *samurai* leaders to effect a political revolution that overthrew the decaying military regime of the *shogun*, the dynasty of the noble Tokugawa family.

The *coup d'état* was called the Meiji Restoration, because it 'restored' the Emperor (the then fifteen-year-old Meiji) as the formal head of government and a symbol of nationalism. The Meiji Constitution of 1889, based on the Prussian model, was described as a 'gracious gift' from the Emperor to his subjects. It declared: 'The Empire of Japan shall be reigned over and governed by a line of Emperors unbroken for ages eternal.' The lack of constitutional restraint to the Emperor's theoretically unlimited powers acted to undermine the early attempts to establish a viable democratic political system, and allowed the unfettered growth of ultranationalism. The *kokutai*, to the ultra-nationalists, was made up of three elements: loyalty to the throne, the mission to dominate Asia and a belief in the special innate qualities of the Japanese race.

Hirohito ascended the 'Chrysanthemum Throne' in 1926 when his father, Emperor Taisho, died after a long mental and physical illness. Five years earlier, Hirohito had greatly enjoyed making a tour of Western Europe. He had become firm friends with Edward, Prince of Wales – later King Edward VIII – and had been deeply impressed by the workings of the British constitutional monarchy. On returning to Tokyo, however, he had been sequestered in the Imperial Palace and, with the inexorable rise of the military, Japan became more and more hostile to the liberal ideas he had absorbed. He conformed to the strict conventions of the Imperial court and took little direct part in the affairs of state.

Britain and the USA had not stood in the way of Japan's early territorial expansion: first the annexation of Taiwan (Formosa) in 1895, then that of Korea in 1910. Many Anglo-Saxons regarded Japan as 'the Great Britain of the Far East', and an Anglo-Japanese Alliance linked the interests of the two island nations closely until 1922. There-after, radical groups in the Imperial Army gained ascendancy, and relations with the West sharply worsened. Japan turned Manchuria into the puppet state of Manchukuo in 1932, and when the League of Nations denounced the action, Japan walked out. In 1937 local units of the Imperial Army staged incidents that led to full-scale war with China.

In this period Japan was in the throes of what was dubbed 'government by assassination'. Anti-foreign sentiment mounted. The Western calendar was dropped from regular use; instead the Japanese were expected to count the years according to the old system of Imperial ages: Hirohito's reign was 'Showa', meaning 'Enlightened Peace' (a pious wish at the time the name was chosen). A host of 'patriotic societies' grew in influence. Their aims were to 'protect' the Emperor and enlarge Japan's overseas empire, in the form of a 'Greater East Asia Co-Prosperity Sphere'. Army officers took part in a series of attempted *coups* and incidents of political violence, in which two prime ministers as well as several other public figures were assassinated. Emperor Hirohito himself took a firm stand against this trend when he ordered the arrest of the leaders of the so-called February Uprising, in which, on 26 February 1936, a group of young army officers seized control of central Tokyo for three days and murdered several leading public figures, including the Finance Minister and the Lord Privy Seal. Their proclaimed goal was to achieve a 'Showa Restoration', by which they meant a government based on the Imperial Way, reflecting the mystical relationship between the Emperor and his subjects. In practice, they wanted to abolish all political parties and democratic institutions.

Hirohito was not present at cabinet or chiefs-of-staff meetings where day-to-day policy, and detailed plans for attacking Pearl Harbor and taking on the Western Allies, were laid. However, his approval was needed for crucial state decisions. Several times he rebuked his senior ministers and military commanders for failing to curb the army's independent actions, or to seek a peaceful settlement with the West over China. But when, in 1941, America insisted on Japan's retreat from China and imposed an oil embargo, the Tojo Cabinet moved irrevocably to war, and, in December, it was in the Emperor's name that Japan declared war on the United States of America and on the British Empire.

Three years and eight months later, when Japan received the Potsdam Declaration, the Cabinet sent a message through neutral Switzerland asking the Allies for clarification of their intentions over the Emperor's status. That was on 10 August 1945. Two days later a reply came, implying at least that the Allies would not depose the Emperor or abolish the Imperial throne. In this President Harry Truman ignored the wishes of the governments of China, the Soviet Union and Australia, all of which wanted Hirohito to be tried and convicted as Japan's arch war criminal. Truman's message, which had the blessing of the British government among others, said that after surrender 'the authority of the Emperor and the Japanese government to rule the state shall be subject to the supreme Commander of the Allied Powers'. This seemed to acknowledge the Emperor's high authority, but also made clear that the Japanese would not be able to decide his exact status themselves. The War Minister, General Anami, instructed the other military commanders that the armed forces must obey the Emperor, whatever he should decide, and the threat of a serious mutiny by 'super-patriotic' younger officers, aimed at upsetting the peace moves, did not materialise. The next time the full Cabinet met in Imperial conference, all its members were prepared to defer in the fateful decision to the Emperor himself.

The nation was told to await a broadcast by the Emperor at noon on 15 August. A plot by a group of army officers to snatch the recording and prevent its being aired was narrowly foiled. Crowds gathered outside the Imperial Palace – where in the past Hirohito had appeared at moments of military victory on a white charger – and listened, crouching on the ground with their heads bowed low. During the war years ordinary Japanese had been forced to make obeisance to pictures of the Emperor at special altars set up in schools and other public places. On occasions when he appeared before his people, all present had to bow to the ground and avert their eyes; children were told that even to gaze on the Emperor's picture would make their eyes burn. Now, in every town and village, people gathered around communal radio sets to hear for the first time in their lives the 'Voice of the Crane'.

Everywhere the reception was poor, and the stylised court language made the Emperor's message hard to grasp. Hirohito never used the word 'surrender' at all. His message went: 'We have ordered Our government to communicate to the governments of the United States, Great Britain, China and the Soviet Union that Our Empire accepts the provisions of the Joint Declaration.' Many had expected the Emperor to exhort them to fight on to the last man, and army officers had to explain to the people that it meant the end of the war. Censorship had kept the nation from knowing how close it had come to total defeat; nor did the populations outside Hiroshima and Nagasaki have any way of knowing what Hirohito meant by referring to a 'new and terrible weapon' unleashed against Japan. 'The situation has developed not necessarily to Japan's advantage', the message continued, but 'We have resolved to pave the way for a grand peace for all the generations to come by enduring the unendurable and suffering what is insufferable.' Certainly it was a roundabout way of admitting the country's total defeat. The self-consciously lofty language, and the assumption that even in these straits Japan held the initiative to create a 'grand peace', reflect the paramount status of the throne.

Until that moment the population had expected to have to die fighting the invaders with swords and bamboo spears. They had been told to 'kill at least one American'. More than forty years later, Japanese people of different stations and beliefs still recall their sense of enormous relief, mixed with anguish. Conscript Japanese soldiers had endured a numbingly oppressive discipline in most parts of the empire as well as at the battlefront, and the reaction of Private 1st Class Matataro Fujikawa, stationed in Korea, was representative of many. He was inwardly jubilant at the news of surrender: 'Now I could get home and see my mother again, alive. I didn't want to die.' Fujikawa returned to his native Sado island, off the northern coast, to resume life as a rice farmer.

Mrs Shizue Katoh had opposed the war and was later to become a socialist member of parliament, yet she felt no joy as the truth sank in:

My husband and I were horrified to see a fool like Tojo start that stupid war, and the terrible acts that were committed, so we never joined in the flag-waving and send-offs for the soldiers. But in spite of everything it was a great shock for me to accept that my country was defeated ... an overwhelming sense of sadness came over me.

After the strict suppression of liberal thought and trade-union activities for more than a decade, the defeat brought a feeling of release and an outpouring of new hopes and aspirations. Some wanted Japan to become a Marxist state, in which workers would for ever be freed from the control of a class of capitalists. Ichiro Suzuki, working at the heavily bombed marshalling yard at Shinagawa in Tokyo, recalls how at the time he thought of the coming struggle for workers' rights as 'a second war' to be fought by the Japanese working class. Other Japanese were equally anxious that the old values would survive.

Among the military, discipline stood firm. Once the Emperor's broadcast had been made, most of the generals of the Japanese Imperial Army carried out their appointed duties to the letter. Outside the palace, many officers joined the crowds of ordinary men, women and children to kneel, sobbing silently. Occasional pistol shots rang out as some of the Emperor's subjects took their own lives. Over the coming days, as the order to surrender spread to military and prisoner-of-war camps across Asia and the Pacific islands, Imperial Army officers prepared to turn over their weapons to the Allies. The War Minister, General Anami, and several of his top commanders committed suicide rather than face a future of shame and likely retribution.

Before the broadcast, Lieutenant-General Seizo Arisue, the former head of Military Intelligence, was detailed to take charge of the demobilisation of the army under American orders. He and a group of fellow senior officers met and debated whether to take their own lives in the time-honoured way of the *bushi*, the *samurai* warrior, faced with defeat or disgrace. They decided to live and try to rebuild Japan from the ruins. General Arisue and his fellow officers, knowing that the Americans, when they landed, would head straight for the army headquarters in Ichigaya, hurried there to burn all the secret documents they could. For four days after 15 August the skies over Kasumigaseki, the area in Tokyo where government buildings are concentrated, were black with the smoke from burning papers.

Rarely has a nation so totally failed in its diplomatic and military goals as the humiliated, exhausted Japan of the summer of 1945. An estimated 2 million Japanese soldiers had died making and defending the empire. Over 600 000 Japanese civilians had also been killed on the Japanese mainland, in Manchuria and on Okinawa. The casualties in China and among the other populations of Asia had been many times higher. Instead of controlling Asia in a so-called Co-Prosperity Sphere and neutralising the West, Japanese forces had been destroyed or surrounded. Japan's war had assisted the rise of powerful communist movements in the region and provoked America to extend its reach across the Pacific. However, Japan had weakened the old European powers' grip on Asia, leaving them vulnerable to newborn nationalist groups in Vietnam, Malaya and elsewhere. Later this 'liberation' of Asia would be held up by some Japanese as an important achievement; but the Imperial Army's atrocities left a legacy of bitterness and hatred throughout Japan's former empire.

In 1945 Japan's immediate fate depended on General Douglas MacArthur, Commander-in-Chief of US forces in the Far East, whom President Truman appointed Supreme Commander for the Allied Powers for the Occupation and Control of Japan (SCAP). A small contingent of British and other Commonwealth forces was also dispatched, and had duties in some provincial areas, but in practice the Occupation was virtually an all-American affair. General Arisue was detailed to arrange the reception for MacArthur, who was set to land at Atsugi air-base south of Tokyo on 30 August. A group of fanatical officers plotted to make a suicide attack on Atsugi, but they were forestalled. The landing took place without mishap. The image of MacArthur as he stepped from his plane, tall and relaxed in an open-necked shirt, with a corncob pipe in his mouth, was one which would imprint itself on the Japanese mind. Well-disciplined Japanese soldiers lined the road along which MacArthur passed on his way to Tokyo. His arrival set the tone for the remarkable co-operation between victors and vanquished that was to be a hallmark of the Occupation. During the next seven years some claimed that not a single shot was fired in anger.

The first Occupation forces found it hard to believe this was the land that had been for so long such a formidable enemy. American photographers who arrived in Tokyo to record events after the surrender were amazed at the scale of the devastation. Most of the old, eastern part of the city had been reduced to rubble. Firebombs had been used to set flame to wide expanses of wooden-built housing. One strike, on 10 March 1945, may have visited as much death and destruction on the Japanese as each of the A-bombs dropped on Hiroshima and Nagasaki. Formations of B-29s carpet-bombed Tokyo on that night and an estimated 100 000 people lost their lives. The Imperial Palace, the former *shogun*'s castle in the centre of Tokyo, was deliberately spared, as were the historic cities of Kyoto, Nara and

Kamakura, which housed many of the treasures of Japanese art and architecture.

Throughout Japan people were dressed in little more than rags. Disease was rife, and many were suffering from beriberi and other conditions brought on by vitamin deficiency and malnutrition. In the last stages of the war food had been severely rationed. Most people in the cities had survived on no more than a bowl of millet a day; some were reduced to boiling grasses and weeds for sustenance. Everywhere they went the American field teams used their invasion supplies to feed communities suffering from hunger. There was very little fuel for heating. The American GIs were greeted by crowds of children who eagerly took the chewing gum and chocolate they threw from the backs of their jeeps.

On the morning of 2 September 1945 the Pacific War officially ended when Foreign Minister Mamoru Shigemitsu signed the instruments of surrender for his government on board the US battleship *Missouri* in Tokyo Bay. One participant recorded how the members of the surrender signing party felt they approached the occasion as 'diplomats without flag and soldiers without sword'. Toshikazu Kase, a diplomat who witnessed the ceremony, was left

> wondering anew how it was that Japan, a poor country, had the temerity to wage war against the combination of so many powerful nations. Indeed, it was Japan against the whole world.... The contest was unequal from the first. The adventure was a product of brains fired by sheer madness. Like Satan's doomed legions, we fell from Heaven through chaos headlong into Hell.

To drive home the message of Japan's new status as an occupied land, MacArthur arranged for 400 B-29s and 1500 carrier planes to fly in formation over the armada of Allied vessels on display in the bay.

The Occupation had revolutionary objectives and methods. Its first task was to disarm Japan and eradicate militarism; the second, to induce the Japanese nation to embrace a democratic way of life. Some extreme methods were considered. The most drastic of all, known as the Morgenthau Plan, would have forced Japan (as well as Germany) to return to being an agrarian society, stripped of all heavy industry, in order to prevent it from becoming a military threat ever again. That was rejected in favour of reliance on democratisation, which was the main pillar of the Initial Post-Surrender Policy for Japan sent by President Truman to MacArthur as his working instructions.

The Americans were also bound by the terms of the Potsdam Declaration, which laid down that the Japanese must be able eventually to choose for themselves their own precise form of government. It said that Japan would enjoy 'a new order of peace, security and justice', based on 'freedom of speech, of religion and of thought'. It also held out to Japan the promise that once its terms were carried out, and the country had succeeded in setting up a peacefully inclined and responsible government, the Japanese could rejoin the community of nations and take their part in the free world trading system. The Americans intended to reform every aspect of the nation's life – including the work of the country's police, law courts, schools and press, as well as fundamental practices in politics and business. The task was recognised as monumental. One unofficial but vivid American assessment was that Japan would have to go through 'the political, economic, social, intellectual and moral equivalents of the French Revolution, Russian Revolution, the Reformation, the Industrial Revolution and the Renaissance.'

A US army training film of the time sought to explain 'Our Job in Japan' to the ordinary GIs. It said that the Japanese had been trained to follow blindly wherever their leaders led them. The problem was 'in the brain inside the Japanese head'. As the image of a human brain floated up on screen, the narrator explained:

> There are seventy million of these in Japan, physically no different from any other brains in the world, actually all made of exactly the same stuff as ours. But the militarists have muddled the modern Japanese mind by playing up the myth of the Sun Goddess and telling them over and over and over again that they were destined to rule the world.... It will cost us time, it will cost us patience; but we're determined that this fact will finally sink in – this is Japan's last war.

The first British diplomat to return to Japan after the war, Dermot MacDermot, recorded a different point in his initial dispatch back to London. He found no popular sense of shame about defeat at all:

> There does seem to be a certain amount of regret at being on the losing side, as if it had been a baseball match. There is not yet any popular appreciation of the blame or disgrace attached to having started the war, or for the way in which it started at all.

This response among ordinary people stemmed from the lack of any real political awareness, or of any democratic institutions in the pre-war years. The great majority of Japanese did not feel that they personally had had a conscious choice in the way the government and army had behaved, and in that sense felt no individual sense of responsibility for 'starting the war'. This collective forgetfulness among the Japanese would become a serious issue in Japan's foreign relations as time went on.

At first the Americans had intended to rule Japan directly using the Eighth Army, with a full panoply of military courts and an American-determined currency. Two days after the formal surrender, Foreign Minister Shigemitsu met Lieutenant-General Richard Sutherland, MacArthur's Chief of Staff. When Sutherland handed him these proposals as the first directive of SCAP, Shigemitsu argued tenaciously against them, saying that if they were carried out there might be immediate and violent resistance at the very outset of the Occupation. The Americans were already having second thoughts about the practicality of imposing direct rule. They agreed that the Occupation's authority would be indirect, and that the Japanese government should continue to function, executing SCAP's orders. This was a vital concession, and represented the first victory for the Japanese in a series of battles of will over the character of the Occupation. SCAP's Proclamation Number One was never carried out.

General MacArthur at once set up a General Headquarters but in effect he ruled by a combination of directness and aloofness, rarely constrained either by instructions from his own government or by the gentle advice that came from his staff or from the Allies. MacArthur enjoyed playing the role of pro-consul: he had ambitions (which were unrealistic) to run for the American presidency when his job in Japan was done. He chose to have dealings with only a select few senior Japanese figures, and some criticised him for being too isolated. He struck up a special rapport, in particular, with the strong-willed man who served as Japan's Prime Minister for most of the Occupation years, the former diplomat Shigeru Yoshida.

The Japanese government moved quickly to create the bureaucratic machinery to retain as much control as possible in its own hands. By the end of August it had already established an agency under the Foreign Ministry called the Central Liaison Office, through which it intended that all directives sent by MacArthur's staff would be filtered and passed on to the appropriate part of the Japanese bureaucracy. By the same token, information or messages from Japanese officials were first sent to the Central Liaison Office to be processed or handed onto SCAP. The effect was to limit the Occupation forces' ability to enforce their own will when they were resisted by Japanese officials, as they often were.

In fact the Americans were impressed from the start with the co-operativeness and efficiency of the Japanese government representatives they dealt with. The demobilisation of the army within Japan proper was completed within only a few weeks. Charles Kades, deputy head of the Government Section, said afterwards that 'they organised quickly and expeditiously and put their best personnel into posts that dealt with the occupying forces.... most of them spoke English as well as Japanese and they seemed to go about their affairs in a very businesslike, orderly, disciplined fashion.' The respect was mutual. Koichiro Asakai, then a young member of the Japanese Central Liaison Office and later Japan's Ambassador to Washington, found the Occupation forces quite reasonable compared with the Japanese military, whom he describes as 'absolutely stone-headed'.

Also critical in determining the course of the Occupation was the sharp division within the SCAP staff between the ardent reformers or 'New Dealers' and the more pragmatic career military officers who saw the Occupation primarily in terms of keeping order and getting things done efficiently. Already in December 1945 MacArthur's own senior officers were arguing over what the priority should be – to reshape Japan from scratch and purge all the old leaders from public life, or to allow Japan to preserve its established social and political institutions, the better to meet the burgeoning communist threat. American officers such as Brigadier-General Courtney Whitney, head of Government Section, urged full speed in demolishing Japan's old structures in favour of Western liberal ones. By contrast, Major-General Charles Willoughby, chief of Intelligence, believed the greatest threat came from communism, not from resurgent Japanese militarism.

Initially MacArthur favoured Whitney and his young reformers, and some 200 000 people were listed to be purged. But delays and obstruction by Japanese officials undermined the original plan. Although prominent wartime politicians were barred from public life, and many officials of various Imperialist and militarist organisations were removed from their posts, others switched their titles to avoid detection. In the civil service, the major instrument of social control, only about 2000 people were purged, mostly from the powerful Naimusho, the Home Affairs Ministry. Some figures in the dreaded *kenpeitai* military police reappeared and took on senior jobs in the reorganised police and in the central government.

In the early days of the Occupation the largest unsettled question, what the Americans intended to do about the Emperor, was still unresolved. MacArthur's first meeting with Hirohito was on 27 September. In his own version of events, MacArthur, behaving with chivalry, ordered that

> there should be no derogation in his treatment. Every honour due a sovereign was to be his. I met him cordially, and recalled that I had at one time been received by his father at the close of the Russo-Japanese War.

He was nervous and the stress of the past months showed plainly. I dismissd everyone but his own interpreter, and we sat down before an open fire at one end of the long reception hall. I offered him an American cigarette, which he took with thanks. I noticed how his hands shook as I lighted it for him. I tried to make it as easy for him as I could, but I knew how deep and dreadful must be his agony of humiliation. I had an uneasy feeling he might plead his own cause against indictment as a war criminal. There had been considerable outcry from some of the Allies, notably the Russians and the British, to include him in this category. Indeed, the initial list of those proposed by them was headed by the Emperor's name. Realizing the tragic consequences that would follow such an unjust action, I had stoutly resisted such efforts. When Washington seemed to be veering toward the British point of view, I had advised that I would need at least one million reinforcements should such action be taken. I believed that if the Emperor were indicted, and perhaps hanged, as a war criminal, military government would have to be instituted throughout all Japan, and guerrilla warfare would probably break out. The Emperor's name had then been stricken from the list. But of all this he knew nothing. . . .

But my fears were groundless. What he said was this: 'I come to you, General MacArthur, to offer myself to the judgement of the powers you represent as the one to bear sole responsibility for every political and military decision made and action taken by my people in the conduct of war.' A tremendous impression swept me. This courageous assumption of a responsibility implicit with death, a responsibility clearly belied by facts of which I was fully aware, moved me to the very marrow of my bones. He was an Emperor by inherent birth, but in that instant I knew I faced the First Gentleman of Japan in his own right.

In fact the British government's policy towards Hirohito, like the Americans', was to spare him; but in the immediate aftermath of the war, and indeed to a lesser extent in all the years until his eventual death in 1989, there was a substantial sector of opinion which harboured a loathing of Japan and this anger was often directed towards the Emperor himself. Prisoner-of-war organisations were determined that Hirohito must be held responsible for the thousands of deaths from cruelty, maltreatment and disease in the Japanese camps. James Callaghan, a newly elected MP after Labour's landslide victory in the July 1945 general election and a future prime minister, denounced the Emperor in his maiden speech in parliament and insisted that, once Japanese disarmament was completed, 'we must get rid of him.'

The issue divided the Japanese, too. Left-wing leaders reasoned that the Emperor system had provided the ideological framework for a Japanese form of fascism, and abolition of the monarchy was the only permanent cure. A leading scholar, Masao Maruyama, describes the pre-war political set-up as a 'system of irresponsibilities' in which the Emperor's *theoretically* absolute powers made it possible for unscrupulous men to usurp his authority in the name of patriotism. Maruyama observed that the oppressive hierarchy of which the Emperor was at the apex and the common soldier at the base led directly to acts of inhumanity by Japanese troops in war and in the prison camps, and that 'their acts of brutality are a sad testimony to the Japanese system of psychological compensation'.

Against this, the standard conservative view is voiced by senior diplomat, Koichiro Asakai. For him

> the Emperor system lasted in Japan more than 2000 years, and it consciously or unconsciously was a centre of stability of Japanese politics. You take away that system and all of a sudden there would be instability, and you never know where the Japanese people will go.

The first opinion poll ever held on the issue of the Emperor, in December 1945, found that 95 per cent of Japanese favoured keeping him on the throne. The American government also saw overwhelming advantages in using Hirohito as an advocate of reform. Writing later in his memoirs, MacArthur claimed, perhaps with his characteristic hyperbole, that the Emperor

> had a more thorough grasp of the democratic concept than almost any Japanese with whom I talked. He played a major role in the spiritual regeneration of Japan, and his loyal co-operation and influence had much to do with the success of the Occupation.

On New Year's Day 1946, Hirohito formally renounced his own divinity, reading out his final Imperial Rescript on the radio. A key sentence in it said that 'the bonds between Us and You, the people, are formed by mutual trust, love and respect, and do not rest on mere legends and superstitions'. Hirohito not only renounced the concept of himself as 'a living deity', a concept which for ten years had been a central part of government propaganda; he also formally denied the wartime belief that the Japanese were superior to other races and hence destined to rule the world. He was able to see the absurd side of the situation himself: in one account, when he returned to the palace he is reported to have asked his wife, the Empress Nagako, 'Do I seem any different now that I am no longer supposed to be a god?'

Little has been officially revealed about Hirohito's private views, but there is documentary evidence that on a number of occasions he expressed a willingness to abdicate. He was dissuaded first by the Americans and next by Japanese government leaders. Many years later a letter written by Hirohito to his son Akihito was published. In it he expressed his remorse over Japan's part in the war and called himself an 'unworthy father'. In another letter which he had delivered to King George VI, via the British mission in Tokyo early in 1946, he claimed: 'I did my utmost to avoid war. Things, however, came to such a pass for reasons of internal affairs that we very reluctantly opened hostilities upon your country.' He regretted the 'great loss of life and property' which Britain had suffered as a result, and undertook to help create a new Japan dedicated to peace and democracy.

The Emperor was protected from any formal inquiry into his own responsibility for the war, but the Allies were determined to make a symbolic association between the Imperial house and the prosecution of war criminals. In accordance with the Potsdam Declaration, hundreds of wartime military and government leaders were arrested, and twenty-eight of them were charged as 'Class A' war criminals – the most serious category. Hirohito's birthday, 29 April 1946, was chosen as the date on which the indictments were lodged, and 23 December 1948, the birthday of his son and heir Akihito, as the day the death sentences were carried out.

The Nuremberg International Military Tribunal served as a precedent for the Tokyo War Crimes Trial. The three main violations were crimes against peace, crimes against humanity and war crimes. The charge against General Hideki Tojo, who had been Prime Minister from the time of Pearl Harbor until 1944, was that he had conspired with others to wage aggressive war. From the beginning some international legal groups were sceptical of the idea of the trials, but seven men were sentenced to death and hanged. In other parts of Asia parallel tribunals were set up, and death sentences were carried out on about 1000 of those they convicted. Some were prison guards who had tortured or executed prisoners; others were officers who had planned the war effort and given orders to others in the field.

The decision to keep the Emperor on the throne, although stripped of political power, smoothed the way for the Americans to introduce a new constitution. It was imposed on the Japanese without real discussion. The Japanese government, headed by Kijuro Shidehara, a career diplomat who had opposed the drift into war, first produced a series of highly cautious draft documents that sought to preserve much of the form and spirit of the original 1889 constitution, which accorded a sovereign position to the Emperor and stressed the obligations of the subjects rather than their rights. MacArthur rejected the drafts outright. Twenty-four members of the Government Section were summoned without notice and told to produce a draft constitution.

One of their number, Beata Serota, a young scholar eager to introduce equality for women into Japan, remembers the awe with which they realised they were to act in effect 'as a constitutional assembly'. They worked in such a hurry that junior members of the group like Serota had to go out on a frantic search of Tokyo's libraries for copies of existing Western constitutions in order to have a basis for their own task.

MacArthur himself laid down three principles to be included in the new constitution: that the Emperor would remain as the symbol of the state, without political authority; that Japan would be stripped of the sovereign right to wage war; and that the aristocracy and other 'vestiges of feudalism' were to be abolished. The rest was left to this small group of American military officers, lawyers and public servants. The job was done in six days, and the resulting draft was shown to selected Japanese Cabinet ministers, including Shigeru Yoshida, who was then Foreign Minister. They were shocked at its radicalism and pleaded for more time to rework their own drafts; but MacArthur was determined to have the matter finished quickly. He allowed his staff to hint that unless the Shidehara government showed instant approval he might not protect the Emperor from indictment as a war criminal. That was enough. On 6 March 1946 a reluctant Cabinet adopted a decidedly un-Japanese constitution for Japan.

MacArthur was not exaggerating when he later claimed:

It is undoubtedly the most liberal constitution in history, having borrowed the best from the constitutions of many countries. From an absolute monarch, the Emperor has turned into a constitutional one, 'the symbol of the state and unity of the people'. The supreme power in the state is now held by the Diet. The Japanese people, for the first time in their history, enjoy the safeguards and protection of a bill of rights. As in our own government, it provides for a separation of powers between the three branches of government.

MacArthur's staff had crafted the constitution to give Japan a combination of the American Congressional system and the British parliamentary one. Japan was to keep its two-chamber Diet, but the Upper House, the old House of Peers, now became an elected House of Councillors. The main legislative power was vested in the House of Representatives.

The most controversial section of the constitution was and still is Article 9, the so-called 'no-war' clause. It said:

Aspiring sincerely to an international peace based on justice and order, the

17

Japanese people forever renounce war as a sovereign right of the nation and the threat or use of force as means of settling international disputes. . . .

In order to accomplish the aim of the preceding paragraph, land, sea, and air forces, as well as other war potential, will never be maintained. The right of belligerency of the state will not be recognized.

The wording appears to leave no room for argument that all and any kind of military establishment is outlawed; yet from the early days Japanese conservatives were to argue that the ban on bearing arms need apply only *after* the achievement of 'an international order based on justice and order'. That phrase was added to the American wording in an amendment passed in the Diet. Japanese legal scholars also wrote articles asserting that a sovereign nation, by definition, has the right of self-defence and hence that any armed forces for self-defence do not violate Article 9. Later, that argument was to prevail. Paradoxically, the 'no-war' clause was destined to remain enshrined in the constitution long after the Americans had themselves sponsored Japan's build-up of formidable military forces. Conservative lobbies, including members of the Liberal Democratic Party (LDP), have 'studied' changing Article 9 but have never commanded the two-thirds majority in parliament needed to scrap it. The 'no-war' clause has probably restrained the pace of Japan's rearmament, but it did not prevent it.

To support the spirit of the new constitution, the Emperor went on a series of tours around the country to meet the common people for the first time. There were moments of great embarrassment, as many Japanese could not overcome their sense of awe at meeting the former 'Son of Heaven' and Hirohito was extremely nervous and shy. Usually the first phrase he could find to utter in these situations was 'Ah so?', meaning 'Really?' His constant repetition of the same sound soon made it a catchphrase.

The sight of the Emperor trudging dutifully round coal mines and factories to meet the people was a visible sign of what the Occupation was trying to bring about: a complete recasting of the Japanese mentality. Shinto shrines lost their state support, although some kept their special affiliation with the Imperial house. Other religions, including Buddhism and Christianity, which had been suppressed or downgraded in the war years, were encouraged to revive. The wartime laws giving the police widespread and arbitrary powers were repealed. Police power was decentralised and the police were taught that they must not only keep law and order but also respect the law themselves, and serve the community.

MacArthur's staff gave priority to changing the whole basis of the educational system. Since the late 1920s the Japanese government had enforced strict conformity to the *kokutai* in schools, work places and, through the ubiquitous neighbourhood associations, in people's private homes; the *kenpeitai* had seen to this with thoroughness. School textbooks taught about the destiny of Japan to rule over Asia, the divinity of the Emperor, and complete obedience to authority. Teachers had been a key instrument of the intellectual deceit imposed by the military government. They had been obliged to teach children the myths about the divine origins of the Emperor and the Japanese islands as though they were historical fact, and to support the government's distortion of the facts regarding the origins and progress of the Pacific War.

The Occupation provided for the election of local education boards and took the production of textbooks out of central government hands. For the first time schools were encouraged to teach the facts about the suppression of the labour movement and economic exploitation in Japan, as well as the truth about Japan's annexation of Korea and the invasion of China. Teachers, who only recently had taught groups of children that the Americans were inhuman devils and that the Japanese were innately superior to other peoples, suddenly switched to expounding the virtues of democracy and admitting that Japan had inflicted untold suffering on innocent people abroad. Until new textbooks could be published the old ones often had to serve: they were heavily censored and some of the history texts were mostly blacked out with the censor's ink.

Most teachers embraced the new order with apparent enthusiasm, turning an ideological somersault and landing on their feet. Kiyoko Ohtsu, a young primary-school teacher when the war ended, described her feelings like this: 'The end of the war brought such a drastic change in the society's value system, I felt that I myself should go back to school to learn all those new thoughts and systems. I was ashamed to face my pupils again.' In fact, very few teachers resigned on grounds of conscience. Some were genuinely glad to be free from the lies and oppression of the war years. Others simply parroted what they were told to say without any real conviction. A strongly left-wing teachers' union was formed to defend the reforms against the conservative Education Ministry, which sought to water them down even while the Occupation lasted.

Teachers were no exception to the general rule that the Japanese people were (and indeed still are) by nature not much inclined to argue over matters of principle. Shigeru Yoshida observed in his *Memoirs*: 'It is perhaps a characteristic of the Yamato [Japanese] race not to say things when they need saying, and to be wise after the event.' In the Occupation years the entire school and college system was re-created on the American model, with nine years of compulsory education up to the age of fifteen. Classes in English and other languages were reintroduced after having been banned for many years.

MacArthur and his staff saw this attempt to remould the minds of the younger Japanese as a key to the Occupation's long-term success or failure. They believed that it would take a generation before democratic values could mature in Japanese society. Although the Japanese were not allowed to censor the press, SCAP imposed its own censorship: Occupation policies were not allowed to be debated or questioned. Stories of feudal Japan that glorified *bushido*, the way of the warrior, were banned. Also prohibited for a time were the martial arts; *kendo* sword-training and *judo* clubs were closed down. In the theatre, everything reminiscent of the old Japanese values – feudal loyalty and the subjection of women – was banned. A prime candidate for censorship was the classic *kabuki* play *Chushingura*, a story about the fanatical loyalty of forty-seven masterless *samurai* who avenge an insult to their lord with a carefully plotted murder and afterwards commit mass *seppuku*, ritual self-disembowelment. A leading film director, Kozaburo Yoshimura, remembers how he and his contemporaries were urged to make films 'about all the bad things the militarists had done in the war'. Swordfights and ritual suicide were out. Anti-war films were in.

The new climate meant a revolution in personal behaviour, too. One of Yoshimura's films, *Waga Shogai Ga Kagayakeru Hi* (*The Day Our Lives Shone*), was a love story between the daughter of a good family who had come down in the world and an ex-soldier who had become a social drifter. At one point the couple kissed on screen – Japan's very first Hollywood-style stage kiss. The actor and actress were so untutored that they had no idea how long to hold the embrace. The director could not give any visual signal because the actors could not see him. Inspiration struck. Yoshimura himself stood nearby and scratched the back of the actress's leg when the pair were supposed to break off.

Some of the most fundamental changes in Japan's physical appearance and social structure came with the Occupation's land reforms. For centuries landlords had controlled the lives of their tenants in the countryside. The feudal class structure as such had been abolished at the time of the Meiji Restoration, but before the war inherited wealth and position counted for as much as it did in some European countries.

The poorly educated peasantry had little to look forward to in their own society, and had fallen an easy prey to grandiose ideas of military conquest. At the end of the war nearly half of Japan's farmland, mostly rice paddies, was worked by tenant farmers. SCAP broke up large holdings and let the tenant farmers buy the land at low prices. Some 4 million families benefited immediately, and the reforms did much to mould Japanese society into one in which wealth was remarkably evenly distributed. Suddenly former aristocrats and landlords lost their land and possessions, with only minimal compensation. Akira Matsui, who had owned large estates, decided not even to go back to look at his property one last time, as 'the compensation offered would barely have covered the cost of the train fare'. The pre-war system of inheritance, which gave everything by law to the eldest son of a family, was abolished. It was blamed for creating a disenfranchised class of tenant farmers.

The constitution gave the Japanese parliament law-making and executive authority through its power to elect the prime minister, and so encouraged the formation of new political parties. An influential segment of SCAP strongly sympathised with the Socialists. Hundreds of left-wing political and trade-union figures were released from jail; several leaders who had fled overseas returned. Foremost among them was Sanzo Nosaka, the communist leader, who had spent sixteen years in exile in China and Russia. He was given a hero's welcome around the country as a symbol of those who had fought, as he put it, through Japan's 'age of darkness' under the military. Nosaka hoped that his party, the only major political group which had consistently opposed the war, would now reap its reward. With many of the top-ranking members of the wartime government and thousands of right-wing and military figures being held as suspected war criminals or banned from public office, it seemed as though the left's day had come; but it was not to be.

The general election of 10 April 1946 was the first major test of the political climate. The majority of members of the wartime parliament were out of the contest, being investigated for possible war crimes or on the 'purged' list. Ichiro Hatoyama, an independent voice among the nationalist-minded conservatives, reorganised the remnants of the pre-war Seiyukai Party, which had been partly financed by the Mitsui business group. Now they called themselves the Liberal Party. A rival group, including many wartime collaborators with the military, emerged from the pre-war Minseito Party, which had been backed by the Mitsubishi business combine. At first it called itself the Progressive Party but changed its name to the Democratic Party two years later. Scores of minor parties and fringe groups also fielded candidates. The

Socialists and Communists quickly organised trade unions and joined in the vigorous campaigning.

The concept of democracy as expounded by the Americans was patently difficult for most ordinary Japanese to grasp. In the country-side, important decisions affecting the community had traditionally been taken by the village heads acting as an unelected council. Since 1940 all political parties had been dissolved and merged into one pan-national organisation, the Imperial Rule Assistance Association. To propogate the American vision, the Occupation authorities sent more than fifty teams of instructors into remote hamlets, where they dis-tributed US government-made films on the lives of figures such as Abraham Lincoln and George Washington; a favourite among the audiences was a Hollywood version of 'the American way of life' entitled *America the Beautiful*.

The population eagerly, if rather shallowly at first, embraced democ-racy, as they did Western fashions. GIs joked that the Japanese treated democracy as a novelty, like toothpaste or soap powder. In many constituencies voters flocked with little thought to support the can-didates whom they knew personally. Mrs Shizue Katoh, who became a socialist member of parliament through that election, recalls how in her first election campaign she visited a factory to discover that the crowd listening to her was made up only of men, with no single woman present in the meeting hall. 'Are there any women in this factory?' she asked, and they replied 'Yes, Yes.' She asked why they didn't come inside, and was told, 'Well, women *don't* come inside.' The candidate was amazed: when she looked, the women of the factory were standing outside the windows, eager to catch everything that was going on.

The 1946 election was a fragmented, chaotic affair; but it served, as MacArthur had intended, as a referendum on the new constitution. All the major political parties endorsed it, at least in public, although most conservative politicians in fact had deep misgivings. It was clear that the great majority of people felt a revulsion towards the war. Most voters were still farmers or first-generation city-dwellers. Women voted for the first time. The main concerns were food, housing and jobs; and most parties echoed the same promises. Only the Communist Party dared to advocate abolishing the Imperial family and turning Japan into a republic.

The election system, adapted from the pre-war one, was designed to make it hard for a single party to gain an overwhelming majority of seats. Each constituency was to elect up to fifteen Diet members to represent it (the maximum number of seats per constituency was later cut to five), and competition was intense. Ichiro Hatoyama's Liberal Party won the largest number of seats, though less than a majority.

Hatoyama was preparing to take over the government when suddenly, as a result of leaks by disgruntled SCAP officers, he was purged – barred from active political life: it was revealed that he had once published a book praising the Nazis. The Liberals offered the party leadership instead to Shigeru Yoshida, who thus became Prime Minister. Yoshida accepted the role only reluctantly, protesting that as a career diplomat he had no experience of national politics; and many expected him to be just a stopgap leader until Hatoyama returned. But Yoshida proved to have immense political skill and staying power; and it was his vision of Japan, not Hatoyama's more openly nationalistic one, which helped to guide the Occupation years.

Shigeru Yoshida led Japan from May 1946 to May 1947 and, after a brief spell out of power, headed four more Cabinets from October 1948 to December 1954. Hatoyama was kept out of the political ring, first because of the purge order and later because of illness. By 1948 SCAP had barred from public office some 200 000 people but the purge was weakened by delay and vacillation. It skimmed the top layers of the bureaucracy and big business, but left the body intact. A great many of those who were disqualified later came back to assume influential positions in business or public life.

Yoshida was already sixty-seven when he first became Premier. A short, stocky cigar-smoker, he was a member of the aristocracy by marriage and had been Ambassador in London in the 1930s. To the Japanese Yoshida quickly became a reassuring figure, steering the nation with a sure hand during one of its darkest periods. He had supported Japan's attempt to take over China, but had also taken a public stand against his country's signing of the Tripartite Pact with Germany and Italy. Towards the end of the war he had been one of a group of leading public figures who had tried to press the government to sue for peace. When the plan came to light Yoshida had been arrested and briefly kept under surveillance at his home. The episode provided him with credentials to lead the new Japan.

Yoshida was representative of the patrician Japanese conservatives who found themselves at odds with the pre-war and wartime military. He was by no means a pacifist, but was strongly opposed to Japan's making enemies of Britain and the United States. To his mind, Japan's leaders in the Meiji period (1868–1912) had shown admirable statesmanship in expanding the Japanese empire by judicious steps, while holding back from actions that would bring the country into conflict with Britain and America. It was by this means, he wrote, 'that a small island nation in the Far East came in half a century to rank among the five great Powers of the world'. He believed in empire for his country, but detested the hot-headed militarists who led Japan to disaster. In his own phrase, Tojo had 'hijacked the nation'. At the same time Yoshida was deeply attached to the Emperor, still believed fervently that Japan had a right to be a major power in Asia, and saw nothing wrong with aspects of Japanese society such as the *zaibatsu* (big business groupings), aristocracy, authoritarian education or the land-owner class.

He felt, therefore, that the Americans had started work in the Occupation 'on the erroneous assumption that we were an aggressive people of ultra-militaristic traditions to be refashioned into a peace-loving nation'. He put the need for food, recovery and independence ahead of any of the Americans' intended reforms. He especially felt that the Americans were wrong in their assessment that Japan's great business combines, the *zaibatsu*, had been in any sense warmongers. He and others succeeded in considerably watering down plans for the dissolution of the *zaibatsu* by arguing that to cripple Japan's strongest industrial enterprises would slow down the country's recovery and make it more dependent on the USA, as well as risking a communist revolution. He argued that outward conformity would best speed up the Occupation and expedite a peace treaty, and felt that the Japanese achieved their objectives most quickly by 'being good losers'.

The Occupation thus pitted two men of very strong character and quite different backgrounds, MacArthur and Yoshida, against one another in a prolonged struggle of wills. MacArthur was, in the first two years of the Occupation, a radical idealist in the tradition of Thomas Jefferson and Thomas Paine. This was the period in which he ordered the release of Communists from jail and supported the growth of the labour movement. These things puzzled and annoyed Yoshida. He wrote later that the agitation of the Communists had done 'untold damage to our body politic', and he saw the encouragement of the labour movement as a grave mistake; he also said of the education reforms that they had only 'sowed confusion in the minds of our bewildered youth'. He resented what he saw as American radicals doing their social experiments in Japan. He and other like-minded conservatives resisted with guile and determination many of the Occu-pation reforms that threatened the old order. In the last years, MacAr-thur gradually began to allow those early reforms to backslide, as his view of the left became increasingly harsh.

There was common ground between the two men on the most fundamental things. Yoshida admired MacArthur's magnanimity and clear vision and appreciated his treatment of the Emperor. He even professed to agree with the 'no-war' constitution, and credited MacAr-thur with saving Japan from partition, the fate of neighbouring Korea.

When the Soviet Union sought to run the Occupation of the northern island of Hokkaido – which represents a quarter of all Japan's land area – MacArthur coldly blocked the move. In the end the Soviet Union played a very limited role in the Occupation, as did the other non-American members of the advisory Allied Council for Japan: China, and Australia, representing the British Commonwealth.

Although in theory Yoshida had to obey any American instructions, in practice he had ready access to MacArthur and he frequently used it to affect the course of events. His wily but determined style won him great respect among some of the SCAP officers, as well as among the Japanese. Matataro Fujikawa, the Sado island farmer, expressed one strand of popular opinion:

> Everything MacArthur achieved was against a background of the fact that he and his side had won; but Yoshida's side had lost. Even so he was able to speak his mind and hold his end up – to me that makes him twice as great as MacArthur!

Yoshida himself thought that the Occupation, despite all its power and authority, 'was hampered by its lack of knowledge of the people it had come to govern, and even more so, perhaps, by its generally happy ignorance of the amount of requisite knowledge it lacked'. He relates, for instance, how the Americans planned to purge all those in the business world who had in their view been warmongers. The SCAP directive said that all 'standing directors' of large firms – meaning all members of the directorial boards – should be removed from their posts. The Japanese side, however, translated 'standing directors' as 'managing directors' – a far smaller number. Yoshida writes candidly of the deception, saying that in this way 'we were able to save many ordinary directors who might otherwise have been so classified from the purge'. This episode, he wrote, 'shows that upon occasion mistranslations serve their turn'.

SCAP sponsored a lively and independent trade-union movement to counterbalance the vested business interests. Workers were granted the right to form unions, to strike and to conduct collective bargaining. In the pre-war period an alliance of conservative business and right-wing political groups had destroyed the union movement by the mid-1930s. The military established a nationwide Industrial Patriotic Association, with councils in each company dedicated to increasing production. The post-war labour movement never wholly shook off the social pressures for 'loyalty and patriotism' dating from the pre-war years. The Americans had a hard time explaining the principles of trade unions to the would-be recruits. Shigekatsu Iwano, a railway driver at the Shinagawa locomotive yard in Tokyo, remembers that when he and his fellow workers were told they would be allowed to form trade unions, 'we were completely ignorant about what they were and really had to learn about them from first principles'.

The economy was in tatters and food prices were spiralling out of control. Wages for the average Japanese worker in the late 1945 were no more than 30 US cents a day. In the autumn of 1945 the rice crop failed. The search for food was uppermost in the people's minds. Rationing was severe and the black market flourished. Trains heading for the northern suburbs of Tokyo were regularly overflowing with people travelling to the countryside to buy extra rice and vegetables on the black market. The United States shipped in large quantities of food, but it was not enough. On May Day in 1946 the most serious of many mass rallies took place outside the Imperial Palace. Tens of thousands of workers roared out the demand for food and better wages. Their banners carried caricatures of the Emperor and the captions made out that he was gorging himself while the workers starved.

Union membership in Japan grew at a rate never seen before in any industrial country – from zero in August 1945 to almost 5 million by the end of 1946. Most of the new union organisations were company-based, but some were industry-wide. The union movement was split from the start between communist- and socialist-led labour federations, weakening its power; but the Communist Congress of Industrial Labour Unions, Sambetsu Kaigi, which was especially strong among public employees, made a determined effort to unseat the Yoshida government.

There was a rash of strikes and sit-ins, in response to mass lay-offs and the uncontrolled inflation which left many people without the means to support themselves. In many cases the workers occupied factories, keeping up production while they pressed their demands for better wages and guaranteed food. Thousands of workers in one railway company took over the running of the trains themselves, repaired the rolling stock and won their demand for a fivefold increase in wages. The communist leadership organised sympathetic unions in coal mines, factories and enterprises across the country. It was a common sight to see red flags fluttering from the roofs of office buildings and factories.

One of the main battlegrounds was the mass media. In turn the managements of each of the major newspaper and broadcasting companies battled with the newly formed trade unions. There were walkouts and other forms of industrial action at each of the major national dailies. The most symbolic struggle occurred at the right-wing *Yomiuri* newspaper, where in the summer of 1946 hundreds of workers occupied the building and held senior management figures hostage. There the free union called a strike over wages and the dismissal of thirty-one workers, but they were outmanoeuvred by the publisher, who had been chief of the Tokyo police during the war. He formed an in-house company union and hired professional thugs to beat up the strikers and throw them out of the offices they were occupying. The strong challenge from the unions sorely tried the Occupation authorities' commitment to freedom of speech and to the labour movement. The Americans leant hard on the press not to give open support to the striking workers on the *Yomiuri*, with the result that newspapers cut back their strike coverage drastically. One socialist paper, the *Jinmin Shimbun*, obediently began to run mostly literary news instead, prompting a contemporary observer to write that it had resigned itself to living in 'a non-political Wonderland'.

SCAP was concerned at the rising union militancy and in late 1946 enacted a law banning strikes by public employees. The unions were determined to show their new power by organising a general strike, and one was called for 1 February 1947. Its declared aims included the repeal of the ban on strikes in the public sector, a minimum monthly salary of 650 yen (about $2), an end to unreasonable discharges and guarantees of collective bargaining rights. Five million workers in 20 000 different unions expected to bring the nation to a standstill. SCAP asked labour leaders to continue negotiations, but the union leaders refused, accusing their American mentors: 'But you were the ones who told us to form trade unions!'

Yoshida, who had warned the Americans against giving so much encouragement to the left-wing and labour movements, bided his time. He believed that when MacArthur saw a sea of red flags waving outside his own window at SCAP headquarters he would order the strike illegal. On 29 January hundreds of thousands of workers rallied in central Tokyo demanding the ousting of the Yoshida government, and the next day MacArthur decided to ban the strike. The strike leader, Yashiro Ii of the railwaymen's union, was forced to go on radio to announce that it had been cancelled. Afterwards he returned to his union office to complain that 'the bastards have done for us'.

Opinion in SCAP itself was split. Some of the most ardent reformers felt that by intervening the Americans had betrayed their original high-minded ideal to hand over the decision-making to the Japanese themselves; also that labour rights were at the heart of the *demokurashii* (democracy) which had stirred the souls of the Japanese but had not had a chance to take root. One of these was Eleanor Hadley, who felt strongly that 'the unions were only doing what they had been told they had a right to do, and that this right was arbitrarily cut off'. However,

Justin Williams in GHQ's Government Section felt that the stakes were too high to take risks. 'If the strike had matured,' he said later, 'the chances are that there would have been a people's republic. . . . It would have been the end of what we call pluralism; it would have been one-party rule.'

Yoshida rejoiced. One of his political secretaries recalled later: 'It was a weight off his mind. Now he thought that MacArthur and GHQ understood the problem and he could work for Japan's recovery with that assurance of understanding behind him.'

The banning of the general strike did indeed signal the start of a major shift of policies and purpose by the Americans in Japan. The 'Iron Curtain' had come down on Eastern Europe. The Communists were fast extending their control in China. In Washington the highest priority was to contain the international communist movement. Socialism in all its forms was viewed with deep suspicion. In Japan, however, another election held soon after the failed general strike forced Yoshida's Liberal Party into opposition, and the Japan Socialist Party took part in two successive Cabinets, in coalition with the Democratic Party, between May 1947 and October 1948. They struggled unsuccessfully to deal with the problems of mass unemployment and soaring inflation. The US Congress was increasingly opposed to the subsidies, running at $1 million a day, being used to build what some of its members saw as a socialist-inclined Japan.

A new set of policies towards Japan was outlined in January 1948 by the US Secretary of the Army, Kenneth Royall. In a speech in San Francisco he declared that Japan must be turned into a bulwark of the free world against 'the communist menace'. He outlined the dilemma like this:

> On the one hand we cannot afford to leave the Japanese war system intact nor forget that there is a danger in retaining in power leaders whose philosophy helped bring on World War II. . . . On the other hand we cannot afford to sterilize the business ability of Japan.

From then on, the Occupation's most important objective would not be to see through the political and social reforms, but to make Japan economically self-supporting.

Royall acknowledged that this new approach was in conflict with the original aims of the Occupation, but now political reform would have to take second place. The new policy was labelled by some as not just a change of emphasis but a 'reverse course'. Many conservatives and former military figures who had been purged were allowed back into public life. Koichiro Asakai, of the Central Liaison Office, recalls that from now on there was a distinct shift in the attitudes of his American counterparts. Whereas before they had treated him and the other officials they met as 'nationals of a defeated country', from 1948 he says 'they took us into their confidence and talked about co-operation'.

Some of Japan's neighbours in the Asia–Pacific region responded with dismay and apprehension to the change of direction. One of the strongest objections came from the Chinese judge who had sat on the bench in the Tokyo War Crimes Trial, Mei Ju-ao. Writing in January 1949, he saw MacArthur and his staff as complacent dupes: 'The American authorities were always honoured, praised and flattered, but they were everywhere cheated and double-crossed.' He claimed that the Japanese government was coming again to be 'dominated by old-time politicians, financiers and bureaucrats', and that 'a return to fascism seems to be a logical outcome of this tendency'. In October 1949 Mao Tse-tung triumphantly proclaimed the success of his communist revolution, and the lines were clearly drawn: Japan would side with the USA in the Cold War.

For the Americans the chaotic state of the Japanese economy was now cause for great concern. The biggest problem of all was inflation. Consumer prices had risen by no less than ten times in the first six months after the surrender, and had kept on rising sharply thereafter, fuelled by shortages, strikes and overspending. The Americans feared that this could lead to more serious social unrest, and they enforced a new set of drastic measures in what was called the Economic Stabilisation Programme. In February 1949 President Truman sent the president of the Bank of Detroit, Joseph Dodge, to Japan. He was given wide powers to carry out his mission – to curb inflation and to report on ways of rebuilding a strong economy. Dodge had earlier performed a similar role in West Germany. The medicine he prescribed was severe. He ordered large-scale lay-offs to improve productivity levels in industry and further undercut the already weakened influence of the trade unions. Public spending was pared down sharply to balance the budgets, and a quarter of a million government officials were made jobless. The 'Dodge Line' resulted in a severe short-term economic recession, but it served its purpose – inflation fell sharply.

By this time the Japanese left was in retreat. From 1949 there was a sweeping 'red purge' of Communists and their alleged sympathisers, among politicians, trade unionists, scholars and journalists. Twelve thousand people lost their jobs. The communist newspaper, *Akahata* (*Red Flag*), was banned from 1950 to 1952. Managements were given tacit or open approval to suppress independent union power. Mac-Arthur, like the Truman administration in Washington, thought that

Japan's rearmament must begin; and in 1950, just after the outbreak of the Korean War, SCAP directed Japan to form a 75 000-man National Police Reserve as the nucleus of a future army. As this directly contradicted Article 9 of the Japanese constitution, the real nature of the Reserve was kept as secret as possible. General Seizo Arisue, who had supervised the army's demobilisation, now helped with its revival.

The Korean War of 1950–3 set the seal on Japan's new role as helpmate to America's strategic needs in the Far East. The sudden onslaught of North Korean forces over the border into South Korea in June 1950 caught the south and the Americans utterly by surprise. In a short time they were driven far into the south-west of South Korea and Kim Il Sung's troops and tanks overran Seoul. The first American reinforcements were sent in from bases in Japan. US presidential adviser John Foster Dulles repeatedly pressed Yoshida to create a force of 300 000 men, but he refused. He was determined to avoid the possibility of Japan's being pressed to take part in the Korean War, and was equally convinced that the building of a strong economy must remain his country's foremost goal.

MacArthur was given command of the UN forces hastily assembled to fight back, and he masterminded a landing behind the North Korean lines at Inchon. However, a push into the north in winter was thrown back by human waves of Chinese troops as the UN forces neared the Manchurian border, and there were many casualties. MacArthur was judged to have challenged President Truman's authority, and was relieved of all his commands, including that of Supreme Commander for the Allied Powers in Japan. His career, which had begun as a West Point cadet in 1899, was at an end. Huge crowds turned out to wave goodbye when he finally left Japan in April 1951. His successor, General Matthew Ridgway, would hold the post of Supreme Commander for the Allied Powers for only a year before Japan regained its independence.

MacArthur believed that his work in Japan was in any case nearly over. He had felt that it would be possible to turn the country from its recent past towards a better future by a policy of firmness and generosity, and his leadership is the key to the relative success of the entire process. It was hardly an exaggeration for the personal representative of the British Prime Minister in Japan to say later that 'MacArthur *was* Japan.' When asked in 1948 about his underlying philosophy in handling the Occupation, MacArthur replied: 'The pattern of my course in the Occupation of Japan lies deeply rooted in the lessons and experience of American history.' He declared grandiosely that '. . . history will clearly show that the entire human race, irrespective of geographical delimitations or cultural tradition, is capable of absorbing, cherishing and defending liberty, tolerance and justice, and will find maximum strength and progress when so blessed'. Some sceptical British observers, however, saw him as an actor hamming it up for home audiences and nicknamed him 'the Hollywood General'.

On other occasions, MacArthur revealed his own doubts about whether those ideas had really taken root in Japanese soil. Giving an account of his mission in Japan to a US Senate committee he said that in terms of political maturity the Japanese were like 'a nation of twelve-year-olds'. This comment enraged many Japanese, and all work on a monument being planned in Tokyo to commemorate MacArthur was halted. In private conversations he also admitted to harbouring grave doubts about his mission. He feared that after independence the Japanese government might simply abandon parts of the democratic baggage so laboriously stowed on board. Long after MacArthur himself died in 1964 the political institutions created during the Occupation are still in place, and outwardly at least are respected. In that sense much remains as a tribute to its architect and mason.

As the Cold War rivalry between the United States and the Soviet Union intensified, Japan became America's favourite son in Asia. The Cold War strained America's resources and hastened the decision to end the Occupation with a peace treaty and simultaneously to sign a bilateral defence treaty with Japan in San Francisco in 1951. The way this was done, and the decision to accord to Japan the status of a key ally through the US–Japan Security Treaty, was a sharp disappointment to the rest of the Asia–Pacific region. John Foster Dulles was given charge of drafting the treaty terms. He had played a part in the making of the Versailles Treaty in 1919 and was determined that the Allies would not make the mistake made at that time towards Germany, of imposing punitive terms which would later fuel a revival of aggressive ambitions.

The price that Japan paid for the settlement with the Western Allies was that it was alienated from China and the Soviet Union. The Soviet Union attended at San Francisco but refused to put its name to the treaty, while neither of the two rival Chinese governments was invited to the peace conference. The Soviet Union was beaten in its bid to turn Japan into a neutral state in its own sphere of influence. In effect the USA exacted from Japan the right to maintain a large number of military bases there, in return for granting early independence. America's allies in the Far East wanted firm guarantees that Japan would not be allowed to grow into a military threat once again, and most had to be cajoled into accepting the San Francisco arrangements. Forty-eight countries did sign the peace treaty and in practice Japan was able gradually to return to Asia under American sponsorship, but it was on terms that were widely resented in the region. Australia and New Zealand voiced very strong concern about the lack of formal restraints on Japan's future military growth; they insisted on having their own collective security pact with the USA, the ANZUS Pact, before they would sign the San Francisco treaty. The Philippines, South Korea and the Republic of China (Taiwan) each acquired their own security treaties with Washington. India and Burma failed to sign the treaty in 1951, though they did later make their peace with Tokyo.

In Japan it was the terms of the Security Treaty that were controversial, because they were decidedly unequal. America kept the territory of Okinawa, far to the south of the mainland, as a trust territory for its own military uses. It also retained a large number of base areas on the mainland, but was free of the legal obligation to commit its own troops to defend Japan in the case of outside attack. In addition, the USA had the right to deploy its own troops on Japanese soil to quell riots or disturbances, if so requested by the Japanese government. Many Japanese feared that the presence of the American bases would make Japan a likely target for Soviet missiles in the event of a nuclear war. Shigeru Yoshida was convinced, though, that it was the best accord that Japan could hope for, and insisted that he alone should sign the US–Japan Security Treaty on behalf of his country.

Independence, when it came in 1952, was greeted with much celebration in Japan. Looking back from the perspective of the late 1980s, Koichiro Asakai expressed the widely held Japanese view that 'it is thanks to the course of events in the immediate post-war period that the Japanese have enjoyed economic prosperity as well as security'. Yoshida himself called the peace treaty 'fair and generous', and was proud of the special relationship that had grown up. He wrote in his *Memoirs* that 'The Americans came into our country as enemies, but after an Occupation lasting less than seven years, an understanding grew up between the two peoples which is remarkable in the history of the modern world.' Japan has made its alliance with the USA the cornerstone of its foreign policy long after America's economic dominance waned. And despite many rivalries and some disagreements, successive American presidents and their advisers have also worked to maintain the original spirit of the relationship.

An assessment of the United States' success in the declared aim of democratising Japan must be more ambiguous. The Japanese, dazed from half a century of state indoctrination, began to embrace the personal freedoms and open debate that was offered; but when the Americans themselves let the spirit of reform die down an older pattern of conformism began to re-establish itself. A radical American journalist who reported on the Occupation, Mark Gayn, reckoned that at the very start, when MacArthur allowed the Japanese government to go on functioning, he set out on the road which led to 'the survival of old Japan'. Gayn recorded in his *Diary*: 'Our worst error in Japan was our original belief that democratic reform would, or could, be carried out by men who hated it.... Before our first Christmas in Japan, we knew that the Japanese machinery of government was geared for sabotage.' In 1948 the same writer judged that 'the spirit of reform is dead'.

The Japanese left, and organised labour, deeply resented the 'reverse course' and have suffered from it. The Occupation years failed to produce a social democratic movement to stand as an alternative to the old guard conservatives, with their history of collaboration in advancing the aims of the war. In practice, left-wing and liberal political ideas were subsumed in the ideologies of Japan's hardline Communist and Socialist Parties, alienating many in the middle ground. At the same time, some Japanese who contributed directly to the Americans' early reform plans felt sorely deceived. Shizue Katoh, the socialist woman Diet member, singled out the reform of the civil service as an area where the Allies should have made fundamental changes but did not: as a result, she said, 'the bureaucrats have stayed just as they were – so arrogant'. Today, after many years of rule by the same staunchly conservative party, many Japanese are doubtful about the validity of their own 'single-party democracy'. The postwar constitution laid down that Japan's sovereignty was with the people, but the Japanese as a nation have remained passive in the face of bureaucratic controls on their lives. Citizens' groups have little confidence that the legal system will administer impartial justice. And in schools, companies and society as a whole there are strong pressures to conform to officially sanctioned goals; these have inhibited the vigorous public debate which alone would firmly underpin the country's democratic institutions.

The decision to maintain the same Emperor on his throne, albeit simply as a 'symbol of the state', was taken in part for reasons of expediency. Clearly, it made the short-term task of the Occupation easier, but at the time many among the Allies believed that a unique opportunity to democratise the heart of the Japanese political system had been missed. Against that, one may argue that if foreign powers had abolished the title of Emperor, there would for ever be the possibility of yet another right-wing *coup* – a new 'Imperial Restoration' in the same spirit as the one attempted by fanatical soldiers in 1936.

It is a matter of record that Emperor Hirohito survived on the throne for forty-four years after the war before being succeeded by his son Akihito, and that was long enough for him to come to symbolise a peaceful Japan. But that continuity has brought with it crucial doubts in post-war Japan about where political responsibility begins and ends. George Atcheson, the former political adviser for the US State Department in Tokyo, summarised those doubts when he wrote in 1946: 'there seems little question that the Japanese people will never learn to follow the fundamental ways of democracy as long as the Imperial institution exists'. One sign of the mentality which would endure in later years could be seen in Hirohito's broadcast on 15 August 1945, where he asserted that in declaring war on American and Britain the nation had acted 'out of Our sincere desire to ensure Japan's self-preservation and the stabilisation of East Asia, it being far from Our thought to infringe upon the sovereignty of other nations or to embark upon territorial aggrandisement'. The Emperor himself never publicly retracted that interpretation of the origins of the Pacific War, and numerous Japanese Cabinet ministers have appeared to endorse it.

MacArthur sought to open up the Imperial household and erase its mystique in the public mind; but with only limited success. In 1945 the Imperial household was forced to give up its enormous private holdings of land, stocks and other assets, but over time the chamberlains and officials there used the weapon of tradition to claw back a good deal of the authority and prestige that had surrounded the monarch under the old, absolutist laws before the war. After the first few years of organised public tours, Hirohito gradually became a remote figure once again. He performed all his duties punctiliously, opening parliamentary sessions, receiving foreign dignitaries and even showing up in the Imperial box to watch *sumo* wrestling tournaments; but in line with the old tradition he studiously avoided expressing any personal opinions and in his final years, before his death in 1989, gave the impression of being held virtually a prisoner of the fustian court officials inside the palace grounds in Tokyo.

More fundamentally, the anxiety of the outside world about Japan's political character derives from the way that post-war Japan, unlike West Germany, never made a clear and unequivocal break with its wartime past. In the 1980s Cabinet ministers several times openly expressed 'revisionist' ideas denying Japanese wartime aggression. The Education Ministry consistently uses its powers to amend approved school textbooks in order to avoid giving Japanese school-children much idea that their country was responsible for destruction and cruelty in the war. Despite the testimony presented at the Tokyo War Crimes Trial, and the outpouring during the Occupation years of liberal and left-wing literature reviling Japanese militarism and fascism, in the minds of many Japanese the question of the guilt of Japan's wartime leaders was left unresolved. The same went for the national values and institutions that fostered the war.

After seven years of foreign occupation, Japan was less changed than most had expected at the time of defeat; and it was about to start an astonishing march towards economic growth and then international recognition. No one person set Japan on its present path, but Shigeru Yoshida perhaps did more than any other. He revealed some of his inner thoughts in a letter to a fellow diplomat, Saburo Kurusu, on 27 August 1945:

> I think that events have reached their inevitable conclusion. If the devil has a son, surely he is Tojo. So far, the manner of Japan's defeat has been quite without precedent in history: we could indeed rebuild Imperial Japan out of this way of defeat. If we excise the cancer of politics which is the military, politics will become clean, the nation's morality will improve and the whole process of diplomacy will be renewed. Not only that, but science will be advanced, business will become strong with the introduction of American capital, and in the end our Imperial country will be able to fulfil its true potential. If that is so, it is not so bad to be defeated in this war. After the rain, sky and land will become brighter.

■ ☐2☐ ■

Comeback

ROADS TO PROSPERITY

In 1952 Masaru Ibuka, the head of a small Japanese electronics company, visited America. One of his aims was to see the work being done on transistors as replacements for bulky and unreliable vacuum tubes. At the Bell Laboratories the doors were opened to Ibuka, and to other engineers visiting from Japan and Europe. He took notes of all he was shown, and drawings were sent back to Tokyo. The next year his company, Totsuko, paid $25 000 for a licence to develop the new device. Ibuka, who became one of the acknowledged father-figures of Japan's post-war industry, recalls how the Americans reacted when he told them what he intended to do with the new technology:

> At last we got our licence, and the Americans asked us what we meant to do with it. I replied, 'We are thinking of making transistor radios.' The Americans told us that could not be done, because transistors could not handle the high frequencies that would be needed. So we were told, 'Whatever you do, don't make radios!'

But by 1955 Dr Ibuka's firm was renamed Sony Corporation and had made its first transistor radios. By 1958 the company had made its first shipments of the new product to the United States.

The story of the portable transistor radio is one of many which show how post-war Japanese companies saw their chance and were alert, informed and well-funded enough to seize it. Sony paid a knockdown price for a key piece of technology, but its in-house physicists and engineers developed the actual product themselves. They did pioneering work in miniaturising the parts and ushering in an age of mass-produced electronic goods. Sony mounted an effective advertising campaign in America for a portable radio that would fit into a shirt pocket. In fact the radios were rather too big for an ordinary-sized shirt pocket, but Sony had their salesmen enlarge their pockets so that the radios would fit into them.

In one product field after another – ships, watches, cameras, television sets, machine tools and cars – Japan caught up with the world leaders and sometimes put them out of business. Later this pattern would be repeated with home video cassette recorders, computers and telecommunications. It was to be an age when manufacturing skills and applied science and technology would divide the world into the wealthy nations and the rest; and those were skills in which the Japanese proved themselves pre-eminent. From the depths of defeat in war, Japan picked itself up so that by 1956 it became the world's leading shipbuilding nation; in 1962 its economy overtook Britain's in size and in 1967 it topped West Germany's to become the third largest in the world. In the 1980s the country's GNP surpassed that of the Soviet Union, and Japanese per capita incomes exceeded America's.

This story came to be known as 'the economic miracle'. A number of factors combined to bring it about: among them a benign post-war Occupation, Japan's distance from regional wars and conflicts, the growth of free trade worldwide, capital dedicated to industrial investment, sound management methods, the influx of new industrial technology, a high level of education and a willing workforce. The additional ingredient which brought all these forces together was 'industrial policy' – the evolution of a calculated policy for fostering national industries, devised by the country's élite and traditionally powerful bureaucrats with the co-operation of private firms.

Japan's sudden rise to the rank of a leading industrial power took the West by surprise because, literally, its like had never been seen before. Between 1954 and 1971 the Japanese economy grew at an average of 10 per cent every year, expanding by fully five times. In the same period investment in new industrial facilities rose as high as 36 per cent of GNP, a level undreamt of in the older industrialised nations. The nearest historical parallel, in fact, was with Japan at an earlier stage of its modern history, when between the ousting of the *shogun* in 1868 and the 1930s the country came from nowhere to become the greatest naval power in the eastern hemisphere. It had then supplied much of the world with textile goods, and had the technology to build the feared Zero fighter. When the Pacific War ended, however, Japan had missed out almost completely on the technological and manufacturing advances made in the West for a decade, but it had a formidable tradition of both craftsmanship and heavy industry on which to build.

By 1967 Japan's post-war transformation was described by the

British writer Norman Macrae of *The Economist* as 'probably the most successful sudden economic growth story of all time'. In what turned out to be a prescient piece of analysis, Macrae drew the inescapable conclusion that Japan achieved its success 'by the most deliberate policies' – among them, careful government direction of industrial investment and export growth, and limitations on protection of domestic industries from outside competition (imports). Some more hostile observers called it a conspiracy to dominate the markets, first of Asia, then of the world. Without doubt, economic growth was planned and carried out with determination by government and businesses acting in close concert. It was conceived as a means of raising Japan's status and influence in the world, through commerce rather than by force of arms. The population as a whole was brought, through education and government advice, to subscribe to the same goal. There was dissent, but it was held back by means of moral sanctions backed by the power of the state.

Japan's great national goal was set in the mid-nineteenth century, and 100 years later it had not changed: it was to 'catch up with' the West. One of the leading industrial planners of post-war Japan, Naohiro Amaya – who later became Vice-minister for International Affairs at the Ministry of International Trade and Industry (MITI) – spells out how from the time of the restoration of the Emperor Meiji to the throne in 1868 – the beginning of the nation's modern history – the aim of Japan's rulers was to avoid the fate of other Asian countries such as India. India had been colonised, and its mainstay industry, cotton, was crushed by being exposed to Britain's free-trade system. Amaya tells how 'India was obliged to specialise in the production of raw cotton and sell it to Britain, which produced cotton goods in its Lancashire cotton mills and exported them back to India'; but 'Meiji-era Japan refused to share the fate of India'. In Japan the government itself therefore promoted government enterprises and adopted interventionist policies that were 'very close to the Stalinist model' of complete state control. Amaya acknowledges that that pattern continued until 1960 when a new policy was born, the aim of which was 'to make Japanese industry self-supporting by liberalising capital transactions and trade'.

Before the guns fell quiet in Asia, Japan's élite government officials had begun to map out a general path to be followed. On 16 August 1945, the day after the Emperor's surrender broadcast, an informal group calling itself the Committee on Post-war Problems held its first, pre-arranged, meeting in one of the few public buildings still standing intact in Tokyo, that of the South Manchurian Railway Company.

The aim was to consider, before the victors arrived, how Japan was to feed its people, start the reconstruction and decide the new national priorities. The committee's secretary was Saburo Okita, who was later to become Japan's Foreign Minister. He recalls how at that time

> everything around was like a scorched planet. Many people were starving. They couldn't stand on railway platforms, they were so hungry, so they just sat on the ground. Everywhere you looked people were dressed in rags. But people thought, even at that time, 'It's miserable now, but in time Japan will get back on its feet again, not through military power, but by new technology and economic power.'

Very quickly this view came to be shared by all those in high positions in the so-called 'iron triangle' of conservative politicians, career bureaucrats and big business which collectively came to rule post-war Japan. There would be many territorial battles among members of this élite group but, apart from a few maverick politicians and a fringe of right-wing activists, all the open advocates of Japan's wartime aims quickly faded from sight. Reconstruction and recovery were the common goals of the élite, and for them it was essential to maintain their economic and social control through parliament, bureaucracy and industry associations. General MacArthur's Occupation staff were too few and too overwhelmed by the size of the task to try to implement detailed economic policies themselves. One senior Occupation figure, Justin Williams of the Government Section, complained that the conservative forces 'resisted anything that was a change. It had been done this way in Japan for generations and they would keep it that way because it worked.'

From the mid-1950s the government laid down the overall economic targets for the nation in a succession of five- or six-year plans, which were frequently updated in mid-term. The aims of the first of these, the 'Five-year Plan for Economic Self-sufficiency' issued in 1955, were to achieve economic independence through a balance in overseas trade and an end to American subsidies, and to come as close as possible to full employment. This meant modernising Japan's production facilities, reducing the dependence on imports, boosting exports and encouraging household savings. Thereafter Japanese industrial planners and business firms proceeded by careful, overlapping stages to raise the scope and technical level of the nation's industry, sector by sector. The government set the investment and growth targets and provided incentives. Competition among commercial firms within Japan was intense, and honed them well for the coming contest in foreign markets. At the same time the Japanese home market was kept closed, or at best unwelcoming, to outsiders. The evidence is that Japanese industrialists and government planners were repeatedly surprised at how quickly they took over the lead from companies in the West.

In 1945 the USA held the undisputed title of world leader, in military and economic matters. From that position the Americans helped to set Japan on the path to become a great economic power. They gave aid and support, and resisted all temptation to take revenge on Japan by gutting its industries. It was a policy of enlightened self-interest: the overriding concern in Washington was to keep Japan on side in the Great Game versus the communist world.

At the end of the war there was strong feeling among some of Japan's former enemies that the country should not be allowed to rebuild its industries. Under pressure from Australia and many Asian nations, the Americans drew up a plan which, if carried out, would have disabled Japan industrially for many years: it was that Japan should be made to pay for its wartime actions with a massive programme of reparations to the countries it had invaded or fought against. At first the Americans set out to see this through. In the early months of the Occupation they not only destroyed ammunition dumps and scrapped guns and tanks, but also closed down hundreds of factories making arms as well as strategic products like iron and ballbearings. Shukichi Fukagawa, a leading radar researcher, describes what happened when a group of Americans visited his factory and demanded to see the equipment: 'They were very impressed with it, but they told us to stop all our experiments. Everything was put out in a field and they blew it up.'

In October 1945 a mission was sent to Japan from America to organise the reparations programme. Its head, Edwin Pauley, based his plans on the ideas that Japan had prepared for war in China and elsewhere by building up an 'overexpanded industrial economy' and that in 1945 it still had more industrial capacity than it needed for a purely civilian economy. He recommended that 1000 factories, including whole electricity-generating plants, shipyards and steelworks, should be dismantled and shipped out to other countries in the Asia–Pacific region. At one section of Japan's biggest steel complex, the Yawata plant in the south-west, every piece of equipment was catalogued and had a number painted on it in white, ready to be taken away. It never was, and Yawata Steel (later incorporated in Nippon Steel) survived to become one of the powerhouses of Japan's industrial recovery.

Many Occupation officials thought the reparations programme misguided and impractical. Sherwood Fine of GHQ's Economic and Scientific Section derided the plans for stripping Japan of its industrial capacity at great expense while Japan itself was, in his words, 'destitute, short of virtually all essential industrial raw materials and painfully short of food'. There seemed to be another powerful argument against the reparations programme: that it might drive Japan to a communist revolution. That possibility seemed real enough in the months leading up to the abortive general strike of 1947. The Japanese officials in the Central Liaison Office did all they could to foil the reparations plans. A few shipments were made, including one of machine tools to China, but the main part of the programme died on the drawing board.

That went down badly in some quarters. The *Manchester Guardian* commented sarcastically that each time the American Reparations Commission visited Japan its plans were scaled down: 'The next time the Commission comes to Japan, I suspect they may recommend that reparations ought to be paid to Japan!' After the San Francisco peace treaty, Japan agreed to settle the outstanding claims for war damage with several Asian states, including Indonesia and the Philippines. That was the start of a massive programme of aid and investment which gave Japan a key role in building much of the industrial infrastructure for those countries. It supplied hydroelectric plants, irrigation and transport systems, and eventually telephone networks across Asia, with mixed government and private-sector funds. The reparations programme helped to produce Japan's first export boom within twenty years of independence.

Ironically, in the early post-war years Japan caused the USA great anxiety because its industries were so weak. American experts were appalled at the shortage of vital raw materials, poor conditions and shoddy management at the factories they visited. Japan's chronic balance of payments deficit meant that the USA had to pump about $2 billion into sustaining the rickety Japanese economy. In 1950 Japan had a large deficit in trade with America, and its exports represented only 1 per cent of all the USA's imports in that year.

The British Commonwealth saw things very differently. Its members wanted compensation for the immense cost of the war it had fought against Japan. In 1945 Britain still governed India, Malaya, Singapore, Hong Kong, Borneo and Brunei, and was seeking to re-establish its influence in other parts of the Far East. France and The Netherlands had similar interests elsewhere in Asia. Until the war, the British finance houses, traders and shippers had been the main link in trade between the East and the West. Now Britain feared that a strong Japan would supplant it in that role. It also feared a repeat of what many had seen as Japanese dumping and other unscrupulous trade practices before the war.

The Americans had little sympathy for the colonial ambitions of the

European powers, and were protective towards Japan. They vetoed proposals by Britain, Australia and other countries to confiscate Japan's gold reserves and impose severe restrictions on its global exports. They poured money and know-how into Japan to put its industries on their feet, and the USA's rich and open market became a magnet for Japanese exports as they grew in volume. The Americans also laid the social foundations for Japan's economic life by doing what the Japanese had been unable to do for themselves: freeing the country from the stranglehold of hereditary wealth. The Occupation was a great leveller. The land reforms had overturned the absentee land-owner class, distributed wealth more equitably and released the energies of millions who had worked on the land for a pittance. They headed for the cities to swell the ranks of the urban workforce. In 1950 one out of every two Japanese gained his livelihood from farming, fisheries or forestry; by 1960 the proportion was down to one in three; in 1985 it was one in ten. A generation after the war, Japan could lay claim to being the most egalitarian society of its size in the world.

In 1945 the prospects for Japan could hardly have looked more dismal. Seven million soldiers were suddenly demobilised, and 3 million were returning to Japan after surrendering at various points across the former empire. With the closure of arms factories and the repatriation of colonists from overseas, some 13 million Japanese were out of work. People flocked back to the cities from the countryside, where they had been evacuated, to find their homes and neighbourhoods flattened. Western witnesses were strongly impressed by the stoicism and energy of ordinary Japanese people. In December 1946 the American journalist Mark Gayn wrote:

> Tokyo constantly amazes me. It was a year ago that the Ginza [Tokyo's main commercial district] was nothing but a succession of brick skeletons, spaced apart by lots filled with rubble. Now the department stores have been repaired, and shops have been erected in the empty lots. ... The big industries may stand idle, but the artisans are busy.

In the early months of the Occupation, when hunger was commonplace, there were frequent demonstrations to demand the basic necessities of life – food, clothing and shelter – and popular resentment at the poor standard of living fuelled strikes in the major industries off and on throughout the Occupation. Yoshida's Finance Minister, Hayato Ikeda, aroused popular indignation when, on being asked what the poor should do if they did not have enough rice to eat, he replied: 'They can eat barley!'

Japan's industrial capacity was by no means knocked out by the war, despite the devastation to the cities and the vast number of casualties.

More than half the country's factories remained undamaged. Raw cotton was imported in bulk from America and mills which had struggled to turn out goods only to meet military orders now came back to life. However, many of them stood idle because of the lack of power and raw materials. Industrial production during the year after the surrender was barely one-tenth what it had been ten years earlier.

Coal production had fallen to only half a million tons a month, more then half of which was set aside to meet household needs. MacArthur had repatriated over 100 000 Koreans forcibly brought to Japan to work in the mines and factories, so labour was desperately short; and there were frequent stoppages over demands by the newly formed miners' unions for better wages and conditions. Miners were given special food rations; but what really got the coal moving again was a system of 'priority production'. This meant pouring American aid money and Japanese tax revenues into the coal industry through a specially created government bank, the Reconstruction Finance Bank. Private firms owned the pits, but the government oversaw the industry closely. Coal output rose sharply.

In due course iron, steel and chemical fertilisers were also categorised as priority industries. This system gave the government powers comparable to those it had wielded from 1938 onwards to mobilise industry, as Japan had gone to war with China and prepared for the wider conflict across the Pacific. The wartime government had virtually extinguished the 'peace' industries – all those not contributing directly to the war effort. That meant that the Japanese civilian population had suffered severe deprivation from hunger and lack of basic amenities during the war years. Similarly, after the war, the government's targets for industry brought much hardship to the Japanese people as a whole through rigged pricing and continuing shortages of basic food and goods. The pattern of Japan's post-war economic growth – favouring heavy rather than light industry and output at the expense of living conditions – was set in the Occupation and remained distinctive features of the Japanese economy afterwards. To paraphrase MITI's Naohiro Amaya, Japan would remain essentially a 'command economy' until about 1960. In this sense the end of the war was not really a turning-point in Japan's economic management; the methods employed were similar to those used for an economy waging war.

As successive Japanese governments opted for a policy of maximising production, and distributed funds lavishly, inflation was allowed to soar. In the seven years of the Occupation wholesale and retail prices both rose by no less than 100 times. The first wave of extravagance took the form of settling outstanding war debts to industry and making army pension payments. Then the government opted consciously to court inflation by pouring all available money into its chosen industries with the aim of getting back to pre-war production levels. Social welfare was a low priority. As in the pre-war years, the social infrastructure, including roads, drains and sewers, was largely overlooked. Half a century later Japanese governments are still grappling with the need to build an adequate network of roads, affordable housing and public sanitation.

Central government control of the country's banks and financial institutions was perhaps the single greatest factor in the economic success story. That control was also the foundation of the government's role as overlord of private industry, which lasted for at least two decades after the surrender. Even in the 1990s its legacy is still strongly felt. Japanese political and bureaucratic leaders were determined not to let Japan rely on the outside world for capital. In the early post-war years the government was overwhelmingly the main source of funds for industry. The Finance Ministry also had sweeping discretionary powers to give or withhold funds to industry, and so maintained a pivotal status within the government.

The Reconstruction Finance Bank had been created in 1947, despite American reservations, with the specific aim of stimulating key industries to regain pre-war levels of output. It was stopped from further lending as part of the 'Dodge Line' – the harsh package of deflationary measures ordered by MacArthur's special adviser, Joseph Dodge, to bring wages, prices and the supply of credit under control. But in 1950 the Americans permitted the formation of an Export Bank, using government funds to stimulate exports of capital goods to support industry and earn much-needed foreign exchange (two years later it was renamed the Export–Import Bank and began also to finance raw-material imports). In 1951 the Japan Development Bank was created to finance industry from public funds.

America supplied a large part of the funds which initially got Japan back on its feet, channelled through the Japan Development Bank and the Export–Import Bank. This aid was supplemented by Japanese government revenues, both from taxes and from the gambling monopolies in horse racing, bicycle racing and national lotteries, which accounted in 1960 for 10 per cent of all the government's revenues. The allocation by MITI of a large part of the government's budget gave it a hands-on control over the economy unrivalled within the government. Yoshihiko Morozumi reached the pinnacle of his career in the much-coveted post of top MITI official, Administrative Vice-minister, in the 1970s. He and his colleagues saw themselves as undertaking a huge responsibility on behalf of the whole country: 'It was up to us', he says, 'to allocate resources, capital and foreign technology, and we made sure that all these were concentrated in several selected and preferred industries.' Morozumi was part of an élite which saw itself as defending something precious beyond compare: the good of Japan in a difficult and dangerous world. 'I worked for my country, and was keenly aware of the national interest,' he says, 'and that was part of the joy of working. Our own interest was much less important.' Morozumi was later appointed president of the important Electric Power Development Corporation, in keeping with the convention that senior bureaucrats take up a lucrative second career after their government days are over.

As part of the industrial policy, rules on commercial lending were deliberately made loose and Japanese companies have regularly borrowed two or three times more from the banks than they have raised from equity flotations. In times of extreme need the leveraging could be much higher even than that. In motorcycles, Honda's strategy in the 1950s was to expand capacity aggressively on borrowed money, flooding the market with new models and leaving its main domestic rival, Tohatsu, standing. The resulting economy of scale in a fast-growing market was decisive, and Tohatsu went bankrupt in 1964. Similar power relationships were evolving around the world. In hundreds of cases Japanese firms were the winners; among the heaviest losers were American and European makers of cameras, watches, electronic goods, motorcycles and cars.

In the early 1950s coal supplied the basis for the large-scale push into heavy industry, especially steel, chemicals and shipbuilding; and from the latter half of the decade a number of new industries, including cars and machine tools, were picked as targets for concerted investment and growth. Special laws were passed to support the development of the Japanese car and electronics industries. Thus by the 1950s the system was in place whereby the government decided on the key industrial sectors and fostered them with subsidies, and where necessary also with protection, until they became strong.

While the political reforms of the Occupation at least changed the constitution and the structure of government, the drive to mould a free-market economy on the Western model was largely a failure. Most of the Japanese civil servants responsible for the economy escaped the purges and then resisted reforms aimed at 'democratising' the economy. The bureaucrats thrived on Japan's tradition of mandarin government. They remained a governing class whose authority could not readily be questioned by others. MacArthur's men, having agreed to allow Occupation policies to be carried out through the Japanese

government's administrative machine, were in practice bound to work
with the officials around them, rather than treating them as one of the
targets of reform. The entrenched power of the officials excited the
suspicion of some contemporary observers. An American political
scientist, John Maki, wrote in 1947:

> If any single organized group in Japan today possesses the power to prevent
> the creation of a peaceful, responsible form of government in that country,
> it is the bureaucracy. More than any other organized group in contemporary
> Japan it is rooted in Japan's pre-surrender past.

John Maki reached the conclusion that the bureaucrats were heirs
to a long and unchanging Japanese tradition of 'irresponsible
government'. He wrote that 'In every period of Japanese history
government was based on the principle of government of, by, and for
the governing groups whether court nobility, feudal lords, or the
modern militarist-zaibatsu-bureaucrat oligarchy.' In the post-war
years the military had been deeply discredited, but the *zaibatsu* and
the bureaucrats kept their prestige and their powerful influence over
society. They engineered a wide-ranging consensus for fast growth at
the expense of everything else, and they crudely promoted Japan's
national interests in the economic sphere.

Continuity was maintained not only in the policies but in the people.
Many of Japan's economic leaders after the defeat were the very men
who had led during the years of war. The man who would be Prime
Minister from 1957 to 1960, Nobusuke Kishi, had supervised the
development of Manchuria in the 1930s, and helped to found Japan's
New Economic Order in Asia. Kogoro Uemura, one of the top civilian
planners of the war effort, became head of the powerful Keidanren,
the Federation of Economic Organisations, and played a key part in
the birth of the grand conservative alliance, the Liberal Democratic
Party, in the 1950s. The LDP's dominance was a guarantee that the
government would not stray from pro-business policies. Yoshihiro
Inayama was another influential figure in pre-war industrial planning
who became the head of Yawata Steel and was president of the Keidanren at the time of his death in 1981. Indeed the senior men in MITI
in the 1950s and 1960s all had their bureaucratic training in MITI's
precursor, the Ministry of Commerce and Industry, during the years
of Japan's military expansion into Asia.

The survival of independent bureaucratic authority was central to
the way that Japan set its priorities in the years after the Occupation
ended. In practice officials in the key ministries, especially those in
charge of justice, finance, industry and home affairs (in charge of the
police), kept wide-ranging powers and remained largely self-directing.

Politicians did not, as in other parliamentary democratic systems, take over open responsibility for policies. Bureaucrats continued to draft laws on their own initiative, and the Diet usually passed them with little scrutiny of the contents, once the wishes of special-interest groups had been satisfied. The system has endured to the present day: each year, when the national budget for the government's planned revenues and expenditure is drafted, there is a long-drawn-out haggle between the spending ministries and the Finance Ministry which has to square the books. The resulting budget generally reflects the power of the various spending departments and their sponsors or allies.

The Allies ruled that the big firms that had controlled a large part of the economy bore a heavy responsibility for driving Japan towards war and that they must be dissolved. The *zaibatsu* had been partners of the military in colonising Korea, Manchuria and parts of China. Nissan became a partner of the puppet government which the Japanese military set up in Manchuria. Mitsui put up much of the capital for the construction of the South Manchurian railway, as part of the policy of colonial development. All the industrial groups had helped actively to promote Japan's 'New Order in Greater East Asia'. During the Occupation the old practice of forcing employees to swear loyalty oaths to the family owners of the big firms was seen as sinister and feudalistic. It was decided in principle that 'excessive concentrations' of economic control should be broken up.

Technically, the centres of the suspect groupings were holding companies, around which there were scores of enterprises active in manufacturing, trading and finance. Altogether there were more than a dozen groups known popularly as *zaibatsu*, but the four biggest – Mitsui, Mitsubishi, Sumitomo and Yasuda – stood out by their size and the great range of their activities. Together they accounted for a quarter of all Japan's economic output, including half of all the banking and machinery manufacture and 60 per cent of all shipping. Mitsui was the largest of all, a vast network of interests run by eleven different branches of the same family. Hideo Edo, an executive of Mitsui, described the shock when the Americans made good their threat and took away all the family shares in the holding company from the safe at Mitsui's headquarters; he described it as like 'water in a sleeping man's ear' – the Japanese equivalent of 'a bolt from the blue'.

The four principal groupings all had their holding companies liquidated; and about fifty other companies were dissolved or reorganised. Mitsubishi Trading Company, like some other giants of the war years, was treated as a showcase: that one firm was divided into 180 different units, and they were obliged to compete against one another for business. But further US plans for dismembering the large firms were quietly forgotten. The attempt to undo *zaibatsu* power was much weakened by fierce attacks by right-wing politicians in the US decrying the weakness of Japanese industry in the face of the communist threat. In practice the old *zaibatsu* companies regrouped in the early 1950s and built new business empires; but the reforms also cleared the way for self-made entrepreneurs to contribute to the economy.

Shigeru Yoshida, the long-serving Prime Minister, was firmly set against the dissolution plans because of the damage he believed it would do to Japan's hopes of recovery. He and other leading politicians had no wish, either, to alienate those who were the most important source of their political funds. Already in the early post-war days, being elected to the Diet was an expensive business. Important firms all contributed to the coffers of particular factions and their leaders as well as to the major conservative parties, in the expectation of future advantage. The Americans were constrained in their anti-*zaibatsu* campaign by the desire not to undermine politicians, such as Prime Minister Yoshida, who could be counted on to maintain a pro-American line.

American proposals for an Anti-Monopoly Law were also strongly resisted, but in 1947 legislation was passed to ban holding companies and outlaw unfair competition. Its spirit was bypassed from the start, and in order to get higher production the Americans themselves actually encouraged the formation of numerous cartels. After the Occupation the majority of the old companies reformed over a period of years. When they did so, it was around the so-called 'core bank' of each business group instead of around private family holdings. The bosses from now on would mostly be professional administrators, engineers and technocrats. The new system was of *keiretsu*, meaning 'business groupings', and was far more efficient than the family-dominated system it had replaced. Now each of the major industrial groupings not only had a bank and other financial institutions at the centre, but an arm covering every major field of manufacturing and service activity. Eventually the areas embraced by the system grew to include a score of industries, including metals, cars, electronics, chemicals and machine tools. The *keiretsu* structure made it possible for a company or group of companies to conceive, design, manufacture, obtain parts for, distribute and sell a new product using its own or allied resources: a concept of 'integrated manufacture' without parallel in any major Western economy. Large and small firms within a grouping shared capital, technical know-how, office buildings, sports grounds and even staff. In the 1970s and 1980s the firms within the *keiretsu* groupings were in control of a quarter of the Japanese economy, the same proportion as the *zaibatsu* controlled in the pre-war period.

48

The Americans presided, in part unwittingly, over the formation of what was in effect a peacetime 'high command' of the Japanese economy. In spite of the early American determination to do away with everything and everyone associated with Japan's wartime expansionism, the country's post-war economic revival was planned and executed using the same central control over the nation's resources as had been used in prosecuting the war. At the heart of this operation was the wartime Munitions Ministry, which after the war reverted to the title of the Ministry of Commerce, and in 1949 adopted its present name, the Ministry of International Trade and Industry. MITI officials acted not only with the discipline of military officers in their own sphere; they also sometimes had the power to let firms prosper or die by determining whether they could acquire a new licence or build a factory. The ministry had sweeping responsibilities for industrial planning, financing, enforcing mergers, setting production quotas and rationing foreign exchange, as well as buying in new technology and allocating it to particular firms.

The laws were framed to give the government control over private industry in the allocation of foreign exchange for imports. They also virtually ruled out direct foreign investment. The American scholar Leon Hollerman said the Occupation-imposed controls resulted in 'the most restrictive foreign trade and foreign exchange controls ever devised by a major free nation'. Naohiro Amaya of MITI reinforces the point:

> Ironically speaking, General MacArthur and the Occupation forces did quite a lot for Japan having the industrial policy. For example, the Occupation forces gave to the Japanese government the Foreign Exchange and Foreign Trade Control Law, which has been the major source of power given to MITI for the implementation of the industrial policy.

In addition, wanting to give Japan every help to become a self-sufficient and useful partner of the USA, the Occupation laid the framework for Japan's economy to be highly protected. Industrial tariffs were set at levels which were among the world's highest. The goal of making sure Japan could pay its way resulted in the creation of dynamic industries which were strongly export-oriented.

As the economy grew, the planners depended more on the efficient flow of funds from the household sector to industry. This was achieved by a policy of encouraging high savings. Consumer borrowing was penalised by taxing interest payments; but interest income from savings accounts was made tax free. Japan's credit allocation policies were strongly biased against consumers. Consumer credit was so scarce that a vast, largely unregulated money-lending industry sprang up, thriving on interest charges as high as 10 per cent a month. Japanese gangsters, known as *yakuza,* made sure the money appeared when lenders decided it was time to be paid. There was no real welfare system in case of sickness or redundancy, and state pensions were quite inadequate to live on; so households had to save a substantial part of their income.

The most favourable rates were offered by the Post Office savings system, and in time the Japanese Post Office became the largest bank in the world. The massive fund – over 7 trillion yen ($28 billion) in 1970 – went into a 'second national budget', called the Fiscal Investment and Loan Programme, a key element in Japan's policy for industry. The FILP was about half as big as the 'first budget', derived from regular tax revenues and the like, and the money could be spent, largely at MITI's discretion, on projects judged to be in the national interest. They included heavy industry, support for uncompetitive small businesses and subsidies for traditional features of Japanese community life, such as public bath-houses. The FILP funds were channelled through the Japan Development Bank to the preferred industries and through the Export–Import Bank in order to finance exports of capital goods and imports of raw materials. The government also gave active support to the three long-term credit banks as sources of funds for industry. The most important was the Industrial Bank of Japan, which before and during the war had been directly under government control.

The role of the central bank, the Bank of Japan, was vital. Its main instrument of control over the commercial banking sector was its power to set rates of interest. Each month the Bank of Japan set the credit ceiling of every high-street bank, controlling interest rates by informal 'administrative guidance', and vetted the banks' programmes of loans and investment. In return, the central bank implicitly guaranteed the loan positions of all Japan's main private financial institutions, and they were enabled to overlend recklessly by the standards of the rest of the world. In some extreme cases, banks possessed funds to cover only 2 or 3 per cent of their lending. Some observers saw the role of Japanese commercial banks in the early 1950s as little more than a channel through which the central bank fed industry with investment funds. The Bank of Japan was nominally independent of the Finance Ministry, but in practice it was obliged to accept the ministry's directions and often had to agree to an official from the ministry being made its governor.

In the early post-war years, however, it was not at all clear that the new industries would ever stand on their own feet. Even large firms such as the Nissan Motor Company reached the verge of bankruptcy.

Sometimes on the weekly pay-day there simply was not enough cash to go round. Japan still represented poor workmanship and quality. Homer Sarasohn, who went from Western Electric to inspire managers in Japan with the new creed of efficiency, recalls that at the time 'If the legend "Made in Japan" was stamped on the bottom of a product you *knew* it was shoddy merchandise!' The Americans saw it as their mission to show the Japanese how to become good managers. Sarasohn himself doubted how much could be done in a short time. He found that thanks to the 'feudal background' in Japanese factories, the man in power would speak only to the person directly below him in the chain of authority. The Americans brought their ideas of management as a science, calling for a rational division of responsibility, training and the right tools. They introduced a concept that had been developed in America's war factories and was destined to be adopted by the Japanese as their very own speciality: quality control.

One American expert in that field, W. E. Deming, became a legend in Japan. He gave hundreds of lectures – many, he recalls, in non-air-conditioned rooms in the torrid summer heat – to eager managers on the vital importance of statistical quality control. Factory managers, he said, should be on the factory floor, not out of sight in a smart office. 'Deming's Wheel', a diagram rationalising the business of production management, was circulated widely. Deming himself treated his wards like promising schoolboys and was always confident of success for Japanese industry because he found his pupils so attentive and quick to learn. Later he would boast: 'I think I was the only man in Japan that believed my prediction in 1950 that within five years manufacturers all over [the world] would be screaming for protection: I think it took four!' Deming's almost boyish dedication and his loyalty to his close Japanese followers made him something of an idol. Among his pupils were many who were to become captains of Japanese industry in the 1960s and 1970s, heading firms like Nissan, Sharp and Nippon Electric Company (NEC). The annual Deming Prize for good management was highly coveted in the 1950s, and is still being awarded today. Deming was never so honoured in his own country.

The Korean War transformed the prospects for the Japanese economy: Shigeru Yoshida called it 'a gift from the gods'. The Korean peninsula lies 9000 miles from the west coast of the USA; but at its closest point it is just over 100 miles across the sea from Japan. When in June 1950 North Korean T-34 tanks rolled across the United Nations partition line into South Korea it quickly became clear that the bulk of the war material and general provisions needed on the American and UN side would have to come from Japan. The old Imperial Army's arsenal, in a huge cave in the hills south of Tokyo, was one of more than 1000 munitions plants reopened on American orders. They were put to work at once, filling fresh orders for guns, mines, flares and all the other necessities of war. The Americans also needed building materials – cement, iron and steel – textiles and army lorries. The Yawata Steel plant in western Japan was the closest to Korea and work went on around the clock. There was continuous competition among the workers at its different blast furnaces to produce more steel for the rails, bridge girders, fences and other requirements. Shigeo Hosoki, who built up the strip-mill capacity at Yawata in response to the large-scale American orders, was only too glad:

> Before I went to the Yawata plant I was in a plant where production was almost at a standstill, and I thought it was much better to be asked to do the impossible. I thought there was nothing so hard for a human being as to have no work.

Many companies which had been struggling for survival sprang to life again. Toyota, for example, was making only 300 lorries a month in the early part of 1950; but with the special procurement orders that figure leapt to over 1500 by the spring of 1951. The company's president at the time, Shotaro Kamiya, described these as 'Toyota's salvation'. He added: 'I felt a mixture of joy for my company and a sense of guilt that I was rejoicing over another country's war.' The government's top economist at the time, Hidezo Inaba, remembers how military procurements amounted to $600 million per year: 'That injection of funds gave us the foreign exchange so that we could import; and the economy started to come into balance ... the Korean War gave Japan its first opportunity, by the hand of fate, to recover.'

In 1952, following the signing of the San Francisco peace treaty, Japan was again an independent country. Once the Occupation forces had gone, overall foreign participation in the Japanese economy was small. Direct foreign investment was very severely restricted. Foreign lawyers were banned from practising. Imports of manufactured goods were limited by quotas and high tariffs, and there was little incentive even for large Western firms to keep offices in Tokyo. The climate of regulation, combined with the language and other cultural barriers, discouraged Western businessmen from setting up new operations in the Japanese market, and other Asian countries could only dream of it. Apart from the injection of capital and technology, Japan's economic planners strove consciously to keep foreigners from playing a large role in the domestic economy.

As the Korean War wound down, with the opposing sides entrenched in positions approximately where they had begun in 1950, the

Japanese economy went into recession. With the windfall American military orders gone, Japan had to rely on strong growth at home to build up industry, but its factories were old and worn out. The answer of the industrial planners in MITI was the same as in the critical years of the late 1940s – to go all out for growth, concentrating on the 'strategic' industries of steel and chemicals which would stimulate others. The strategy paid off quickly. Demand picked up again dramatically in 1955–6; the upturn in the economy generally was nicknamed the 'Jimmu Boom' after Japan's first, mythical, Emperor. In 1956 a government white paper on the economy proclaimed that the 'post-war period' was over, because industrial output had again reached its high pre-war level.

After independence, the Japanese government undid the remaining parts of the Occupation structure which interfered with its own plans for the economy. It passed new laws authorising MITI to create cartels among small businesses as exceptions to the Anti-Monopoly Law. By the 1980s the Fair Trade Commission, supposedly a watchdog, had smiled on the formation at various times of some 2000 cartels because they were legally authorised. MITI reorganised itself to ensure that the scope of its various departments exactly matched the various industrial and commercial sectors in the economy. It created a series of deliberative councils on what was called the 'rationalisation' of industry, which in time became the forum for comprehensive planning of goals for the economy. Major manufacturers and trading firms were under strong pressure to take their place in the *keiretsu* structure or risk going under; and MITI cut down the number of general trading firms, from over 100 to about 20. The complex of government-backed banks and laws to allow the state direction of industry was completed with the setting up of the Japan External Trade Organisation (JETRO) to be what one writer called 'an international commercial intelligence service'.

Gradually six giant conglomerates emerged around the big commercial banks: Mitsui, Mitsubishi, Sumitomo, Dai-ichi Kangyo, Sanwa and Fuji. Cross-holdings of stocks among member companies of the same *keiretsu* made them all practically immune from outsiders' attempts to take them over. Also, the system helped to ensure that, although the number of contestants in the marketplace was generally regulated, there was usually strong rivalry among several firms in every sector. This system of 'competitive oligopoly' became a major factor in keeping the leading Japanese businesses internationally competitive.

The Americans left Japan with the management of what outsiders quickly dubbed 'Japan Inc.' already in place. Ordinary shareholders had scarcely any idea of what it meant to exercise their rights. Law and custom ensured anyway that they had little chance to challenge or even to have detailed information about the activities of publicly listed companies. Japanese standards of financial accounting and reporting have always been loose. Many companies have no outside directors, and rely for capital less on equity than on bank loans. This encourages firms to put capital appreciation of the company's stock above shareholders' dividends. The habitual secrecy of Japanese firms was an important reason why the disturbing pollution cases of the 1960s were able to develop into such horror stories without public outcry.

It could also be dangerous openly to challenge this nexus of corporate self-interest. Gangsters would regularly act as sanctioned lawbreakers, extorting money from companies under the threat of exposing embarrassing facts during their annual general meetings. Once terms were agreed, these 'specialist' gangsters ('shareholders'-meeting specialists' or *sokaiya*) would scare the shareholders into silence and the meetings would be over very quickly. That practice, which today has been contained but not stopped, is one way in which the rule of law has been undermined. Powerful economic concerns have on occasion allied themselves with members of the criminal underworld, while law and order stand aside.

Consumer groups were co-opted by the business establishment and it took them years to pluck up any courage to criticise openly either the government or big business. Price- and quota-fixing among firms became common and had the approval of officials: government permission was regularly needed for commercial business decisions.

In parallel to the policy of high spending on industry went a calculated programme of importing technology, using precious foreign exchange for the areas which seemed the most promising. In 1950 MITI had published a shopping-list of the strategic technologies it was after, and over the next fifteen years Japanese firms acquired almost all the licences needed, although some contracts limited their right to export the finished products for a period of several years afterwards. In almost every case the attitude of Western companies and governments was open to the Japanese approach. The rights to nylon were bought from the US firm DuPont, allowing the textile industry to move from cotton into synthetics. The plastics and petrochemical industries were built up with technology licensed from ICI, Dow Chemical and others. Know-how in machine tools, electronics and aviation was bought from North America and Europe. In total, it is estimated that Japan paid only about $10 billion between 1950 and 1980 to acquire all the foreign technology it needed. The government itself determined which firms would have the benefit of the imported technology, so strengthening the sense of obligation between officials and businessmen.

Even the co-ordinated industrial policy and supply of funds for industry might have failed to produce sustained results without good industrial relations. The taming of union power, in the course of a decade and a half of protracted conflict, was a crucial element in forming the character of post-war Japan. For the most part, working people looked on their company as a means of survival, and strong 'company loyalty' was a direct result of employers' banding together to prevent movement between companies. At the end of the Occupation Japan's resurgent left-wing labour unions were already much weakened from the 'red purge' and the joint effort of government and industrialists to discredit left-wing labour leaders. All public employees, including railway- and power-workers, were banned by law from taking industrial action. That did not stop them from staging 'strikes for the right to strike', but it was rare for services to be seriously disrupted.

In the period from the late 1940s to the mid-1950s there was a succession of strikes in key industries, including coal, electric power, steel and cars. At first the newly formed and active industrial federations took the lead, mobilising workers in whole industries for better pay and conditions. Their power was formidable, and in some cases their leaders were influenced by Marxist ideas of proletarian revolution and workers' control of the means of production. Ordinary workers were impelled by the desire to improve their meagre wages, and many were also fired by the idea that in the 'new Japan' the old guard who had run industry when Japan was at war should not be allowed to regain control.

The nationwide mood of confrontation came to a head in the strike at Nissan. In the summer of 1953 the national car-workers' union federation, Zenji-roren, took on three car firms in a battle over wages and managerial control. When the union's Nissan branch called an indefinite strike, the company was prepared. There was a series of pitched battles at the plant and outside between union activists and the police, helped by hired toughs. Both sides knew that the outcome would be important for the fate of the whole union movement. For three months production was halted as the tense confrontation continued. The Zenji-roren staged rallies with thousands of angry Nissan workers. Meanwhile, the employers' organisation, Nikkeiren, arranged a massive bank loan, and extracted agreements from Toyota and other rival companies not to poach Nissan's market share while the dispute continued. There was more solidarity and far more muscle among the companies than among Japanese car-workers. Nissan's management seized the initiative, locking the workers out of the plant and barricading themselves in.

At the same time the company backed the formation of a new union, made up only of Nissan workers. Its slogan was 'Those who truly love their union love their company.' During one fracas at the factory the leader of the militant union was arrested, and the new in-house union gradually converted all the employees to its side. Since that time Nissan has never lost a single day's output at any of its domestic plants through strikes. Nobutake Shikanai, leader of Nikkeiren who co-ordinated the tactics of the nation's top managers through the Nissan strike as well as others, has no doubt about the importance of that one victory: 'If the management side had lost,' he says, 'then in Nissan and elsewhere the communist-led unions would have had a big say in the running of the country, and Japan would have lived in misery.' As it was, he considers that the bruising experience of confrontation laid the foundations for Japan's later economic success. He describes the violent labour disputes of the early post-war years as 'like an infectious disease which, once contracted and survived, leaves the individual stronger and immune from the disease. Today's success was achieved only by the blood, sweat and tears that were shed on both sides in those years.' It was a monumental victory for the management side. The industry-wide car-workers' union was broken.

Strikes similar to the one at Nissan occurred at Toyota and other motor firms as well as in other major industries. In 1960 another turning-point came in the coal industry, where a number of pits were being closed. At the Mitsui coal mine at Miike in Kyushu, a severe dispute went on for almost the whole year. The strikers held out with support from the local community, demanding the reinstatement of dismissed workers, until eventually the company called in the police and local gangsters. They stormed the yard where hundreds of miners were gathered, beat them with wooden staves and drove them out. The union was crushed.

Coal was declining, but steel was the centrepiece of the country's drive to succeed in heavy industry. A series of disputes and strikes in the industry in the late 1950s led to the eclipse of militancy among the steel unions. The company unions of the leading steel firms became co-operative with management. They joined those of the main heavy-industry and car companies to form a new umbrella organisation, the International Metalworkers' Federation Japan Council. The IMF-JC negotiated directly with the management side each year during the wage-bargaining season and hammered out an overall level of wage rises in the leading sectors of industry. The wage settlement came to be based on the prevailing levels of inflation and productivity. Not only did the militant labour movement go into a long-term decline; organised labour faded from the scene as a dynamic force. For a quarter of a century from 1964, no Japanese prime minister deigned to meet a labour leader during the *shunto,* annual spring wage 'offensive', season.

On the factory floor and in offices conflict was gradually ironed out as Japan's prosperity took hold. Union–management battles continued sporadically through the 1950s, but in an age of high growth – averaging more than 10 per cent per year – larger enterprises were able to satisfy most of the unions' demands. Smaller companies discouraged employees from joining unions. Union membership reached its peak at about 40 per cent of the workforce in the mid-1950s and then declined. Today more than half of Japan's workforce has never belonged to a union. By the 1960s the majority of company unions were docile, company-organised affairs, where labour and management generally saw themselves as being on the same side, intent on producing prosperity for their companies. During the annual spring and autumn wage offensives, the unions would put up a great show of presenting hardline demands to management on wage levels and fringe benefits; in practice disruption of output was usually minimal. In the early 1970s an American scholar, James Abegglen, calculated that 'the direct cost of strikes in Japan in recent years has been about one-seventieth the cost of strikes in the United States'.

In the public sector the Japan General Council of Trade Unions, Sohyo, combined some of the most militant unions in the country, such as teachers, railwaymen and municipal workers, and allied itself closely with the Socialist Party. Sohyo would play a leading role in left-wing political and social movements for several decades, and would remain the most militant part of the labour movement; but, under the American-inspired laws, public workers were legally banned from striking. Although its members did stage regular strikes for the right to strike, bringing chaos to Tokyo's transport system in spring year after year, Sohyo, like the Socialists, stayed limited in its influence.

Thereafter the net gradually closed in on the freely-formed unions and they were replaced almost everywhere by 'enterprise unions' which were generally co-operative towards management. The trend was encouraged by the companies themselves but union leaders were also comfortable with this pattern of organisation, as it allowed white- and blue-collar workers in the same firm to bargain together for wage rises. In practice there were many other advantages, too, as the larger companies, in exchange for industrial peace, offered their employees housing and a whole range of social benefits that were not to be had from the state. In most enterprises capable employees could expect to join middle-management and leave the union in mid-career. Leading firms stressed loyalty in exchange for lifelong benefits. That developed into a system of 'lifetime employment' which eventually all major manufacturing firms adopted for their male graduate employees. Women were almost completely excluded from the system until the 1980s, and are still effectively segregated in career terms by many employers.

MITI's industrial march was centrally planned in great detail, but carried out with flexibility. Japan's approach in long-range sectoral planning of the economy was similar to that of the socialist economies of the Eastern Bloc: the difference was that in Japan competition was fierce, even though the government took care to limit the number of players in many sectors to avoid 'excessive competition'. Private firms were strongly motivated to increase their profits and prestige, and they proved to be endlessly inventive in every aspect of manufacturing and doing business. Japanese business leaders and government officials took pride in their ability to co-operate among themselves, and many of the plans succeeded spectacularly well.

Steel, described in those days as 'the rice of industry', was at the centre of MITI's attention in the 1950s. At the start of the decade Japanese workers took seven times as long to make a ton of steel as their American counterparts did, and twice as long as steelworkers in Britain. In 1951, MITI put out its 'First Development Programme', involving the use of Japan Development Bank loans for specific steel projects, earmarking funds for the smallest details. In the early 1950s Japanese experts toured the USA by invitation to learn at first hand about modern steelmaking. At Yawata Steel the company newspaper proclaimed the ultimate goal in banner headlines: 'WE MUST BE WORLD NUMBER ONE.' MITI's own projections for output proved far too modest. In 1955 its provisional twenty-year plan foresaw a target of some 25 million tons as Japan's steel output in 1975; but already in 1972 that target had been outstripped by almost four times. By the mid-1970s, despite the narrowing of wage levels, Japan had overtaken the USA and European steel firms in productivity.

The government helped the steelmakers to achieve the economies of scale they needed to stay profitable. The 'Big Five' steelmakers rivalled one another in building brand new integrated mills, into which raw materials could be shipped, and the whole process of iron- and steelmaking was laid out for maximum efficiency. Land was short, so they looked to the sea for new territory, reclaiming land in a massive civil-engineering effort. Kawasaki Steel was the first to build out into Tokyo Bay, on land provided by the government. The work was done in such a hurry that the seawater was still being pumped away as the foundations were being laid. With help from MITI the steel firms bought up whatever technology they needed from the United States, West Germany and elsewhere. The Japanese moved quickly when they learned that a small firm in Austria, Lintz Alpine, had developed a cheaper, faster method of steelmaking using blown oxygen. Tomokatsu Kotani of Yawata Steel was a member of the Japanese delegation that visited Austria. Recalling that occasion, he reflected: 'They probably thought that Japan would not be able to master this method, and would get nowhere; but ten or twenty years later the Austrians who sold the technology probably thought they sold it to us too cheaply.'

MITI's approach to the steel industry illustrates its approach to managing and guiding industry as a whole. Ministry officials gave the orders directly in the years 1951–5, kept a tight rein on the investment money in the 'Second Modernisation Programme' in 1955–60, and from 1961 onwards they allowed the individual firms to set their own investment programmes through what was called 'voluntary adjustment'. The level of direct official involvement was progressively looser in each period, but in practice MITI's word continued to be law even when it came in the form of administrative advice or 'guidance'. How forceful MITI's non-legal sanctions could be was clear when, in 1965, Sumitomo Metal Industries, one of the lesser members of the Big Five steel firms, objected to plans for an across-the-board cut in crude-steel production for all the major producers. MITI brought Sumitomo into line at least temporarily by threatening a cut in its allocated quota of coking coal. In 1970 MITI achieved a long-standing ambition by bringing back together Yawata Steel and Fuji Steel, which SCAP had split into two in the Occupation. The new giant, Nippon Steel, was meant to be strong enough to dominate the home market and to match any competition from the West.

In shipbuilding, too, Japan's industrial planners and the leading firms set out to take first place in the world, spurred by the loss of almost all Japan's merchant fleet in the final months of the war. In the 1930s Japan had been the world's third largest shipbuilder. The atom bomb dropped on Nagasaki had been meant to destroy the port's industrial base, including the huge Mitsubishi shipyards there, but it had fallen 4 miles short and those yards had survived virtually unscathed. Around the country, many other slipways had withstood the American bombing. Straight after the war the yards were banned from producing steel-hulled ships of any kind, and were forced to turn out wooden fishing boats instead. But then in 1949 the ban was lifted, as America resolved to do whatever necessary to foster Japan as a strong ally.

When General MacArthur gave the go-ahead for Japan to set about rebuilding its merchant fleet, the country was blessed with one outstanding asset above all: a fund of trained and eager naval architects and shipbuilding engineers. Unlike Britain, the world leader in the industry, Japan trained its shipbuilders at university level; and even in the immediate post-war years the flow of trained graduates continued at a steady pace. Dr Masao Kinoshita, a naval architect who worked his way up to become president of Hitachi Shipbuilding, recalls how the young people who worked under him were obliged during the four fallow years to take jobs as tutors or lecturers wherever they could. He calls them a 'reserve army', waiting for the time when Japan could once again build large ships. When the first orders came in, the big shipyards were already preparing to update their techniques.

That they did to extraordinary effect. When it became clear that efficiency could be greatly increased by using welding rather than riveting, Japanese shipbuilders made the transition much more easily than their counterparts in Britain and other European countries. There were no craft unions to stand in the way of introducing new techniques and work practices. American help was crucial. Japanese study teams toured American and European yards to acquire skills which they then applied at home. Kure, the naval shipyard where the giant battleship *Yamato* had been built during the war, had its fortunes lifted when an American firm leased the yard to make bulk carriers cheaply. One of the managers, Masaru Nagaoka, remembers how the US firm brought over its best experts of all kinds, including welding trainers and outfitting experts, as well as all the necessary plans for building various classes of ship. The technique the Americans brought with them – called 'block construction', in which sections were welded at ground level under cover and then lifted into the building-dock when they were ready – was already revolutionising building-times for large ships. After detailed study, the Japanese took it all in and then set about making their own improvements.

Shigeichi Koga was head of the Nagasaki yard of Mitsubishi, which led the way in standardising the production orders. Ships were being made there, like off-the-peg suits, according to a range of standard models – of 80 000, 140 000 or 240 000 tons. 'Whatever size of ship was wanted,' he recalls, the model for it existed already:

> The workers already had it all in their hands, and without even having to look at a blueprint they would say 'Ah, yes: one of those!' and go and do their job straight away. That way of thinking was one of the most important factors in our success.

With wage levels well below those of rival yards in the West, Japan quickly attracted large orders from all over the world. The boom in world shipping went on with only shortlived interruptions from the end of the war until the oil 'shock' in 1973. To the Japanese engineers, the bulk carriers and oil tankers which came into demand in the 1960s were the easiest class of ship to build. Koga describes them as 'technically extremely primitive – like huge matchboxes, not really like ships at all'.

In Britain, meanwhile, shipyards struggled to maintain their order books. At the turn of the nineteenth century, Japan's leaders, full of admiration for British technology and world leadership, had placed orders on the Tyne for their great warships, such as the *Mikasa*, the flagship which had led the Japanese navy to a celebrated victory over the Russian Baltic fleet in 1905 during the Russo-Japanese War. The Japanese Imperial Navy had been modelled largely on the Royal Navy and, for Japan, in shipbuilding Britain had always been the target to beat. Young Japanese shipbuilders like Masayuki Ozono of the big firm, Ishikawajima-Harima, who graduated before the war, found his teacher lecturing him:

> After your graduation you'll very soon get married, but I advise you not to become absorbed with your married life; you are destined to build many large ships in your time, and I want you to do your best. Now England makes more than half the world's ships, but Japan must replace Britain as the world's top shipbuilder.

It took barely a decade after the Second World War for that ambition to be fulfilled. By 1956 Japan had overtaken both Britain and Germany, and led the world in shipbuilding. Shigeichi Koga himself visited Britain in 1955, but no yard would show him round; so, he recalls,

> I went by myself to the River Clyde, where there were shipyards on both banks, and for three days I took photographs and measurements by eye. That way I got a pretty clear idea of what was going on, even without going inside. I could tell that not much had changed. What the British did they did very well, but in a completely traditional way.

Among the British, war memories and the trauma of decolonisation had left a legacy of antipathy towards Japan, and a caricature image was built up of the Japanese as a nation of irredeemable copiers and industrial cheats. It was a miscalculation. Koga's mission to Britain was one of many examples of enterprise, and the Japanese themselves certainly saw it as following the spirit of self-help which a century earlier they had avidly studied from the works of Adam Smith and Samuel Smiles – even if the Japanese preferred their self-help through collective rather than through individual endeavour. Japan had become a society which accorded the highest respect to manufacturing skills. At the same period the old world of Europe was increasingly absorbed in its own debates about ideology, class and social justice. America was pre-occupied at home with the civil rights movement, and abroad with defending the 'frontiers of freedom' around the world in the interval between the Korean and Vietnam Wars.

By 1960 Japan had succeeded beyond all expectation in becoming a major force in heavy industry. To many Japanese it seemed that there was no longer any economic frontier that could not be crossed. In that year the nation acquired a new Prime Minister who came to personify Japan's fastest period of economic growth. Hayato Ikeda had been both MITI and Finance Minister, and had overseen the birth of the government banks as midwives to industry. He came to power on a slogan which then seemed headily ambitious: 'Double Your Income'. The goal was meant to be achieved in ten years; in fact it took only seven. Masaya Ito, Ikeda's press secretary, summarises the appeal of the new government's line to the masses of people in the factories and teeming cities:

> It was saying that if you all work hard we, the government, will see to the results of that hard work, look after you carefully through economic policy and make absolutely sure that things will get better: your salary will go up, your income will double.

It was a social contract on a grand scale.

The Ikeda government reaped the fruits of the much-increased government revenues after the boom years of the late 1950s, and it clearly identified heavy industry as the main means to achieve the nation's goals. The National Development Plan, announced in 1962, was a blueprint for building up heavy and chemical industries along the Pacific Industrial Belt. The plan was carried out so thoroughly that by 1970 the four designated regions – the Kanto area (around Tokyo), Tokai, Kinki and Seto Inland Sea – were producing more than 90 per cent of the country's industrial output from about a quarter of its land area.

But Japan was storing up trouble for itself with its single-minded pursuit of 'market share' and productivity. Trade conflicts loomed large in the newly re-established ties with Western Europe. The first was over textiles. Japan's cotton industry had dethroned that of Lancashire in the 1930s; and in the Occupation years Britain had done its best to prevent Japan from again challenging this key British industry, by arguing for quotas and minimum prices on Japanese exports. The

Americans supported the Japanese industry, however, maintaining that now it was committed to fair competition, higher wages and good commercial behaviour. The disagreement was never resolved and Britain's suspicion led it, together with other European nations, to impose restrictions on Japan's re-entry in 1955 into the world-trade system as a member of the General Agreement on Tariffs and Trade (GATT).

In 1957 when the Japanese Foreign Minister Aiichiro Fujiyama visited London, he was met by a spirited ITN television reporter, Robin Day. Day intercepted him at London airport and challenged him to say whether his government was going to ban the practice of copying British designs and labels in Japanese products. When the minister gave an evasive answer, Day held out both his hands, clutching an object in each, and persisted: 'This is a British packet of ballbearings and this is an almost identical packet of ballbearings made in Japan: a deliberate copy. What do you have to say about that?' The interpreter backed off in horror, muttering that the questions were 'discourteous' and 'treachery'. The fractious interview illustrated the frustration that the British public felt towards what was seen as a 'copycat' Japan – and an unrepentant copycat at that. In the 1960s Japan's overseas trade was growing at twice the speed of Europe's and its exports took an increasing share of the market in steel, ships and cameras from European firms.

The years of Ikeda's premiership coincided with a new stage of Japan's economic progress: the start of its tortuous adjustment to world standards of free trade and investment. Towards the end of the 1950s many of Japan's trade partners in the West had begun to show signs of real irritation at its closed market and its export successes. The American government was incensed at the market inroads made by 'one-dollar blouses' from Japan. European nations were concerned about the inroads being made by Japanese exports of textiles, shoes and other cheap goods. At the end of the 1950s only about 20 per cent of Japan's imports were free of bans or quotas. In 1959, at a meeting of GATT in Tokyo, there was a chorus of demands for Japan to open its markets and make its currency freely convertible.

The Japanese press dramatised the threat to the country's cosy insularity, likening the times to the arrival in 1853 of Commodore Perry's 'black ships' – the US naval flotilla that sailed to Japan to demand the opening of the country to foreign trade and investment. Prime Minister Ikeda set a target for the liberalisation of 80 per cent of Japan's imports by 1963, but in that year the International Monetary Fund insisted on a figure of 90 per cent. Britain also drove a hard bargain before it would agree in 1963 to sign a basic treaty of commerce and navigation with Japan. The British government insisted that Japan must undertake to remove its export subsidies. Ikeda gave the required undertakings and the next year Japan was admitted as the first Asian country into the 'rich nations' club', the Organisation of Economic Co-operation and Development – though with limits on its full participation pending the wider opening of its markets.

Even after most quotas were removed and tariffs were reduced, foreign firms often complained that they were confronted with a maze of administrative barriers to doing effective business in Japan. Foreign investment was allowed only when the government was satisfied that it would meet an important need, and would not threaten established domestic interests. The first large outside firms to set up in Japan in the late 1950s, such as Olivetti, Coca-Cola and the oil companies Mobil and Esso, were not allowed to remit any of their earnings from Japan abroad. During the 1960s a growing number of joint ventures between Japanese and foreign firms were permitted, but foreign ownership of existing Japanese firms was limited to 25 per cent. Even after a phased liberalisation programme was announced in 1967, MITI let in competition first in areas where none could seriously be expected, such as motorcycles and wooden clogs. The process of screening investment applications was slow, and infuriated many foreign businessmen. Only in 1979 did the government change its official policy on inward investment from 'prohibition as a rule' to 'prohibition as an exception'; and overall foreign ownership of corporate assets in Japan remained below 2 per cent throughout the 1980s. In recent years, when Japan has been criticised for having closed markets, some of its political and business leaders turned out conveniently to have forgotten the past, and attributed the small market share of Western firms in Japan to their lack of effort and interest.

The scorn felt in the West for the rise of the Japanese 'economic animal' was expressed by President de Gaulle of France, who, after a visit in 1963 by Prime Minister Ikeda, asked, 'Who was that transistor salesman?' Yet the belief, common in the West, that Japan's factories were sweatshops peopled by exploited, unwilling workers was wide of the mark, and some thoughtful people did describe the reality of the country's industrial culture. In the first of his sweeping reports on Japan in 1962, Norman Macrae of *The Economist* concluded that 'those Englishmen who think of Japan as a backward country of adaptable but unskilled labour are talking nowadays through their hats as far as Japan's new and younger workers are concerned'. Macrae described Japan's young generation as 'more technologically skilled than their contemporaries in Britain'.

The reality was also recognised in a Confederation of British Industries report published after a study tour of Japan in 1961. The authors found that 'industrially Japan has graduated to first-league status'. The reactions of those British visitors is instructive, as it shows a group of Western industrialists striving to comprehend an economic system made up of many alien elements. They took note of the high rate of personal savings, the in-house company unions and the closeness between government and industry, but did not think to suggest that any aspect of this might be worth closer study at home. They acknowledged some positive aspects of what they had seen, though: for instance, that 'a cheerful and keen acceptance of work' was apparent everywhere.

One of the emerging strengths of Japan's distinct structure of industry was what came to be known as the 'dual economy'. Smaller firms supplied the larger in a well-understood hierarchy, and in general the larger the firm, the better the pay and the job security. The British industrialists reported on the problems associated with the system of sub-contractors, who supply larger firms with the parts they do not wish to make themselves. They wrote that 'in matters of delivery and payment, sub-contractors are clearly driven on a very tight rein', and they found the system wanting because it contributed to a shortage of highly specialist component manufacturers. They did not point out the benefits of the vertical division of labour to the Japanese economy as a whole, including price flexibility and the protection of the leading-edge firms from market changes. In practice, when times were bad the sub-contracting firms would bear much of the burden, cutting their profit margins and adapting their product lines quickly to meet new demands.

The Japanese themselves made much of their unique institutions. MITI men were fond of speaking about Japan's three economic 'sacred treasures': lifetime employment, promotion by seniority and enterprise unions. Lifetime employment was limited to the larger firms, but it was an ideal to which all aspired. It gave security to both employers and employees, but depended on trust, not on any written contract. Promotion and wage payments according to years of service, like the in-house unions, served to cement the sense of loyalty to a particular firm. Japan built up what were in effect a series of pyramids of power in industry. At the top, the board members were susceptible to pressure from the government and often included members of the élite top rank of the bureaucracy. On their retirement private firms recruited them eagerly and for high salaries because of their ability to exercise influence in the halls of power: the custom came to be known as *amakudari*, meaning 'descent from heaven'. At the base of the pyramid were recruits from the best universities. Since life gave each Japanese male only one chance, the competition to enter prestigious and growing firms was fierce.

Eijiro Saito, president of Nippon Steel and later of the Keidanren, summed up the traditionalists' view of the relationship between an employer and employee as 'like that between a parent and child'. The Japanese economic model grew out of a social ethic peculiar to the East. The Japanese took the tradition of paternalism out of their feudal past and adapted it to the modern company with astonishing results.

Japanese-style corporatism had its paragon in Konosuke Matsushita, founder of Matsushita Electric, a newly emerging electronics firm based in Osaka. Matsushita summed up what the firm was about: 'Matsushita makes people: it also makes some electronic goods.' The firm's company song had great play in the West. Its refrain was:

> To build a new Japan
> Let us put our strength and minds together
> Endlessly and continuously
> Like Water Gushing from a fountain
> Grow, industry, grow,
> Harmony and sincerity – Matsushita Electric!

It was all too easy for some in the West to disparage such a cloying corporate embrace; but the sense of the 'company as family' matched well with Japan's old traditions of clan and class.

Konosuke Matsushita became an archetype of the Japanese entrepreneurial capitalist. His life story was proof that Japan was a meritocracy, in which a person of ambition and ability could create an industrial empire even in his own lifetime. Born in Osaka, Matsushita left school at ten to become an errand-boy. At the age of twenty-three he started his own electrical company. He sat out the Depression, he claimed, without sacking any of his more than 100 employees. From the 1960s, when the consumer electronics industry grew at a dizzying rate, his strategy was to win a commanding market share of products for the mass market, concentrating on reliability and skilful marketing rather than on leading the market with new products. In quick succession, between the 1950s and the late 1960s, the company turned its hand to mass-producing rice cookers and vacuum cleaners, transistor radios, hi-fi sets, tape recorders, air conditioners, calculators and colour TVs. Matsushita is a classic case of a company investing aggressively in order to achieve economies of scale and thereby push out most competitors.

The keys to this success were stable financing, a government industrial policy for electronics in which Matsushita occupied an important place, and an unwritten contract with the workforce that what was good for one must be good for all. The workforce in his Osaka factories was made up largely of unmarried women who could be depended on to leave and get married before they reached the seniority to demand much better wages or job prospects. Often they would return to the production line, still on relatively low wages, after rearing their children. Matsushita Electric grew into the world's largest consumer electronics company, with its founder as a rather exaggerated father-figure. Indeed his fond nickname was 'Father of Japanese Management'. Konosuke Matsushita advanced a homespun philosophy based on the simplistic slogan of 'Peace and Prosperity'. His ideas did not make converts in the West, but they were an integral part of his company's successful bid to be the biggest in the world in its field.

MITI's worldwide search for technology to foster a new generation of industries began to bear fruit during the 1960s. Some Japanese firms paid no royalties at all, but bought samples of the best products on the market and took them apart to study and imitate the way they worked. Patents were in any case cheap. In every field the Japanese scoured the world to collect the best processes and master them. The Nikon company, which had processed the lenses for gun-sights in the war, adopted techniques widely from German firms and began making 35mm cameras. Takateru Koakimoto, who spent a lifetime in the company and eventually became its president, remembers how one of the first models was, in effect, a hybrid of parts already being made overseas, with lens, body and method of film-insertion from Contax, and range-finder and shutter taken from Leica. By a process of trial and error, the quality of the products was gradually improved. Soon Nikon was making high-quality cameras on a production line, some-thing which the Germans could not then do. In time Japanese camera production overtook that of Germany.

In 1969 the Sato government announced a 'New National Develop-ment Plan' which further extended Ikeda's aim to build industrial complexes in the regions, and the infrastructure to support them. Priority was still given to steel mills, oil refineries, and chemical and heavy-machinery plants. Although the plan held out 'the balance between nature and human life' as one of its principles, the effect was to concrete over ever more of the Pacific coastal plain, and to worsen the already serious congestion and pollution problems.

Many ordinary Japanese workers shared the goals of their companies unquestioningly. The spirit of collective effort is clear from the opinions of a random selection of employees in Nippon Steel, inter-viewed in 1989. One said: 'I went to America and Canada and found that, just as in England, they were always taking tea-breaks, morning

67

and afternoon, and were hardly ever at the workplace. Japanese workers are far more hard-working.' One of the growing number who thought that Japan's successes stemmed from superior inventiveness as well as application said: 'In foreign countries workers only do what is asked of them; but Japanese workers go off and think about problems and do research on their own initiative.' Japanese workers in most parts of private industry had lost their status as a strong countervailing power towards employers. They had almost lost the power to say 'no'. But some at least had gained instead the satisfaction of material reward for the first time in their lives, and a sense of being brought into the process of decision-making at their own place of work.

Eijiro Saito of the Keidanren puts Japan's economic performance down to the special ability of his fellow countrymen to work together towards a common goal:

> In Japan we were all in the same boat, so we helped each other. Everyone realised that if they didn't work together they could never be happy – rather like members of a large family. Perhaps that is why we were accused of being selfish: we did stick together. I think this consciousness of all belonging to the same race played a large part in Japan's economic recovery.

★

In Japan today there are few obvious reminders of the time when the nation humbly put out its begging-bowl to the United States. The world's biggest banks, stock exchange, steel mills and population centre (Tokyo and its satellite cities) are all in Japan. Land prices are so high that only the richest individuals or companies from outside can contemplate owning land or renting space in central areas of Tokyo. Homer Sarasohn, one of the American teachers of Japanese business pupils during the Occupation, claims most Japanese have forgotten, or have not been taught, about the debt they owe to America's past generosity:

> I think the Japanese do *not* appreciate the contribution that was made in those days by the American people to the Japanese economy and the rehabilitation of their production base ... and there are, I think, attempts to rewrite history on the part of the Japanese government.

At the same time, Sarasohn sees the rich irony of the way that the tables were later turned against the USA: 'What the Japanese learned about management after the Second World War,' he said, 'they learned from the Americans: and the Americans forgot their own lessons.'

Japan's economy simply does not fit any of the classical economic models described by economists in the West. In the post-war period Japan almost totally rejected public ownership of industry, yet government officials directed the precise pace of growth in most major sectors for about two decades, and in the early years industry depended on government funds for a third of all its needs. Economic targets were centrally planned, but there was cut-throat competition among firms to win larger shares of the market. There were, in effect, approved oligopolies in various sectors, including the steel, textiles and chemical industries; but in the newer industries like electronics, where the market was changing very fast, newcomers could and often did succeed.

The government entered into 'sweetheart deals' with a variety of major sectoral interests – such as rice and livestock farmers, the tobacco industry and the distribution trades – to protect them from competition and sustain prices; but at the same time manufacturing industry achieved world-beating standards in terms of high productivity and low unit costs. Private firms, with a few exceptions, did what officials in MITI and the other ministries said, but had enough say to stop the bureaucrats from ruining their business. MITI men like Naohiro Amaya also acknowledge several serious policy failures, including the over-protection of the coal industry, which led to needlessly high energy costs in Japan; but those were the exceptions.

The difficulty in grasping the Japanese model was expressed by the American academic James Abegglen. He described the organisation of Japanese manufacturing firms in detail in his book *Japanese Factory*, published in 1958, but found that influential American businessmen could not accept it:

> I reported that Japanese large companies did not fire people, paid people basically in terms of seniority rather than merit, that the unions were enterprise unions, so-called, taking in only the employees of the company, [but] the conclusion was you simply couldn't run companies that way. After all if you couldn't fire people you couldn't deal with cyclical changes in demand, if you promoted people on seniority how could you possibly reward merit?

Yet the hardest aspect of the Japanese system for outsiders to understand was the opaque decision-making process. The LDP Diet members, the civil servants and the business leaders together formulated Japan's stand on each international issue that arose. Behind them was an array of business and other pressure groups, each seeking to hold its corner against all encroachments. In agriculture the powerful Central Union of Agricultural Co-operatives, Zencho, pressed the Ministry of Agriculture every year for more protection and subsidies; because of the decisive power of the farm vote the government complied. Rice imports have been banned between 1952 and the present day. In the matter of beef imports, the Union of Livestock Co-operatives exercised similar control, keeping quotas low and prices several times higher than the world average. By agreement with the Health and Welfare Ministry, doctors stopped the import of drugs and equipment which might take away their livelihood, and foreign suppliers of sophisticated drugs and medical equipment were among the losers. The tobacco industry, a government monopoly, successfully kept out most imports until the 1980s, and has prevented any serious official anti-smoking campaign.

Even the lowly could become a powerful pressure group by banding together: the loose community of *burakumin,* the former outcast class that still runs the slaughtering and tanning trades, twisted the government's arm to keep tight quotas on imported shoes and handbags. In a host of areas prices were fixed by collusion among the directly interested parties – the producers, the power-brokers and officials, and those in the distribution trade. Consumer organisations acquiesced with barely a murmur of protest: they were apparently persuaded by the arguments of the officials and politicians that the interests of Japan were identical with those of Japan's manufacturers. As a result, Japanese consumer prices have grown to be among the highest in the world.

Japan's 'economic miracle' is now taken for granted, but it was not preordained. Another former industrial planner of the élite Ministry of International Trade and Industry, Taichi Sakaiya, described the trade-off that led to Japan's becoming 'the greatest exponent of standardised mass production the world has ever seen'. It was done, he acknowledges, by encouraging uniformity and stifling individualism. 'Uniform levels of knowledge and skills would ensure efficiency in the mass-production factory,' he wrote, 'while a uniform product culture would make for an excellent consumer market for the output of the factories.'

In 1971, as Richard Halloran of the *New York Times* saw, the Japanese were 'the best-dressed, longest-lived, wealthiest nation in Asia'. Japan stood high in the table of world economic powers. The effort had indeed been rewarded. Most Japanese were still proud of their separate traditions, and sentimental about what many of them perceived to be the special merits of their national way of life. Although they chafed at the 'exam hell' which their young had to go through to matriculate into the system, and the life of unremitting work that most people had to accept for the sake of a moderate standard of living, nevertheless for most the price paid seemed to be well worth it.

To many elsewhere, Japan's industrial paradise appeared to be more like a purgatory. The national priorities were clear from an Economic

Planning Agency report, the *Economic Survey of Japan,* which found that in 1970 the 'social capital' in Japan – including houses, property and public amenities – was barely half that of Britain, and only a quarter that of the USA. But Japan's example was an inspiration to other countries in Asia, as well as to much of the developing world. One of Japan's post-war prime ministers, Masayoshi Ohira, who presided over the 1979 Tokyo economic summit, summed up the twin factors which above all else produced Japan's economic miracle: 'The beginning was thanks to the Americans' guidance and generosity,' he said. 'The rest was of Japanese doing.'

3

Brave New World

THE 1960s

On the afternoon of 10 October 1964, the world's attention was fixed on a young athlete in the Olympic stadium in Tokyo. Yoshinori Sakai was then nineteen years old. He had been born in Hiroshima on 6 August 1945, the day the atom bomb was dropped. As the Olympic flame shot up towards the sky, loud applause broke out around the stadium. The pictures were carried live across the Pacific by satellite to America. The world was witness to Japan's symbolic return to the community of nations. In Sakai's own words: 'The whole population of Japan, all 100 million people, took pride in the fact that the Olympics marked the end of the post-war period, and that from now on we would be building a new Japan. I think that pride was what made the Olympics such a success.'

When Sakai was born Hiroshima was an inferno of death and many of Japan's other cities little more than expanses of rubble. In the years since then Hiroshima had been rebuilt into a thriving provincial capital, Tokyo had grown to be one of the world's most dynamic cities, with a population of 10 million, and in less than one generation the country had emerged as an outstanding example of national reconstruction. Emperor Hirohito, the man who had announced Japan's surrender and escaped the Western Allies' will for vengeance, now declared the Tokyo Olympics open. Japan's decades of deepest shame were over.

The Olympics had been awarded to Tokyo in 1940, when the military government had wanted to stage an event as grandiose and nationalistic as the Berlin Olympics of 1936, but those games had been suspended because of Japan's invasion of the Chinese mainland. The 1964 Olympics, the first ever to be held in Asia, were the culmination of years of feverish preparation. In Tokyo two new ring-roads and three raised expressways appeared, ready to carry athletes and spectators to the various venues. New sports facilities blossomed. The citizens of Tokyo were schooled to accord the maximum courtesy and hospitality to the officials, athletes, journalists and spectators who suddenly converged on the capital. In the last frantic days pile-drivers were still tearing up roads around the clock, bulldozers were rearranging the landscape, while lorries stood near the major competition sites taking the earth dug from the city's bowels to dump it out of sight.

The Olympic stadium was now the largest sports arena in Asia. The Budokan, or Martial Arts Hall, had been specially built to house the first-ever judo competition in the history of the Games. The architect Kenzo Tange had designed two important Olympic sites that were widely admired for his linking of traditional Japanese forms with modern engineering techniques. His inverted egg-shell gymnasiums appeared as cover photographs on countless international magazines, much to the delight of the Japanese government. In addition, modern roads, subway lines, an airport monorail, hotels and housing projects had been given priority in the crash programme to redevelop and clean up Tokyo's unsightly and improvised post-war urban sprawl. The result was an enormous success, both as a sporting event and as a public-relations exercise. The efficient organisation and warm welcome by the host nation moved Avery Brundage, the American chairman of the International Olympic Committee, to congratulate the Japanese on staging 'the greatest Olympics ever held'.

For the period of the games, Japan was swept with a fever of ambition to win medals, as though the nation's survival depended on it. Passions reached their peak over the women's volleyball competition. Volleyball is a game almost all Japanese girls play at school and the Japanese media lavished attention on the self-appointed mission of the coach, Hiroumi Daimatsu. He had been a platoon commander during the war and used the harsh discipline he had learned in the front line of battle to bring his team to the peak of their form through a five-year training programme. The Soviet Union had long been dominant in the sport, but the Japanese were determined to exhibit their superior 'fighting spirit' and, when the two nations duly met in the final, the Japanese women surpassed themselves. They beat the Soviet team in three straight sets, leaving the sports commentators, spectators in the hall and millions watching on TV weeping with excitement. The captain, Mitsue Nakamura, expressed the all-embracing urge to succeed as 'a sort of psychology of hunger, in sport as in everything. We knew it was not enough to be content with second best: we felt we absolutely had to give our all.' The national effort paid off. Japan –

helped by a clean sweep in the judo events – was rewarded with fourth place in the medals' league, behind the two superpowers and West Germany.

The Japanese also seized eagerly on the Olympics as a chance to show off their progress to the world. The most ambitious single project they spawned was the construction of the 'bullet-train' line between Tokyo and Osaka. With a cruising speed of 130 m.p.h., the bullet trains were the fastest and smoothest in the world. Japanese and foreigners alike were thrilled to see Mount Fuji as they sped by in air-conditioned luxury; some visitors from abroad were equally amazed by the disciplined service of the uniformed girls who came through the carriages every few minutes offering a selection of food and drink, their bird-like call of *Aisu kureemu, purin'* ('Ice cream, pudding' – the Japanese term for crème caramel) echoing through the carriages. Japanese railway engineers had not only improved on existing European technology for high-speed rail transport; they had overcome daunting obstacles to lay the tracks along the earthquake-prone Pacific coast. The bullet-train route coincided with Japan's historic Tokaido (eastern sea-route) highway. In 1964 the Tokaido became an even busier commuter corridor than that between New York and Washington or London and Manchester. The seconds-accurate timing of the arrivals and departures was so reliable that for years after the opening of the line Japan National Railways offered a refund to passengers if their train was late.

Japan was then a country which encompassed the very new and the antique side by side in striking contrast. The Kanto plain, including the Tokyo metropolitan area and the surrounding prefectures of Kanagawa, Chiba and Saitama, already contained one of the world's greatest concentrations of industry. The region around Nagoya, 225 miles to the west, was Japan's Detroit: there the Toyota Motor Company had its congregation of factories and employed 20 000 people. Osaka, a further 120 miles west along the Pacific coast, was the headquarters of Matsushita Electric, as well as of a clutch of smaller rival firms such as Sharp and Sanyo. The prospect of the Olympics had encouraged millions of Japanese families to buy colour TV sets in the year before the games began, and the firms making them were expanding fast. Meanwhile, inland in the villages of the Japan Alps in central Honshu, in the old farming region of Tohoku to the north, on the western main islands of Shikoku and Kyushu and along the coast of the Sea of Japan – known as *ura nihon*, 'the back of Japan' – life followed the same hard pattern as it had done for centuries. Farmers and their wives, sons and daughters sowed the rice-seeds in spring, transplanted the seedlings one by one by hand in the humid early summer heat and harvested the crop in autumn before the annual round of thanksgiving festivals and the long, frozen winters.

After the first, introspective, post-war decade, Japan had begun to make an impact on the Western world again. In 1956 it had taken its seat at the United Nations, after earlier being vetoed by the Soviet Union. Japanese-made transistor radios were 'vogue' products of the 1950s. Western audiences admired the work of Japanese film-makers, especially Akira Kurosawa, whose *Rashomon*, an enigmatic story of truth and illusion set in feudal Japan, won the top award at the 1951 Venice Film Festival. The image of Japan as a warlike nation peopled by subservient masses was receding; in its place came a new stereotype of the earnest and indefatigable factory- and office-worker, the foot-soldier of Japan's industrial revolution. The image matched one version of reality, but Japan had dimensions that such a simplistic picture missed. The average 9 per cent annual economic growth in the decade before the Olympics brought a dramatic rise in living standards for nearly everyone in the country. Dr Saburo Okita, one of the brains behind the government's 'income-doubling' plan and the sprint for growth in the 1960s, later described the age as one which saw 'the arrival of the mass-consumption society and the almost limitless desire for better living'.

Economic growth had altered the face of Japan. The rural influx, and the wholesale rebuilding of bombed-out residential parts of Tokyo, led to a massive house-building programme, and to a crazy scramble for flats in the new apartment blocks known as *danchi* ('collective zones'). They were so much in demand that public lotteries were held to allocate them. Mrs Fusako Matsumaru was one of the lucky ones who got into one of the cheaper, government-subsidised blocks: 'After thirty tries, you got priority, and that's what I was after; but after I'd tried about twenty-eight times I managed to get in anyway.' The multistorey flats were small: two or three rooms of between six and eight straw *tatami* mats (each measuring 6 by 3 feet); but the running hot and cold water, family bath and flush toilet were all wondrous luxuries to their new occupants, most of whom arrived from run-down and draughty wooden houses. In the suburbs and the countryside most houses still depended on the night-soil man who came to clear out the contents of the latrines into 'honey-buckets' to be used as fertiliser in the fields.

Inside the new flats were the first tangible fruits of the hard grind of the post-war years. Typically, the rooms were sparsely furnished; normally only the living room was carpeted, the other rooms being floored with the plain, elegant *tatami*. Thin *futon* mattresses for sleeping on were laid down at night and gathered up again in the daytime to allow the bedrooms to be used for other purposes. Shoes were always removed in the porch and exchanged for slippers. Furniture very probably consisted of only a chest of drawers, bookshelves, and a desk for each child to do his or her homework. Often the only sizeable table was a square one in the centre of the living room; it also served as a heater. This was a Japanese invention, called a *kotatsu*. An electric heater would be fitted to the underside of the table and family members would gather round close together; a blanket or cloth draped over the table top served to keep the heat in and the sitter's legs warm. Most buildings had no central heating, and cooking was from a small gas range. Sometimes space was set aside for a miniature household altar, bedecked with a small bell, a few other Buddhist ornaments and a small vase of flowers. People of the older generation would pause in front of it for a moment to offer up a prayer for the spirits of their parents and grandparents. But the *danchi* were designed for 'nuclear' families of parents and at most two or three children.

The cramped space had to be meticulously organised in order to accommodate a range of household goods that were unknown until the Occupation years. Saturation advertising encouraged the idea that each family had to have a TV set, refrigerator and washing machine; by 1964 90 per cent did possess a TV set and more than half owned the other two items as well. These were known as 'the three sacred treasures' of the household, an ironic popular corruption of the phrase used to describe Japan's real 'sacred treasures': the mirror, sword and jewel which are the symbols of the Emperor's authority. Japanese women wanted each of the gadgets immediately they appeared on the market; and as they, not their menfolk, generally managed the household budget, they usually got what they wanted, spending part of the mid-year or year-end bonus and saving the rest.

The spartan simplicity of the average Japanese household has changed somewhat since those times, as families have acquired many more possessions and more rooms have been converted to Western style, with carpets and standing furniture. But in the 1950s and 1960s the novelty for the new flat-dwellers was exhilarating. Fusako Matsumaru confessed: 'I used to get carried away and rush around looking for things to wash, looking for things to put in the washing machine.' Many housewives would load up the machine at least once a day just because it was there. Likewise, by 1964 half the nation owned cameras made in Japan. The hand of MITI and the economic planners could be seen in this: prices were fixed to encourage mass purchases of certain goods. Once the firms had had a chance to recoup their investments through heavy sales, the profit margin would be reduced and the commodity tax rate on the product would be raised, ensuring the government extra income.

The *danchi*-dwellers, uprooted from the age-old cares of blood relations and the village or neighbourhood community, became a bedrock of Japan's emerging middle class: well educated, modest in their aspirations and apolitical. Vandalism was almost unknown in the new housing estates, and is still rare today. The social stigma attached to failure to uphold standards proved an effective form of pressure. Tokyo's housing estates rarely became slums of the kind that appeared in post-war cities in the West or in other parts of Asia where populations were housed in high-rise buildings.

Outside the public *danchi* a modest three-room flat in Tokyo proper cost over seven times the average annual income of a production worker. Such was the pressure for affordable homes that soulless dormitory cities, known as 'bed towns', were built outside the twenty-three wards of Tokyo proper – west along the Tama river, north to Saitama prefecture, and south in Kawasaki and Kanagawa. It became the norm for working people in the Tokyo area to spend an hour or more commuting each way to and from work. The road system was hopelessly inadequate, and the main roads were generally choked with traffic, much of it heavy goods vehicles. Workers commuted by rail, and on the platforms the crowds grew so thick that people learned to form queues for two or three consecutive trains at one time. Professional 'pushers' crammed harassed men and women into the carriages while warning sirens blared at ear-splitting levels. To Western eyes the scenes seemed grotesque, even comic. The reality for those involved was highly stressful and often physically painful; yet open quarrels and complaints were extremely rare. For good reason, the Japanese gained a world-beating reputation for enduring discomfort in silence.

Even as modern buildings and facilities appeared, the old way of life survived: traditional communal bath-houses still attracted a steady stream of local people; workers digging up the road at midnight wore split-toed rubber shoes and worked without let-up. Most first-generation city-dwellers brought their sense of region and their dialect with them. Partly because of the crampedness of the homes, most residential areas were well served not only with bath-houses and *sushi* (raw fish) bars, but with eating, drinking and entertainment places of all descriptions, in keeping with the Japanese custom of easy drunkenness and the systematic relief of stress. The evening and night life of Japanese cities was – and is even more today – a world of sensual pleasure known to the Japanese as *mizu shobai*, 'the water business', because it is so ephemeral.

The rustic-style eating-places and *nomiya* (drinking houses) were a man's world. Japan, indeed, was still a country run by and for the male half of the population. The household head had one paramount role: to go out and earn the family's income. It mattered little what time he came back. He would anyway expect his wife to leave him a traditional meal of rice, fish and pickles, with bean-paste soup, and she would most likely stir even after midnight to make it hot whenever the man of the house reappeared. He would be expected to stay at work until after the boss left, whatever time that might be. He would go to work seven days a week without thinking twice about it. He would observe all the ceremonial niceties life required of him: the customary deferences at work, and among the family – if work permitted – an annual pilgrimage to the graves of ancestors.

What he did for the rest of the time was of little concern to his wife. The marriage was likely to have been arranged, anyway, by his and his wife's parents. True 'love marriages' were the exception; most were more of a contract for the exchange of life's essential services. The woman's role would be to have children, bring them up and look after the family finances. Except in high society – among the old aristocracy and diplomats – couples were not expected to go out for social occasions together. When the husband had time and money he would generally be out drinking with his workmates; he might well be enjoying the company of a bar hostess or *mama-san*, the professional soothers of men's cares. Japan had emerged from the Second World War with one foot still in the feudal past. Women might have the same rights as men in the constitution, but mostly they had little idea of how to exercise them. When guests came to the home, the wife would kneel down and serve refreshments. If a tradesman or visitor needed the family seal to be affixed to a document, the wife would probably fetch it for the head of the household to use. Children were admonished to be quiet, and most had only a fraction of the aggressiveness of their counterparts in the West.

The shift in population undermined the strong traditional sense of family. Before the war most Japanese had lived in extended families, with three generations under one roof, mostly following the Confucian rules which placed the male above the female and the older above the younger. Everywhere in the regions young people were now rushing to seek a better life in the cities. Families broke up as their sons and daughters were recruited by the big industrial firms to work on the assembly lines of the new factories. The companies sent group recruitment trains around the country to transport the schoolleavers, most of them fifteen years old, into the cities. Mr Jonai and his wife Toyo, rice and mushroom farmers living in Iwate prefecture in Tohoku (the north-eastern district of Honshu), sent both their sons off to Tokyo in that way. Mrs Jonai saw off the elder boy, Kiyoshi, who was leaving with almost all his classmates – 300 school-leavers on one train bound for the capital. The mothers who went to the local station to wave goodbye to their children were constrained by a thick rope from going on to the platform. Mrs Jonai, like the others, was distraught when the train pulled away:

> All the children were looking out of the windows and everybody was shouting out at the tops of their voices – 'Work hard! Don't get ill!' ... And when the whistle blew, all the children just burst into tears. I felt so sorry for them that I just ran along, dashed along the station towards them and chased after the train as far as I could.

The young people who settled in the cities generally lived frugally, sending part of their earnings back to their parents in their home town or village. Most of today's inhabitants of Tokyo were born elsewhere, and the word for home town, *furusato*, meaning 'old village', is still redolent with nostalgia to many Japanese.

The scale of the migration turned large areas of the countryside into depopulated backwaters in the two decades after 1945. In the village of Yamagata, where Toyo Jonai and her husband stayed behind with their only daughter, local people and others from the surrounding villages met often to discuss their predicament. Many felt bitter about the disintegration of whole communities, but as there was no prospect of other work for young people in the area, Mrs Jonai says, 'We thought we really had no choice. There was nothing we could do because we had no help from the government. We reckoned in the circumstances it was better for the children to go out and get a job, learn a trade and then come back.' In reality the great majority never would go back, except during major festivals like the *bon* (Festival of the Dead) in mid-August and the traditional New Year celebrations.

The employees in the fast-expanding factories had little hope of finding homes close to their work. The great majority went into company dormitories for several years, and the company's horizons became their own. Conditions were severe. Kiyoshi Jonai once wrote to his mother that he was so sick that he could not hold down any food, but he was told to go to work as usual. His mother recalls:

> I opened the letter and could see it was all stained with my son's tears. I was badly shaken. So I wrote a letter to the dormitory chief saying 'He's only a child and he's sick, so please look after him!' I sent the letter off

thinking that my son might be cross with me, but I was so worried, I had to do it.

Hard work and long hours were still the norm among all classes and among people in all walks of life. Masumi Sasaki, a chemical-worker, worked hours that were only what was expected in large manufacturing firms: having started before eight in the morning, 'it was usually after eight in the evening before we would get off work, and we only had one day off a week, normally a Sunday; but often we had to work on Sundays as well. One of my friends once did a six-month stretch without once having a single day off.'

Centuries of feudal tradition lived on in people's relationships at work. It remained very common for a factory-worker to rely on one of his superiors to be the matchmaker in an arranged marriage to a woman employed in the same workplace; the couple would take at most a three- or four-day honeymoon, then return to a company flat where they would spend the rest of their working lives. Each year the husband would travel away from home on only one overnight trip – the company outing; his wife stayed behind. Holiday allowances depended on seniority: most employees were entitled to at least two or three weeks, but actually took only six days at most. To be away from the place of work while others were present was seen as a form of disloyalty, and could affect a person's promotion prospects.

The spirit of rebellion against such a regimented way of life was rarely expressed openly by those caught up in it. Company workers generally stayed with the same employer until retirement. After the labour-management showdowns of the Occupation years, sackings were very unusual, and were taken as a sign of failure on the part of the firm as well as the individual. However Japan's youth did seek to mark itself off from the older generation through a show of unorthodoxy. In 1956 a popular author, Shintaro Ishihara, published *Taiyo no kisetsu (Season of Violence)*, a novel which depicted the pleasure-seeking and sexually liberated lifestyle of some among the post-war generation known as the 'Sun Tribe'. The book was about the sons and daughters of the rich, but the way the characters ostentatiously rejected the values of obedience and unquestioning self-sacrifice of the older generation caught the mood of the time. Ishihara himself became a popular idol and began a high-profile career in politics as a spokesman for Japanese traditional values, but also as a critic of the modern political establishment.

Gradually the benefits of economic growth were felt even in the most backward areas. Eishi Takahashi, the mayor of Yamagata village, described conditions there in 1952:

We had no electricity at all, and of course no doctor in the village. The roads were closed off during the winter months and once every three years or so the crops failed because of frost damage. Because of all the difficulties, children were often absent from school for long periods.

Electricity gradually reached the whole of the Tohoku region, and a drive to improve health and hygiene in the villages, as well as to eradicate cholera, typhoid and smallpox, took doctors and nurses into the country areas. Miyoshi Ohba, who was a nurse in the local medical team seeking to eradicate intestinal parasites, described how they would 'take a big metal cooking pot into the garden of the public drinking hall; we tipped packets of de-worming powder into the pot and got everybody to drink two teacupsful of the medicine.' Afterwards the villagers would proudly display 'masses of worms hanging on sticks ... There were people who'd come along and say: "Look, I've got 120 here", and they would still be wriggling, hanging from the pole.'

With the baby boom immediately after the war, Japan's population grew from 70 million in 1945 to 100 million in only about twenty years. Families were actively encouraged to restrict themselves to two children, which was also all that most couples could afford. Abortion was a common form of birth control. Japanese women accepted the likelihood that they would have to go through that ordeal at some time, and there was little or no social stigma attached to it. Government figures showed that in 1955 seven births were prevented by abortion compared with only three by contraception. This ratio had been reversed by the mid-1960s; in time condoms became a common form of contraception, but the Japan Medical Association and the Health and Welfare Ministry combined forces against the introduction of the birth-control pill, arguing that it was unsafe or unsuited to Japanese women, and its use has never grown to be widespread. Other scientific methods of contraception were slow in gaining general acceptance, although for centuries the 'rhythm' method of natural contraception had been widely practised, with some success.

In this as in other things, including the household finances, women had to take the main responsibility, while men were indulged. Miyoshi Ohba says her medical team started from the premise that Japanese men dislike condoms.

They'd say it was like getting into the bath in gumboots or shaking hands with gloves on. ... As it is the woman who has most to lose, we encouraged women to think of putting on the condom for their husbands, and also to learn more about sexual technique in order to give their husbands greater satisfaction.

Mrs Ohba recalls how in her country area the family-planning team thought up the idea of a 'love box' containing various hygiene supplies, including contraceptives. It was passed from one married woman to the next wrapped in a traditional *furoshiki* wrapping-scarf, and anyone could take what they wanted and put cash into the box in exchange without embarrassment.

After the fierce confrontation between the right and the left in the immediate post-war years, Japanese society settled down to a fairly uniform acceptance of national goals. The foremost aim became that of national self-improvement, and achieving it meant the subordination of matters of conscience – including discussion of the war Japan had lost and individual concerns – to the drive to make Japan economically strong. The left – the union movement, liberal intellectuals and the self-styled left-wing political parties – had sought to create a government system more attuned to the wishes of working people than to big business, but they had suffered badly from the débâcle of the banned general strike in 1947 and the 'red purge' that followed. The civil service was in close sympathy with the conservative-minded, pro-business politicians who were in power continuously from 1948 onwards.

The instruments of social management and control were considerable: the government ministries with their advisory panels; the big corporations, which could command the loyalty of small and medium business through a network of obligations; and most fundamentally of all, the community organisations, such as parent–teacher associations and local chambers of commerce, where official policies reached down to the grassroots. The leading news media were effectively co-opted, with only a few exceptions, into the same consensus. The media were well represented on the multitude of government advisory panels which embodied the nation's goals.

One outstandingly influential committee was the Education Ministry's central advisory panel, made up of a cross-section of civil servants, teachers, civic leaders and men of the media. The committee set out the collective thinking of the authorities in a series of all-embracing guidelines. One draft policy paper published in 1965, *The Image of the Person We Expect*, sums up what it calls the 'ideal type' of young person that schools should strive to turn out in order to regain lost values, and to counter the pacifist tenor of the Basic Education Law, passed in 1947 under the influence of the Occupation. The three cardinal elements mentioned were a 'free and constructive' nature, a 'correct form of patriotism' and being part of 'a loving home'. Many teachers baulked at the idea of the state seeking to define a single ideal set of Japanese attributes, as had been done in the Emperor's Rescript on Education in 1889, a document that provided an ideological basis for wartime ultranationalism. The teachers protested that for the state to instil patriotism meant a drift back to the pre-war atmosphere of forcible conformism, while the pious idea of a rich homelife was directly at odds with the ethos of schools, where rote learning and exam performance were stressed above all else.

Films and books of the period evoke the severe social and generational strains caused by the abrupt changes. Yasujiro Ozu's classic film *Tokyo monogatari* (*Tokyo Story*, 1953) captures the claustrophobia of life for a young professional couple in a dismal flat in the Tokyo suburbs. When the husband's parents come to stay it is not only the physical dimensions of the flat that cause embarrassment: the confines of the mental world the harassed young couple inhabit is also plain. Akiyuki Nosaka's *Erogotoshi* (*The Pornographers*, 1963) is an account of the bizarre lives of a group of sex-merchants in the underworld of Tokyo. Kobo Abe's novel *Tanin no kao* (*The Face of Another*, 1964) tells of a man who tries to regain the love of his wife by putting on a plastic mask to hide his own burnt and disfigured face. Some films of the period contained haunting images of isolation and discord: one such is Hiroshi Teshigahara's *Suna no onna* (*Woman of the Dunes*, 1964), another Abe story, in which a lone butterfly-collector falls into a hole in the sands of the Tottori coastline, on the Sea of Japan, and is held captive by a woman who makes him question the basis of his previous existence. After failing in an attempt to escape, he gives up and accepts a claustrophobic life struggling to hold back the encroachment of the sands above his sand-pit.

In the 1950s Japanese life and attitudes took on many of their present characteristics. It was as though work, sex and drink acted as three 'opiums' of the Japanese people, leaving little time for reflection. On the outskirts of every city there sprang up a host of special 'love hotels' where couples could go to be alone. Often the clients would be married couples seeking the privacy they could not find even in their own homes because the thin walls of their tiny suburban flats allowed every sound to be heard. Prostitution, although technically illegal, grew into a huge industry, run by a distinct class of professional gangsters to whom the police turned a blind eye.

Kenzaburo Oe, a leading writer and novelist, articulates well the mood of the age. He recalls that

> there were a series of 'movements' to create a new, special sense of identity and impose it on Japanese people.... The government had slogans about how much was expected of you as Japanese. The government and the

83

Ministry of Education resolved to get people to be aware of their national identity – not exactly going back to the pre-war period, but getting them to sing the national anthem, respect the flag and think of the Emperor as part of a wonderful Japanese tradition.

The response was divided, Oe says: young adults like himself, who had been children in the war, 'reacted against it and refused to have a sense of identity imposed on us'. But the older generation, which had been scarred in the war and had lost confidence, responded to the call for a new national purpose. Oe calls them the 'silent generation', which wanted above all to rebuild Japan:

> They didn't emphasise their own sense of identity, or speak up for themselves either within Japan or abroad; they were the heads of families who got on with their work in silence. . . . That generation was the backbone of Japan's post-war economic advance.

Post-war Japan has one of the highest rates of literacy anywhere, and its leading daily newspapers established themselves as the most widely read in the world, after *Pravda* in the Soviet Union. They all strove to capture the 'middle ground' of public opinion, each wanting to maximise circulation and each claiming to be the true voice of the nation. The uniformity and the horror of extremes in the press reflected the emerging Japanese national ethos. It also contributed much to it. Japanese journalists saw themselves as loyal and chosen members of an élite, and as part of the Establishment. As in industry, competition among the major companies was tightly regulated. Since before the war a system had evolved whereby separate 'clubs' of reporters kept a permanent watch on every source of official information, enabling them to pass on official messages without delay. The system remained with only minor changes after the war. The press was not in any position to challenge the 'economism' of post-war Japan. Planned and joint coverage was the norm. Interviews with the nation's decision-makers were always deferential. Scoops were very rare. The pattern has changed little up to the present day.

Television too added its powerful voice to sustain the national consensus. It also brought new entertainment into the people's lives. 'Westerns' were popular, but they never replaced the home-grown equivalent: tales of brave and cunning *samurai* from Japan's feudal past. Ever since 1966, a serial drama has been broadcast at 8.15 a.m. each weekday of the year on NHK, Japan's public broadcasting service; and it became part of the collective imagination of the Japanese. The first of its kind, *Kumo no jutan* (*The Carpet of Clouds*) broke all comparable records for audience viewing. It told the life story of

Japan's first woman pilot in the period between the two world wars. The pattern of the plot, including a series of setbacks and triumphs over adversity, had powerful appeal for Japanese audiences who had lived through hardships themselves. From then on NHK kept up the tradition of pulling at the heart-strings of the viewers – mostly women who stayed at home after their menfolk had left for work. The daily serial came to be a regular homily to the nation on the virtues of hard work, thrift, and loyalty to seniors and benefactors.

In the countryside television was like magic – 'a vision from heaven', Toyo Jonai called it. Everyone in her village, including the children, would gather round in her living room and watch until after ten o'clock every evening. 'We were so excited: you could see what was happening in Tokyo and how things were there; and it was through TV that I first got to know the name of the Prime Minister!' The Japanese quickly became among the world's most addicted television viewers. It was normal for the set to be left on all day in the living room of ordinary homes; a TV set would also usually be on with the sound up in many of the eating- and drinking-places where most males would go regularly to unwind at the end of a working day. The fare was mostly banal: *samurai* dramas or westerns, interspersed with quiz shows, news and sport. One influential social critic, Soichi Oya, excoriated his countrymen, saying in 1956 that television was turning the Japanese into a nation of 'a hundred million idiots'. The jibe was hardly disputed; but standards remained generally low, with the five commercial channels in the Tokyo area competing furiously to find the lowest common denominator in television entertainment.

The nation could be brought together by symbols, and the marriage in April 1959 of the Crown Prince Akihito was a genuine national celebration. Millions of Japanese went out and bought television sets in order to watch the wedding. After Emperor Hirohito's orchestrated tours of the country during the Occupation, the Imperial family had again become cut off from ordinary people. But the romance between Akihito and Michiko Shoda, the daughter of a wealthy businessman, was covered with great enthusiasm by the Japanese media. Akihito was hardly a dashing figure. He had opted to take up the same unexciting life hobby as his father, the study of marine life. But the press made the most of the couple's meetings on the tennis courts at Karuizawa, Japan's most fashionable resort town where John Lennon and Yoko Ono also spent their summer holidays. There was also some spice in the fact that Akihito was going against the stuffy conventions of the Imperial court in choosing as his bride a commoner, rather than allowing the palace chamberlains to select the future Empress from among the daughters of the former nobility. Cheering crowds lined the streets of Tokyo as the royal couple rode in a horse-drawn carriage on their wedding day. It was the biggest live event that Japan's TV stations had ever broadcast. For once the monarchy was displaying a real human touch and enjoyed true popularity rather than perfunctory respect.

The Japanese 'wedding of the century' created a so-called 'Michy boom'. Mothers took Princess Michiko as a model as they aspired to turn their daughters into *ojo-san*, well-bred young ladies. Their manner should be deferential, their bearing perfect, their dress tasteful; their knowledge of society and the arts, both Japanese and Western, should be deep. It was one of a succession of fashions that swept the country, keeping the nation's mind almost miraculously fixed on the same target or set of targets at the same time. There were booms and fads for each useful electronic gadget that came on the market, for hulahoops, indoor bowling, and for Japanese pop singers imitating their Western models.

The media, headed by a few smart opinion-leaders, had a riotous way with language. Social types were characterised as 'tribes' or *zoku*. In the late 1940s the 'Setting-sun Tribe' was identified: those, like the old nobility, who had lost out from the war. During the Korean War the 'Expense-account Tribe' came on the scene – the squads of company men who bought their way into others' favour. After Shintaro Ishihara's 'Sun Tribe' in the late 1950s came the 'Thunder Tribe' of hell-raising motorcyclists – who despite their name were much less anti-social than their Western equivalents, the Hell's Angels. In the 1960s came the 'Roppongi Tribe', the smart set in the newest enter-tainment area, and the 'Idle Tribe' of youngsters who gathered to watch the world go by in the streets of pulsating Shinjuku, in Tokyo's west end.

English and French words were plundered in large numbers, warped and twisted into new sounds and meanings to excite the Japanese masses and to describe phenomena which summed up the mood of the moment. The *salariiman* (salary man, or company white-collar worker) became firmly established in the language, as did the OL – the 'office lady'; her role was to serve tea rather than to take part in business meetings. Apartments became *apaato*, department stores *depaato*. A second job became *arubaito* from the German 'Arbeit', bread became *pan* from French 'pain', and even rice was often referred to as *raisu* rather than the native word, *gohan*.

Japan was such a uniform society that passing fads seemed to take hold of the nation's consciousness one after another. There were wild crazes for baseball players who topped the batting league, for *sumo* wrestlers who won the Emperor's Cup in major tournaments, and an

■ *1* The remains
of Tokyo after the
US fire bombings,
Summer 1945.

■ *2* Hiroshima
remembers:
offerings at the
children's
monument in the
Peace Park on the
anniversary of the
dropping of the
A-Bomb.

■ *3* Unconditional surrender: the Japanese delegation signs the instrument of surrender in front of General MacArthur on board the *USS Missouri* on 2 September 1945.

■ *4* Return to the fold: Prime Minister Yoshida addresses the San Francisco Peace Conference, 7 September 1951.

■ *Opposite 5* General MacArthur and Emperor Hirohito at their first meeting on 27 September 1945.

■ *6* Kenzo Tange's innovative architectural design for the Olympic swimming pool in Tokyo.

■ *Left above 7* Twin symbols of Japan: Mount Fuji and the bullet train. The superfast service between Tokyo and Osaka began in 1964, in time for the Tokyo Olympics.

■ *Left below 8* Large-scale public housing projects, such as this one in the suburbs of Osaka, started in the 1960s in the major cities.

■ *9* In step again: Japan's Olympic team marches into the Olympic Stadium for the opening ceremonies of the 1964 Games.

■ *10* Student demonstration against the US-Japan Security Treaty's revision in front of the Diet building in Tokyo, 1960.

■ *11* Appeal from the right: Yukio Mishima addressing unenthusiastic Self-Defence Forces personnel shortly before his suicide on 25 November 1970.

■ *Overleaf 12* Pollution victim: photographs such as this by the American W. Eugene Smith made Minamata a symbol of the excesses of Japan's post-war industrial growth.

ongoing delight in the Nichigeki cabaret – for years its provocative slogan 'Topless Japanese Girls Completely Fascinate You' confronted every passer-by in the fashionable Yurakucho district. Tokyo was a mental universe in which new stars and supernovas were created almost by the week, dazzling the earthlings who gazed at their brief passage across the sky. It was a frivolous aspect to a society otherwise intent on the deadly sober pursuit of economic goals. The linguistic jokes and love of social sensation were a sign of new confidence as well as of the increasing size of paypackets. By the early 1960s most Japanese people were beginning to feel prosperous for the first time in their lives.

There was a heavy price to be paid for the economic achievement which had brought the heightened living standards and expectations. In their headlong quest for fast industrial growth and world status, the Japanese had devastated their own natural environment. Factories had been built in and around Tokyo and the other major cities with little or no thought for pollution control. By the late 1960s Japan was probably the most polluted country in the world. In built-up areas traffic exhaust and factory emissions combined, especially on sunny days, to produce photochemical smog, and by 1970 this had become a serious health hazard. In the Tokyo area 'smog alerts' were put out whenever the air pollution reached levels at which it was judged unsafe for children to stay out of doors. Sometimes the air was so thick with iron particles that if one held a magnet to the dust it would cling to the magnet. Kiyoshi Jonai, working in industrial Kawasaki, south of Tokyo, recalls that the air 'smelt revolting because of the pollution and gases; when it was hot and sunny your eyes would prickle and your head would hurt.' The atmosphere in the industrial centre of Kawasaki was the worst of all. Masumi Sasaki, who worked at the Asahi Chemical company, recalls:

> the sky was very dark and often there would be a sudden evening shower. You'd get soaked with the little drops of black rain all over you, and the rain was full of soot. It was really dirty and would turn you all black!

In 1953 fishing families in the city of Minamata on the southern island of Kyushu began to suffer from what local people first termed the 'strange disease'. Cats were seen jumping about madly and throwing themselves into the sea. People who had eaten local fish felt numb and then started to experience muscular spasms and slurred speech. Dozens of babies were born with brain damage. The victims lost control of their bodily movements and writhed in agony. By 1959 there was clear evidence that the local aluminium plant owned by the Chisso company was the source of the disease. For several years it had been allowing deadly methyl mercury waste to be poured as effluent into Minamata Bay.

As the symptoms of the disease grew apparent, other residents would avoid the affected people, mostly members of fishermen's families. Among the victims was a boy, Tomiji Matsuda, who went blind after being fed prawns from the bay. From the age of six he was unable to control his limbs and became entirely dependent on his family. His sister Yukiko, who looked after him when he was small, was shocked at the superstitious reaction of the people the family knew: 'People would walk by us and then spit out once they had passed by. Nobody would have any contact with us.'

In the city there was still much reluctance to close down the plant, since Chisso was by far the biggest local employer. The company took full advantage of its position and at first denied responsibility. Victims and their families staged a sit-in outside the company gates for over a year, demanding compensation; eventually they forced a showdown with the firm's management, shouting accusations in an open meeting. Support groups initially received very little encouragement from elsewhere, but overseas publicity, notably in the moving photographs of the American Eugene Smith, helped to increase public awareness, and the company offered meagre compensation of 300 000 yen (then about $830) to the families of those who had died. The great majority were too poor to refuse and did not know how to pursue their claim in any other way. Once the company had agreed to negotiate with the Minamata Sufferer's Association on individual claims, it did make compensation payments to about 2000 people, but it rejected thousands more. In the early stages the government gave the victims no help and no hope of other redress. Some of them sued Chisso, but the court battle was long and hard. It was not until 1973, twenty years after the first sufferers fell sick, that a court ordered the company to pay full appropriate compensation, but to only 138 people. Altogether over 350 had died and thousands had been crippled or had their lives ruined. Only then did the government take strong steps at national level to curb industrial pollution and clean up the environment.

Likewise the Minamata events were a test of the ability of Japan's new media to see an issue of great public interest and to report on it adequately. For many years little was written anywhere in the national press because of the built-in pressure on the economic reporters of the main media not to write anything damaging to the interest of industry. Their newspapers were all striving to become a respected part of the Establishment, and that meant not rocking the boat. It was only in the late 1960s that the full story of Minamata came out, after general reporters from the head offices of the national press began to investigate the issue dispassionately. Suddenly, the newspapers' policy changed when they realised that they could sell more copies with stories about the horrors of industrial pollution.

A so-called second Minamata case occurred in Niigata in the mid-1960s. The symptoms were the same, and the waste from a chemical plant owned by a large company, Showa Denko, was identified as the cause of the illness, which led to over seventy deaths and payment of compensation to more than 600 people. Cadmium pollution, dating from the war years, was still affecting local people. This terrible disease came to be known as *itai-itai byo* ('ouch-ouch disease'). The victims' bones became so brittle that they could be broken merely by being touched. Other serious pollution cases included arsenic poisoning among people working in or living near arsenic mines. More than twenty people died and altogether more than 60 000 were officially recognised as suffering from chronic arsenic poisoning. The Inland Sea, lying between Honshu and Shikoku islands, became one of the most contaminated stretches of water in the world. Heavy industry had been encouraged to concentrate there under successive government economic plans since the late 1950s, and many factories discharged untreated effluent into its shallow waters, polluting the rich fish, shell-fish and seaweed grounds.

The Basic Law for Environmental Pollution Control, enacted in 1967, failed in practice to oblige either the government or industry to take steps to prevent pollution. It stated that a balance should be struck between the protection of the environment and economic develop-ment. But a series of lawsuits from the late 1960s resulted in successful claims against business firms, and led to some tightening of the law. After the social trauma of the Minamata disease and other much publicised pollution cases, the issue also threatened to turn the elec-torate against the ruling Liberal Democrats, and in 1970 the govern-ment set itself specific environmental quality standards for air, water, soil and noise pollution. By 1978 some 64 000 people had been awarded compensation for medical costs and loss of earnings under the law, but many people still criticised the government for arbitrarily limiting the number of designated diseases and areas covered by it.

The 'oil shock' of 1973 provided a new spur to industry to save energy and to move away from the pollution-prone heavy and chemical industries. That shift took place at a remarkable pace, and Japanese firms came to be among the world leaders in making pollution-control equipment of all kinds. Still, the legacy of Japan's uncontrolled rush for industrial growth is that tens of thousands of people are still having treatment for pollution-related diseases, and Japan's most populated areas are among the unloveliest examples of modern living to be found anywhere.

While society was being shaken and changed by rapid industrialisation, the Japanese performed another miracle of sorts: the creation of a multi-party political system in which a single party monopolised power. Japan was governed by ten successive LDP Cabinets under three Prime Ministers – Nobusuke Kishi, Hayato Ikeda and Eisaku Sato – all of whom had been trained as civil servants in the conservative tradition. A stable political environment was essential for economic growth, and growth helped to ensure that the Liberal Democrats went on being returned at the polls. From 1948 onwards all Japanese Cabinets were broadly conservative in complexion. This was partly thanks to the disproportionate weight given to the rural vote in Japan's multi-seat constituency voting system. That inequality was an important factor favouring the Liberal Democrats in national elections, and only the most half-hearted attempts were made to rectify it.

Successive Japanese governments were formed on the basis of the same beliefs: a capitalist economy, social stability at home, active opposition to communism in all its guises, and close, friendly relations with the United States. Prime Minister Shigeru Yoshida set the tone during the Occupation with his 'Yoshida doctrine', which meant putting rice before guns. He knew that no other state was about to offer Japan the kind of protection and market opportunities that the United States of the 1950s and 1960s was prepared to give. The American need for military bases in Japan in the Cold War years meant that the USA absolutely needed Japan as well, and that gave successive Japanese governments considerable leverage. It also tempered Washington's complaints over the slow pace of Japanese rearmament and the country's closed markets. Once, when advisers urged President Eisenhower to get tough with a recalcitrant Japan, he replied: 'Don't let Japan reach a point where they want to invite the Kremlin into their country. Everything else fades into insignificance in the light of such a threat.'

Anti-American feeling has surfaced from time to time in the postwar years, sometimes as an oblique means for ordinary Japanese to assail their own government. In 1954 there were scattered protests over an incident that seemed to show the Americans being insensitive. The USA tested a hydrogen bomb on the Bikini atoll in the Pacific in March of that year. Twenty-three Japanese fishermen aboard their boat were close enough to see the blast and reported seeing 'a ball of fire' rising in the air which seemed to burn their eyes. When the crew of the *Lucky Dragon Number Five* returned to Japan, their hair was falling out and all were suffering from severe radiation sickness. Later in the year the boat's captain died.

In spite of such moments of resentment towards America, Japan remained deeply dependent on Washington, and the path towards full independence was tortuous. From 1950 onwards conservative politicians led by Yoshida, in alliance with the mandarins of the Finance Ministry, firmly rejected American pressures to rearm quickly. However, soon after the start of the Korean War Japan had set up a paramilitary force of 75 000 men, the National Police Reserve, and in 1954 Yoshida made the controversial announcement to the Diet that it was to change its name to the 'Japanese Self-Defence Forces' and expand its size quickly to 200 000 men. Yoshida explained his government's reasoning, that the Self-Defence Forces would not run counter to the 'no-war' clause in the constitution because they would be purely defensive in nature. Japan was to have 'an army without offensive power'.

By then Yoshida's reign was about to come to an end. His political power began to wane after his triumph at the San Francisco peace conference. He was growing impatient with his critics on all political sides and had to fight another election in 1953 after a row in which he had used unparliamentary language, shouting at an opposition member *'Bakayaro!'* (*'You fool!'*) in an argument over Japan's basic diplomatic stance. Yoshida's Liberals only just managed to remain the largest party in the new Diet. His arch-rival Ichiro Hatoyama was doing his best to remove him from office, and when a number of conservative politicians were caught up in a scandal involving shipbuilding kick-backs the Prime Minister took responsibility and resigned. It was December 1954. One eyewitness to Yoshida's departure was Masayoshi Ohira, who would himself serve as Premier in the 1970s. He recalled that

> it was a bitter cold day and only a few of us braved the bone-chilling wind outside the Prime Minister's official residence to bid Mr Yoshida farewell. It was a cruel and sad finale for Mr Yoshida, who during his six years and eight months in power had shown himself to be a truly outstanding leader.

In 1967 Yoshida died and was accorded the rare honour of a state funeral.

As it turned out, Yoshida founded a political dynasty of pro-American, bureaucrat-trained politicians which would dominate the political stage for another two decades. Ichiro Hatoyama became Premier, but he headed a conservative camp which was deeply split between his Democrats and the Liberal Party which Yoshida had led. The Socialists, who had themselves been split into two groups, saw their chance. They had strengthened their position in the Diet and in early 1955 came together again as a self-styled 'class-oriented mass party' committed to achieving a workers' revolution. It looked distinctly possible that the Socialists might become the largest single party at the next election and claim power for themselves. The bitter feud between the two conservative camps was put aside. Senior aides to Hatoyama and Yoshida, who for thirty years had refused even to drink a cup of tea together, kicked off the parley that led to the establishment in November 1955 of the Liberal Democratic Party.

The LDP was first and foremost a broad alliance against communism and socialism. Its founding goals were all-embracing: 'to stabilise the national livelihood, advance the country's welfare, restore Japan's international prestige by establishing true independence, and strengthening the conditions for a lasting peace.' But the 'Mission of the Party' contains a strong streak of nationalism. It blames the nation's troubles in part on what it calls 'the mistakes of Occupation policies'. It says that, as a result of the drafting of the post-war constitution, and the educational and other reforms, 'the national sentiment and patriotic feeling of the nation were unjustly impaired, and the national power of Japan was weakened'.

In its official founding documents the party commits itself to amending the constitution and to revising the laws passed during the Occupation, and looks forward to 'the eventual withdrawal of the foreign armed forces from Japan'. The significance of this pledge was above all that the party meant to revise Article 9, which formally bans the armed forces. With this the seeds of still more entangled contradictions were laid in Japanese politics. Just as its armed forces had been born illegitimately, outside the constitution, now Japan's key political organisation was set up with the intent of ultimately discarding the constitution, although the outside world saw it as the formal guarantee of Japanese good behaviour. Hatoyama personally wanted to see Article 9 revised, but backed away from attempting such a controversial move while in office.

Later, after the LDP had settled in as the natural party of government, critics claimed that it in fact was neither liberal nor democratic; nor was it a party in the Western sense, as it monopolised power in the same way as the communist parties in single-party states. The LDP was an expression of both the genius and the besetting weakness of Japan's political tradition. From the start the party was not much concerned with any particular political set of priorities, but with the effective management of conflicting interests within a stable framework. This it has done according to unwritten but implicitly understood rules of patronage. Its claim to govern rests above all on the premise that it can handle this role to the great satisfaction of the greatest number in Japan, while securing an even higher standard of prosperity for the nation as a whole. The LDP was born as a collection of lobby interests and has kept that character ever since.

In 1957 Japanese politics again heated up, with the election of the wartime minister, Nobusuke Kishi, to leadership of the party and the post of Prime Minister. The Socialists could not realistically attack the conservatives over their handling of the economy, which was performing extraordinarily well. But over the other main issue of the time, the relationship with the USA, and especially the prospective revision of the US–Japan Security Treaty, the LDP and the new Premier were deeply vulnerable. The Socialists and Communists united with the trade unions, with many university teachers and other intellectuals, and with the active student movement to attack the revision terms. The result was the most acute political and diplomatic crisis in post-war Japan.

The security pact which Yoshida had signed in 1951 had a strong flavour of the 'unequal treaties' imposed on Japan in the mid-nineteenth century by the Western powers. The US military, with bases in many parts of Japan, had a privileged status, and even the theoretical right to put down disturbances. These terms, and occasional crimes of violence committed by GIs, brought objections from both the left and the right that the Occupation was continuing, in spirit if not in name. In Moscow and Peking the official media were every day denouncing Japan as a 'running dog of US imperialism' and 'a military colony of the USA'. The Socialist Party leadership stuck to its line that the Security Treaty had to be torn up; some in the party, reflecting a widely held view of the liberal left, could not stomach the obduracy of their own side, and in 1959 they split off to form the Democratic Socialist Party.

Kishi, with the fervour of a convert, acted as the most pro-American of all Japan's post-war leaders, but he saw that the 1951 Security Treaty now had to be revised. The negotiations were difficult. The Pentagon felt that the bases in Japan and Okinawa were too strategically valuable to be the subject of any bargaining, and Congress was reluctant to budge on the issue. As the demonstrations gathered steam, Kishi himself voiced the view in private that in Japan 'it is generally felt that the US has no interest in Japan other than military'. After lengthy negotiations, the revised treaty was signed amid much fanfare in Washington in January 1960, and both governments saw it as proof of a new and secure relationship. As the two nations' flags flew side by side, Dwight Eisenhower, who had commanded the Allied forces in Europe, was heard by one of those standing near him to comment proudly: 'To think that I would ever feel as I do today about the Japanese!'

The new treaty was an improvement from the Japanese point of view. It committed the United States, 'in accordance with its constitutional provisions and processes', to defending Japan in case of armed attack, and took away America's right to intervene militarily in Japanese domestic affairs. The USA also kept the wording it wanted. American troops based in Japan were to be used not only for Japan's own protection but 'to maintain peace throughout the Far East'. A leading socialist politician, Masashi Ishibashi, found two strong reasons for rejecting the close alliance with America: one, that 'Japanese defence forces would be used in effect as frontline troops for American military strategy', the other that, if the Americans were again to fight a war using Japanese bases as they had done in Korea, 'Japan would become involved in an American war.' For Ishibashi, it was also a source of shame that the Japanese Prime Minister in charge of the treaty terms had once been arrested as a war criminal. Even though he had not been tried, 'we were worried that people elsewhere would think that the Japanese hadn't really searched their souls about the war at all'.

After the signing in Washington, the treaty had to be ratified by the Diet in Tokyo, where the combined forces of the left took to the streets to show their hostility both to the treaty itself and to the way it was being pushed through against considerable popular opposition. Once again, as during the threatened general strike in 1947, the streets of Tokyo were filled with crowds of angry demonstrators. The students made a ritual out of snake-dancing around the US Embassy, the Diet and other key places. Over several months there were many street battles between them and the police.

On the night of 19 May 1960, after weeks of high tension and almost daily demonstrations, the government was set to force a vote. Opposition MPs seized the seventy-six-year-old Speaker, whose presence was essential for such a vote, and held him in the basement of the parliament building. This provoked the LDP members, using their superior numbers, to go and physically drag the old gentleman back into the chamber. There were violent scuffles and the police were brought in to prevent the opposition members from blocking the corridors. Then the LDP, using its overall majority, opened a plenary session and voted to ratify the treaty while the opposition members were absent. The public was outraged. The voting itself was legal but the arrogance shown by the LDP in spurning their opponents and using physical force against them deeply shocked the Japanese sense of fair play and consensus. The most influential Japanese newspaper, the *Asahi Shimbun*, which then had well over 10 million readers, wrote a front-page editorial calling on Liberal Democrats to revolt against Kishi and make him resign.

The next month President Eisenhower was due to visit Japan to set the seal on the new, more equal relationship between the two Pacific allies; during that interval the anti-treaty demonstrations reached a crescendo. A nationwide series of strikes went ahead on 4 June. The next week Eisenhower's press secretary, James Hagerty, and the President's advance party landed at Haneda airport. Their Cadillac was besieged by thousands of demonstrators who threatened the occupants and danced and banged on the car roof. US Ambassador Douglas MacArthur II – the nephew of General MacArthur – was in the party and recalls that Hagerty was 'as cool as a cucumber. He pulled out his little pocket Kodak and started snapping pictures of the demonstrators through the windows of the ambassadorial car.' MacArthur himself was impressed with the way the students contented themselves with shouting and beating the car when 'they could have torn open the doors and taken us apart if they'd wanted to.' Still, the American party had a close escape. A helicopter was sent to rescue them; it landed safely inside the American Embassy compound, but at the very moment that it touched down one of its blades fell off, damaged by the missiles the demonstrators had thrown.

To Satoshi Kitakoji, the leader of the militant student federation Zengakuren, parliamentary politics had failed. The students decided to try to 'block the treaty revision by physical means and overthrow parliament'. On 15 June there was a huge rally and demonstrators surrounded the Diet building. Some tore down one of the gates and invaded the grounds. In the head-on clash with the riot police that followed, a twenty-two-year-old woman student of Tokyo University, Michiko Kamba, died. The scenes were relayed on television and proved to be the catharsis of the whole drama. There were no further large-scale demonstrations. Japan's seven most influential newspapers issued a joint statement condemning the use of violence for political ends and calling on the opposition parties to return to the Diet. It is a measure of the importance of the press within the Japanese body politic that the advice was heeded. The Americans announced that following the Hagerty 'incident', Eisenhower's visit was being postponed. The Security Treaty came into force on 23 June and on 18 July Kishi gave up the premiership to his Finance Minister, Hayato Ikeda.

Later Kishi maintained that the anti-treaty rioters had been unrepresentative of the general public mood: 'During the 1960 riots you could have found far more students carousing on the Ginza,' he claimed. But the LDP learned a lesson from the story: thereafter it would do its utmost to avoid using its superior numbers in parliament to ram through bills or motions in the face of opposition boycotts, for fear of exciting the same public censure as in 1960. It had been a salutary lesson in other ways, too. The conventional picture of Japan as America's prize student in Asia, eager to follow Western political and economic precepts, was now seen to be a fond myth. President Eisenhower, who received a rapturous, if orchestrated, welcome in Taipei and Seoul, was unwelcome in Japan. It was time to rethink the relationship after the first post-San Francisco decade. Eisenhower's postponed visit never took place, and neither of his two successors, John F. Kennedy and Lyndon B. Johnson, visited Japan. For the rest of the 1960s the USA treated Japan with caution on political and trade matters, wanting at all costs to prevent any further structural damage to the relationship. Japanese prime ministers regularly made the pilgrimage to Washington, but not until Gerald Ford's visit in 1974 did an American president go to Tokyo.

The protests against 'Anpo' (the Security Treaty) stand out as the largest political movement in Japan's post-war history. Japanese scholars called them 'the high-water mark of participatory democracy in post-war Japan'. After the forced passage of the treaty bill, 13 million people signed petitions demanding fresh general elections; 6 million workers supported these efforts with work stoppages. Hundreds of thousands of Japanese citizens, many of them completely new to political activities, demonstrated in Tokyo streets and around the Diet building. The emotion was not directed against the USA as such; Satoshi Kitakoji, the student leader, says the aim of the protests was to block Japan's rearmament: 'There was no reason for the Japanese to kill Americans or vice versa ... we have to have good relations.' A leader of the Tokyo University students, Satsuki Eda, became head of a small opposition political party, the United Social Democratic Federation, which strongly affirms the need for Japan to keep its close ties with America. 'To me,' he says, 'being against the Security Treaty was not anti-American. America was the symbol of freedom, democracy and prosperity, and its existence gave us a dream.'

The crisis over Anpo was a mass show of opposition to the national goals set by the power élite and to the methods used to achieve them. In the end, though, the protestors failed to break the mould set by the LDP and its backers. The disillusionment was very deep. Many students and young members of the intelligentsia joined in the demonstrations less because of the treaty itself than out of a sense of frustration at the 'managed society' they lived in. To them the treaty was a symbol of how Japan had opted to barter independence for prosperity. Students from Tokyo University and other top colleges knew they were destined to join the Establishment – or, as they themselves said, the 'manipulators' – who were exploiting the docile Japanese majority and people in developing countries alike. Those students were among the most forceful leaders of the anti-Anpo demonstrations. After the turmoil died down, a deep political apathy took hold of the majority of Japanese.

Throughout the months of unrest the political climate was so inflamed that Nobusuke Kishi had to be kept under close police guard wherever he went. His personal secretary, Tsutomu Wada, doubted whether he and his boss would come out of the crisis alive: 'In my heart I wondered when we were going to be assassinated. . . . Mr Kishi in practice lived each day surrounded by millions of demonstrators, and he staked his life on getting the job [of passing the revised treaty] done.' Kishi was unharmed in the months of greatest violence, but shortly after he stepped down he was attacked and stabbed in the leg by a right-wing fanatic who thought he had let the nation down.

There was more to the season of political violence in 1960. In October, with elections only a few weeks off, several political party leaders addressed the same meeting at a public hall in Tokyo. The socialist leader, Inejiro Asanuma, unveiled his party's policies, including the immediate recognition of red China, to a chorus of boos and hisses. A young member of a right-wing association ran up to the rostrum and stabbed Asanuma to death with a short sword in full public view.

The echoes of pre-war fascist violence, when several leading public figures were assassinated for standing in the way of the right-wing revolution, were all too obvious. The shock was felt inside Japan and out. An editorial in the *New York Times* commented that: 'The streak of violence that continues to lurk behind the façade of Japanese democracy has been revealed again.' Many in Japan and abroad felt that to some extent the Socialists themselves were guilty of creating a climate of lawlessness and extremism by orchestrating the earlier months of street turmoil. At the same time it was widely recognised that, as a result of the somewhat artificial political framework since the war, the Japanese had not as a nation fully digested the experience of the war and the defeat, or yet built up a fully functioning system of representative democracy.

A fresh alarm broke out early the next year over yet another right-wing outrage, when a seventeen-year-old self-styled 'super-patriot' broke into the home of a leading publisher intending to murder him for publishing a story insulting to the Imperial family. The youth found his intended victim out, but he injured the man's wife and stabbed a housemaid to death. The offending work had by general consent little literary merit. It was a short story in the form of a fantasy about the gory deaths of the Crown Prince and Princess and it had appeared in a monthly magazine, *Chuo Koron*, a recognised forum for debate on major political and social issues. The incident showed all too clearly that the forces of ultranationalism which had taken Japan to war still commanded the faith of some of the tens of thousands of active members of right-wing associations. One of their most prominent figures, Bin Akao, head of the Patriotic Party, publicly defended the assassination attempt, saying that Japan's established press was under the influence of communist thought and that right-wingers 'had no choice but to resort to violence to fight back'.

The far right appeared to be set back by the public disapproval of its methods, yet the magazine incident if anything served to strengthen its power to dictate the limits of political debate by intimidation. The 'chrysanthemum taboo' – open discussion of the Imperial family system – was confirmed. This became clear later in 1971 when another intellectual magazine, *Shiso no kagaku*, also issued by the *Chuo Koron* publishing company, suppressed its own series of essays on Japanese politics and the Emperor system out of fear of terrorist reprisals from right-wing activists. Without consulting its staff, the management ordered all copies of their own special issue to be destroyed. The episode was the symbolic beginning of a system of self-censorship on the part of the Japanese press; ever since then, sporadic incidents of right-wing violence against leading news media as well as against liberal intellectuals have limited the free expression of controversial ideas in Japan.

Hayato Ikeda, Prime Minister from July 1960 until 1964, was a reassuring figure, in contrast to Nobusuke Kishi. Ikeda sought to lower the political temperature with his economy-first policies and his plan for doubling the average income of Japanese people in ten years. However, America's entry into the Vietnam War in 1965 meant a fresh round of struggle between the same forces that had faced one another in the Security Treaty conflict. The chances of the protests affecting events in any real way were remote, and there was a strong element of ritual in the anti-war demonstrations by tens of thousands of citizens, who clashed with gladiatorial riot police. In 1968 dozens of protestors and riot police were injured in demonstrations over the entry of the American aircraft-carrier *Enterprise* into the American base at Sasebo near Nagasaki. The protests were both against the fact that the *Enterprise* was nuclear-powered and against its presumed arsenal of nuclear weapons; a strong anti-nuclear movement rallied to the support of the protestors in Nagasaki, but to little effect. The Japanese government remained stalwartly behind the USA throughout the Vietnam War.

The Liberal Democrats maintained their comfortable parliamentary majority during this period – enough to stave off the threat from the combined opposition, but well short of the two-thirds needed to change the country's constitution. The same groups of people – students, left-wing *kageki-ha* or professional 'radical groups', and trade unionists – would demonstrate for a whole basket of causes: American disengagement from Vietnam, banning the bomb, wage increases twice as high as inflation, and the independence of Japanese universities. Civic anti-war groups came together in a mass movement known as Beheiren, the Citizens' Committee for Peace in Vietnam, which held frequent demonstrations against the Vietnam War and Japan's support for the US war effort. But some left-wing factions were committed to using violent means for the same end, and they kept up a series of bloody feuds with the police.

The issue which brought together the ideological left, activist students and local working people was the government's heavy-handed decision in 1966 to build a new international airport on farming land at Narita, 35 miles east of Tokyo. Local farmers were incensed that the decision had been taken behind their backs and were determined not to move. They were quickly joined in their struggle by a host of other organisations, including the Zengakuren students' federation. Over the course of a decade there were scores of pitched battles on the site itself as the police gradually took over more of the designated land. In 1978 Narita airport at last opened, but the planned bullet-train line from there to Tokyo was abandoned because of repeated sabotage, and Narita's capacity has been pathetically limited by continued physical resistance to its expansion. Even in 1990 it still has only one runway.

There was widespread student dissatisfaction, too, with the autocratic way in which universities were run and also with the overt way in which education was being made to serve the dictates of the conservative government. In 1968–9 groups of radical students captured part of Tokyo University and the authorities had to call in police with water-cannon and helicopters to clear the campus. No one was able to graduate from Japan's most prestigious university that year. Classrooms were barricaded and professors were heckled or even assaulted. Students insisted that the concept of theoretical democracy and freedom that they had been taught to admire in their secondary education bore little resemblance to the manner in which Japanese politics and big business operated in the 1950s. As one student activist said later, he saw the need to act when we find that something is wrong. It was not the kind of democracy we learned about at school. My way of thinking developed through friends or teachers, or when I went to a May Day demonstration without understanding it and became enraged after I was beaten by a policeman. Then I discussed with my friends how to change such a world.

Criticism of the universities and their sponsors intensified. Students, who had been through the competitive 'examination hell' to get there in the first place, knew that after graduation most of them were destined to fit into the expanding corporations and government offices of an increasingly rich Japan. It was hardly an inspiring prospect. To conform to company norms and behave as a diligent *salariiman* for the next thirty years in the same organisation, subject to a slow progress up the age-determined escalator of promotion, was enough to make many turn, at least during their student years, against the 'system'.

The forces of the far right mostly kept to themselves during these turbulent years. Indeed, the only right-wing threat to Japan's constitutional order turned out to be at least as much a piece of personal exhibitionism as it was a political gesture. At its centre was the widely acclaimed writer, Yukio Mishima. His own interest, and much of his writing, focused on Japan's metamorphosis after the war from a nation of warriors embodying the ancient spirit of Yamato (the oldest Japanese kingdom) to an effete and money-grubbing society in which most individuals had lost all self-respect. That anyway was Mishima's characterisation. He produced a series of impressive if sometimes self-indulgent works, from his autobiographical novel *Kamen no kokuhaku* (*Confessions of a Mask*) to his final tetralogy *Hojo no umi* (*The Sea of Fertility*). Mishima became a national figure not only for his literary and theatrical work, but for his open espousal of ultranationalist dogma about the sanctity of the Emperor and the Zen Bhuddist concept of the 'unity of thought and action'. This he mixed up with his own brand of black romanticism. He took pleasure in astonishing his high-society friends, both Japanese and Western, by practised displays of the proper routine for committing *seppuku*.

Mishima had friends among Japan's top LDP politicians. He formed a small private army called the *Tatenokai* ('Shield Society') in imitation of pre-war rightist societies, and gained permission for its members – who apart from himself were all impressionable college students with right-wing leanings – to wear designer military uniforms and go on training exercises with the Japanese Self-Defence Forces. On 25 November 1970 Mishima and his closest followers, including his alleged homosexual partner Masakatsu Morita, went for an arranged meeting to the headquarters in Tokyo of the Eastern Army of the Self-Defence Forces. Nobody will every know whether he really believed it possible, but Mishima planned to incite a military rebellion to restore Japan's greatness. He was carrying with him a manifesto which ended with the words: 'Let us restore Nippon to its true state and let us die.... I will show you a value which is greater than respect for life. It is not freedom, not democracy. It is our land of history and tradition: Nippon!'

Once inside the commanding general's office, Mishima's band took him hostage and tied him to a chair. He demanded that all the soldiers be summoned to hear him address them from the balcony above the parade ground. When several officers tried to restrain him, Mishima used his choice *samurai* sword to slash into them, inflicting serious wounds but not killing them. Wearing his double-breasted Tatenokai uniform, he harangued the men of the barracks, calling on them to rise up with him to amend the constitution and restore the greatness of the Emperor. Otherwise, he said, the Self-Defence Forces would be 'American mercenaries', defending a constitution that denied the existence of a Japanese army. 'I thought that the Self-Defence Forces were the last hope of Nippon, the last stronghold of the Japanese soul,' he shouted. 'But Japanese people today think of money, just money. Where is our national spirit today? The politicians care nothing for Japan. They are only greedy for power!'

The soldiers below heckled and shouted back abuse. Mishima made a last, despairing appeal for them to rise up, but the jeers and catcalls only grew louder. He shouted *'Tenno Heika Banzai!'* ('Long Live the Emperor!') and went indoors. There Mishima knelt down and plunged a sharp dagger into his abdomen. In agony, he was finally beheaded by one of the others. Then, in his turn, the chosen friend, Morita, was executed in the same way, after making only an abortive attempt at ripping open his own stomach.

Reactions within Japan were of horror and widespread disbelief. Prime Minister Sato remarked when he learned the news that Mishima 'must have been crazy'. Foreign literary figures who had known the writer weighed in with their analyses of his motives. The vast majority of younger Japanese rejected his philosophy and laughed at his Emperor-worship. Certainly many on the right were with Mishima in despising society's materialism and lack of national pride, but reaction to his sensational death allayed suspicions that in the 1970s Japan would revert to the xenophobia of the 1930s. Mishima became a martyr to the ultranationalist cause, but his example was cited in only two other isolated and minor cases of rightist violence in the ensuing decade.

On the extreme left, though, there was more student bloodshed. In the 1960s the Japanese student movement gradually lost its earlier unity and some elements spun off into self-destructive coteries. Breakaway factions fought the police, hijacked planes, and slaughtered innocent people and finally each other. In March 1970 Rengo Sekigun (the United Red Army) hijacked a Japan Airlines aircraft to North Korea, where several of its members settled, until years later they declared they were broken-hearted for their own country and wished to return. In February 1972, the group was traced and besieged in a mountain lodge near Karuizawa, about 100 miles north of Tokyo. Two policemen were killed in the shoot-out that followed, and the siege led to the discovery of the torture and death the previous year of fourteen of their own members accused of 'ideological crimes'. Frustrated in Japan by their inability to raise revolution, the remnants of the band then set themselves up in the Middle East and collaborated with anti-Israeli groups in the region. In May 1972, United Red Army terrorists opened fire on unsuspecting passengers at Lod airport in Tel Aviv. Twenty-four people were killed.

Throughout the 1970s Rengo Sekigun kept up a regular spate of terrorist attacks, of which the bloodiest was a devastating time-bomb explosion at the Tokyo headquarters of Mitsubishi Heavy Industries, the country's leading arms manufacturer, which killed 8 people and injured over 300. They struck at widely scattered targets in Europe and South-east Asia as well as in Japan. However, the group's base of support gradually faded, and many of its later actions were planned as a means of extorting the release of its jailed members. They succeeded in securing the release of five in 1975, after occupying the American and Swedish Embassies in Kuala Lumpur; two years later they hijacked a Japan Airlines plane in Bombay and negotiated the release of nine more of their comrades, as well as a $6 million ransom. A dozen United Red Army members are still at large at the time of writing, and their photographs are displayed at immigration points and police stations throughout Japan.

Other left-wing factions remained Japan-based. Among the most violent and enduring has been the Chukaku-ha (Central Core Faction), which was spawned from the student movement of the 1960s. Its attention gradually shifted from the Vietnam War and US bases in Japan to the struggle against Narita airport, Japanese big business and the Imperial family. On 'International Anti-war Day', 21 October 1968, thousands of people belonging to New Left factions of the Zengakuren students' federation went to Tokyo's busiest railway station, Shinjuku, and tried to sabotage cargoes of fuel intended for US military use. They set the station alight and throughout the evening conducted a pitched battle, hurling stones at the riot police, who replied with tear gas. There were over 500 arrests.

In the 1980s the Chukaku-ha and other splinter groups developed sophisticated missiles and kept up a steady stream of attacks at intervals of months or years on the Imperial Palace grounds and other Imperial facilities, the US Embassy in Tokyo, and other Establishment targets; these did little damage, but drew some attention to their presence during the 1986 Tokyo economic summit, and during the ceremonies to mark the death of Emperor Hirohito in January 1989 and the accession of his heir Akihito in the following eighteen months.

Japan's worst decade of political extremism coincided with the decade of America's war in Vietnam, but it had its roots in Japan's own political soil. In the 1960s many new groupings sprang up to join forces against the bureaucratic dead hand that could be seen all too often in the governing of Japan. Many of these pressure groups or citizens' movements were born out of concern over local issues of welfare and the environment which had been largely ignored during the years of heady economic growth. Most of these were not so much anti-Vietnam War or anti-Security Treaty as pro-ecology and concerned to improve the environment. Their zeal met with only limited success.

One issue during this period united all sides in Japan in rare agreement: the call for the return of Okinawa, the island group 1000 miles south of the Japanese mainland. Eisaku Sato, premier from 1966 to 1972, called America's possession of the islands a symbol of Japan's defeat and an obstacle in the relationship of the two countries. However, the Pentagon viewed Okinawa as essential to its task of actively confronting the forces of communism everywhere. The Kadena air-base there was used for bombing sorties against North Vietnam, and was irreplaceable as a strategic outpost in the northern Pacific. Just as at the time of the talks on revising the US–Japan Security Treaty, the government had the daunting task of wringing concessions out of the United States, while the parliamentary opposition was able to champion the strong public demand for Japan to stand up to the Americans on an issue of national concern. Violent street-fighting broke out in October 1968 when radicals chanting for the immediate return of the territory clashed with police equipped with tear gas and water-cannon. Large-scale demonstrations under New Left auspices were organised by Beheiren. Students, workers and housewives were united in a people's movement against a host of targets inside and outside Japan. A common slogan was 'Oppose the War, Oppose the Treaty, Return Okinawa'.

The Americans reluctantly saw that they would have to hand back Okinawa. At a summit meeting in Hawaii in 1969, Eisaku Sato won from President Nixon a firm commitment on its return, but without any date being fixed. Washington was determined that in exchange for the territorial concession Japan would be made to give ground on a number of trade disputes, especially over textiles. Richard Nixon asked for sharp restraint in Japan's textile exports to the USA, and Sato, anxious not to disappoint the American President, gave the impression that he had agreed. Later, however, Sato ran into powerful resistance from the textile industry and from MITI, which had direct responsibility for the matter. When, as the Americans saw it, Japan failed to deliver its side of the bargain, the Nixon administration felt betrayed. Thereafter exchanges between the two governments, in particular in the prolonged textile talks, were often caustic, and the Nixon team chose not to consult Japan on vital policy matters. A crucial failure of communication in the Nixon–Sato summit appears to have played a part in this worsening of relations: after listening to Nixon's request on textiles, Sato replied saying, 'Wakarimashita.' The word means, literally, 'I understand', and it can signify positive agreement; but apparently Sato meant to say only that he understood Nixon's concern and would *try* to ease the situation. It was a textbook case of a Japanese politician not only using his own language loosely, but opting under pressure to try to please both sides.

Negotiations over the terms for Okinawa's reversion were by their nature complex, and they took almost two years to complete. The Americans kept the huge Kadena air-base and other facilities there, but had to remove stocks of nerve gas. It was commonly believed in Japan that they were using Okinawa to stockpile nuclear weapons, and the political opposition stridently demanded guarantees that they would be removed. The Japanese government had to be content with verbal assurances from the Americans, in line with the US policy of 'neither confirming nor denying' the presence of nuclear arms at their military bases. A great deal of public suspicion remained among the Japanese on this score. The opposition charged, and many ordinary Japanese believed, that their own government was allowing American submarines and ships to enter Japanese ports carrying nuclear missiles, and that this would apply to Okinawa even after its reversion. Sato pressed ahead in the knowledge that Okinawa's return would anyway be seen as a triumph for his administration.

There was genuine emotion in Japan when, in June 1971, Sato signed the agreement with the United States to effect Okinawa's reversion to Japan. Many believed him when he called it 'the end of the post-war period', but the euphoria was shortlived. The very next month President Nixon and his National Security Adviser, Dr Henry Kissinger, showed how little Japan counted in their calculations by announcing that the President would be making a trip to China in the new year. The Japanese Ambassador in Washington at that time, Nobuhiko Ushiba, said he was 'flabbergasted' when he heard the news. He protested to Secretary of State William Rogers, 'We were working closely together to maintain the seat of the Nationalist government [Taiwan] in the United Nations: what happened to our common endeavour?' Edwin Reischauer, America's Ambassador in Tokyo from 1961 to 1966, was more scathing. He called the handling of the episode 'sheer stupidity on our part', and said of Dr Kissinger:

> He tended to neglect Japan because he thought so much in terms of sheer military balance of power, and Japan did not seem to figure much in it; so he and the rest of the Administration tended to overlook Japan's sensitivities and they went ahead with the approach to China after he'd promised to consult with Japan on this for many years.

In practice, though, once the shock had been digested, the American opening to China served Japan's needs admirably. Trade links with Taiwan stayed as strong as ever, and Japanese business soon realised that the mainland, the world's most populous country, might one day be a fabulously large consumer market. In the words of Michael Oksenberg, President Jimmy Carter's adviser on China later in the 1970s, 'President Nixon opened the door to China: Japan walked in.' The Nixon visit to China in February 1972 was followed in September that year by a similar visit by the Japanese Prime Minister of the day, Kakuei Tanaka. Chinese leaders began being driven around in Toyotas, and Japan's trade with China quickly dwarfed that of any other country – to such an extent that by the end of the decade the Chinese were pleading for Japan to rein in its exports and cut its ballooning bilateral trade surplus.

Meanwhile the Nixon administration had come to see Japan as a major problem in terms of trade. America's deficit with Japan, of $4 billion in 1971, was also causing much anger in Congress, and American industrialists were complaining loudly about Japan's alleged dumping of steel and colour TV sets. A major factor in the imbalance was the yen–dollar exchange rate, which under the Bretton Woods system of fixed international currency rates had been pegged at 360 yen to the dollar ever since 1949. The second 'Nixon shock' came in August. Without any advance warning, President Nixon announced the decision to float the dollar and impose a 10 per cent surcharge on imports into America. The dollar's value plunged against other major currencies and by the end of the year was worth only 308 yen. Some international economists had seen such a move coming, but Japanese business leaders appeared thunderstruck. The country's export industries lost much of their price advantage at a stroke and some small firms went out of business. A senior official of the Keidanren, Masaya Miyoshi, says that at the time 'Japanese people thought we were treated very badly'. The carefully laid plans for transforming the Japanese economy around the fixed exchange rate were, he said, 'shattered' by the shock.

The sense of crisis reflected the small-country mentality which still stubbornly flourished in Japan. The delicate interaction of government ministries with a multitude of business lobby groups meant that a painful experience for any one group would quickly lead to national leaders voicing the same concerns on behalf of the nation as a whole. In reality, the currency adjustment was long overdue and the hardship was limited to textile and other exporting firms which depended heavily on the American market. Even the business spokesman Mr Miyoshi was eventually to see the move as a 'blessing in disguise', because it enabled Japan to upgrade its economy even more efficiently than would have been possible with the undervalued yen.

There was, however, no escaping the fact that the Nixon administration had singled out Tokyo for rough treatment. But the damage to the political relationship was tempered by that dependency. America not only took fully 30 per cent of Japan's exports; it was still Japan's mentor, and in many ways a role model. In practice Japan had precious few friends other than America as the 1970s dawned. Partly because of war memories in the region, and partly thanks to its role as loyal lieutenant to the American superpower, there was a measure of hostility to Japan's emerging economic and military strength. To the north and west lay China, which needed Japan's economic helping hand, but whose official media went on railing day after day against its partnership with America and its alleged 'rearmament'. After Tanaka's trip to Peking official relations were restored, but the visit was not wholly a success: Tanaka appeared to gloss over Japan's sense of responsibility for the Rape of Nanking and the years of humiliation inflicted by the Japanese army on China, using the lightweight phrase *'Meiwaku o kakemashita,'* meaning 'We are sorry to have caused you trouble.' The Chinese had expected a much more fulsome expression of apology.

Further to the north, the Soviet Union took every opportunity to humble Japan. State-to-state relations had been restored in 1956, but still the two countries had been unable to agree on terms for signing a peace treaty because of a territorial dispute. Japan insisted first on the Russians returning the small but strategically important group of islands to the north of Hokkaido which Stalin's army had seized in the closing days of the war. Moscow had no intention of doing so. At the Yalta conference in February 1945, Roosevelt, Churchill and Stalin had agreed secretly that the Kurile island chain would be handed over to the USSR following Moscow's entry into the anti-Japan military alliance.

The Japanese government was obliged to renounce all claim to the Kuriles in the San Francisco peace treaty, but the Japanese argued tenaciously that the 'northern territories' of Etorofu and Kunashiri, Shikotan and the Habomai group were offshore Japanese islands, and distinct from the Kuriles proper. After the return of Okinawa, Japanese demands for the return of the 'northern territories' intensified, but the Soviet side was unyielding. The islands guard a strait which gives the Russians secure passage for their naval ships and submarines to and from Vladivostok, the headquarters of their Far Eastern navy. Nobuhiko Ushiba, one of Japan's top diplomats, had no hesitation in calling the Russians 'the most hated nation' among the Japanese in the 1970s.

A short distance across the Sea of Japan to the north-west, North Korea, under the self-styled 'great leader' Marshal Kim Il Sung, branded Japan along with America as an 'enemy of peace-loving peoples'. North Korea and Japan had never established diplomatic contacts at all after the war and hundreds of thousands of pro-North Korean ethnic Koreans living in Japan were a constant reminder of the problems surviving from the bitter past. At least with South Korea Japan had formally overcome the wartime legacy of hatred, and had restored full normal relations in 1965. Nevertheless, popular animosities on the South Korean side were so strong that no top leaders from either nation exchanged visits, and South Korean industrialists, knowing their country was materially many years behind Japan, feared economic domination.

In South-east Asia the Japanese had bought a form of forgiveness from the Philippines, Indonesia and Singapore by agreeing to war reparations and help in the economic sphere, but deep suspicions remained over Japan's intentions. By 1972 its economic domination was so marked that when Prime Minister Tanaka toured the region he was met by fierce anti-Japanese demonstrations. Residents in Jakarta, Bangkok and Manila protested in their thousands at Japanese firms' pollution and rapacious business attitudes. In Jakarta crowds carried placards reading 'Tanaka Go Home' and 'Stop the Japanese Economic Invasion'. Eight people were killed when the demonstration turned into a riot against the 'ugly Japanese'.

□ □ □

At the end of the decade Japan hosted an international event designed to celebrate the collective success of the whole nation. In the Senri Hills outside the second largest city, Osaka, the world fair entitled Expo '70 was more than anything an ostentatious exhibition of Japan's new-found wealth, and a monument to Japanese materialism. Japanese companies and public organisations mounted the lion's share of the exhibitions that were staged under the loose theme of 'progress and harmony of mankind'. The pavilions housed garish and eye-catching shows of mechanical marvels and three-dimensional side-projections. Electric cars sped about the Expo compound, driven by pert Japanese hostesses in uniform. It was like a Japanese festival: showy, raucous, a celebration of the Japanese spirit. Expo attracted vast crowds, who queued patiently for a glimpse of moon rock in the American pavilion or art from the Soviet Union; 64 million people, all but 1.7 million of them Japanese, visited the park area over six months. The event was a triumph for Japan's self-esteem, and for man's ability to survive the discomfort of crowds.

Environmentalists were dismayed at the terrible consequences of the nation's 'success'. Those on the radical left had despaired entirely of their country. Minoru Morita, the student leader, gave this verdict on the Japan of the 1960s:

> we had created a monstrous society for ourselves. Our environment was contaminated, our water polluted by industrial effluents and our natural environment was destroyed. In this setting the Japanese people were concerned with nothing but economic gain. They'd lost all humanistic ideals.

Some soberly felt that Japanese public life had reached a nadir of self-serving rhetoric and that the seedling of Japanese democracy needed careful nursing if it was ever to grow into a healthy plant.

Despite this, the great majority of Japanese were proud of the nation's achievements and confident about the future. America might be the society whose dream of affluence was recognised across the world, and the British had invented the 'Swinging Sixties', but more than any nation the Japanese had reason to savour the taste of their new-found prosperity. Masaya Ito, one of Prime Minister Ikeda's confidants, summed it up like this: 'Much had happened along the way, there had been pollution and so on; but we'd really achieved a lot, we'd got ourselves to a good position.' At the same time he was anxious about the future, like other members of a generation of Japanese who had literally taken their country from rags to riches: 'I was a little afraid. I thought, "How much longer can it go on growing?" It was like a magic teapot that just kept on pouring.'

4

Shocks and Scandals

THE 1970s

Eiji Yamagata had never expected to attend a Cabinet meeting. He was merely a civil servant, although a senior one – head of the Natural Resources Agency, in the many-sided Ministry of International Trade and Industry. When the Arabs announced in mid-October 1973 that they would cut off oil to 'unfriendly nations', however, Yamagata found himself at the eye of the storm which at once hit Tokyo. The government needed to know in a hurry how long it would be before Japan's oil stocks ran out. He was the official directly in charge, and was summoned to a meeting of the Prime Minister and other Cabinet ministers.

Yamagata carried bad news. Initial estimates of Japan's oil stockpiles had been too optimistic. In reality the country had enough for only forty-nine days' consumption, of which forty-five days' worth was 'running-stock', already in the distribution chain. Actual reserves of oil amounted to a mere four days' supply.

Yamagata sat down with the robust fifty-five-year-old Prime Minister, Kakuei Tanaka, and his colleagues, including the suave Minister of International Trade and Industry, Yasuhiro Nakasone. He recalls their reaction:

> I explained the situation to these eminent people and they were all extremely shocked. Indeed everyone was in a state of total shock because they thought the Japanese economy would collapse, and that they would be heading towards a catastrophe in terms of running the country.

Mr Tanaka's trusted secretary, Shigezo Hayasaka, remembers his master's reaction:

109

When Tanaka was told there were only four days' supply left he slammed his fists on the table in anger, saying, 'How could such a stupid thing have happened!' Then Tanaka calmed himself and told the rest of his Cabinet firmly and in a loud voice, 'We have money, so even if the price is high we can still buy oil. The world is not coming to an end. Everyone must keep calm: don't panic.'

The 'oil shock' stopped the unfolding Japanese miracle in its tracks, and for a time looked as though it would derail it completely. The world's largest importer of oil suddenly found itself short of the lifeblood of its industries. In the rest of the industrial world there was little sympathy towards Japan's plight. But none of the European nations depended, as Japan did, on imported oil for as much as 75 per cent of its total energy needs. The manner of Japan's recovery was, in the words of the future Prime Minister Takeo Fukuda, 'a kind of miracle'. It was evidence to a watchful world that Japan's economic and social systems contained a potent mixture of discipline and flexibility which would make the country into the world's most resilient economy only a few years after it had received this body blow.

In early 1973 the Japanese economy was going through a very rough patch. That spring the balance of payments dipped into the red as the price of many raw materials rose, fuelled by a spate of commodity shortages. The substantial balance of payments surpluses Japan had accumulated since 1965 meant that money was plentiful. The government itself had led a bonanza of spending in which the private sector had eagerly joined. After international exchange rates were allowed to float in the early part of the year, the Japanese government used up a large part of its foreign currency reserves in buying dollars internationally in order to slow down the yen's appreciation. The money supply had grown out of control and the result was an inflation rate which reached double figures by the summer. Everyone in Japan wanted their share of the benefits of twenty years of fast growth.

Some of the problems were those of success: the stock market had soared by 60 per cent since the new year on hopes of a new wave of growth. But there was a mood of uneasiness and apprehension. The effects of years of government in the interests of big business had led to some of the world's most shocking cases of industrial pollution. The Tanaka government, which had come in the previous year amid high hopes and a record public support rate of 60 per cent, had quickly led Japan into a trade deficit, spiralling prices and a failing economy.

Kakuei Tanaka had swept to power in July 1972 after an internal LDP leadership contest. Tanaka's key campaign pledge was to carry out his own grandiose plans for regional development, published under the title *Building a New Japan: The Remodelling of the Japanese Archipelago*. The scheme called for every part of Japan to be linked in a network of eleven bullet-train lines so that a person could travel the length of the country within a single day, and for the building of new industrial centres in outlying areas, to reverse the large-scale migration from the countryside to the cities. The bullet-train lines would run like a backbone through the Japanese islands from north to south. Tunnels were to be built through the sides of the Japan Alps on the main island, Honshu, to form other lines reaching out in every direction like ribs from the main trunk. National highways would become another set of arteries, with minor roads criss-crossing the country like veins. The plan foresaw the building of a tunnel under the seabed connecting Hokkaido and Honshu, as well as three long bridges to link Honshu with Shikoku island.

The idea caught the public's imagination, but it was spoiled by the greed of speculators. Big construction and real-estate firms had grown immensely rich by buying land designated for future development. Many thousands of people in the regions sold their ancestral land cheaply to speculators. Land prices in Tokyo had risen by 36 per cent in one year and rented living space there had become the most expensive in the world. It was an age of sharks and insider dealing and sudden killings on the markets. The government's support rate fell to 25 per cent. One sign of the public mood was the appearance of a book, *Nihon chimbotsu* (*Japan Sinks*), which became a 3 million copy bestseller in 1973. A film of the same title appeared in the autumn of that year and became an overnight sensation. It showed earthquakes and volcanic eruptions leading to the submersion of the Japanese islands beneath the waters of the Pacific Ocean.

The nervous mood sprang partly from the knowledge that Japan's prosperity rested on a precarious base. The country depended on imports for almost all of its raw material and energy needs, and for half its food. In the summer of 1973 America abruptly announced a total embargo on its exports of soybeans: Japan depended overwhelmingly on the USA for its supply of one of the nation's most essential foodstuffs, and reacted with shock. The US government resumed shipments to Japan, but the psychological damage was already done. The Japanese feared that with a worldwide shortage of grain, American wheat exports to Japan might also be curtailed. Japan depended on the Middle East for 85 per cent of its oil, but conspicuously lacked a network of alliances or established friendships to guarantee this supply. It was deeply dependent on the United States, but the Nixon administration took the relationship for granted. That had been amply demonstrated by the twin 'Nixon shocks' of 1971: the sudden decision to devalue the dollar and the volte-face to open links with communist China. The Japanese feared that if and when some real disaster struck they would be exposed and alone.

So it proved. King Faisal of Saudi Arabia, among others, had warned the Japanese clearly that they would have to come off the fence over the Arab–Israeli dispute or face serious consequences, but Japan doggedly held to a middle course. It voted for the United Nations Resolution 242 calling for Israel's withdrawal from the lands it had seized in 1967, but also followed America's lead in supporting pro-Israel resolutions which denied the Palestinians' case. The Tanaka government trusted in the framework which had always protected it in the past, and took few precautions to secure its oil supplies.

In the spring of 1973 the MITI Minister, Yasuhiro Nakasone, visited four Middle Eastern countries, including Saudi Arabia and Kuwait, in an attempt to win a guaranteed future supply of oil. The trip appeared to go well. He promised that Japan would use its industrial skills to help those countries in their nation-building efforts, and pledged that Japan would not join any oil-importing countries' club. Japan had two big advantages: the lack of any record as a colonial power in the region, and its now recognised industrial might. Also, Japanese oil firms had a reputation for offering a generous share of profits to to the Gulf states where they were drilling for oil and refining it. Still, on the key issue of the Arab–Israeli dispute Nakasone could offer nothing more than neutrality. It would not be enough.

On 6 October, Israel's Yom Kippur holy day, Egypt and Syria launched a joint assault on Israel. Immediately eight other Arab countries joined in the war. After two weeks of fierce fighting, Israel repelled the initial attack and it was clear that it would not be dislodged by force from the Arab territories it had occupied since 1967. At that point the Arab oil cartel used its weapon. The ten members of the Organisation of Arab Petroleum-Exporting Countries (OAPEC), which had never before been able to enforce decisions on production and price levels, now acted as one. They announced on 17 October that they would cut their collective output of crude oil by 5 per cent a month for the next twenty months, unless Israel withdrew from the occupied territories. They slapped an immediate embargo on exports to the USA. Oil prices soared, with Petromin, the Saudi oil company, raising its price by 70 per cent and the American oil majors by 30 per cent before the end of October. Japan and oil-importing states also faced an oil embargo unless they demonstrated full support for the Arab cause in the war. The deadline for them was 24 November, when the Arab oil ministers were due to meet again in Algiers. Dr Henry

Kissinger, the newly appointed US Secretary of State, began his 'shuttle diplomacy' to stop the war and end the threatened oil embargo, but the Arab nations now seemed resolute and united.

Japan faced the possibility of economic starvation. Given its over-whelming dependence on imported oil, the impact of the inevitable shortfall both on industry and on households would be immediate. An actual embargo would mean the swift closure of many large factories, mass unemployment and a drastic shortage of food and basic goods. To head this off Japan would have to come down clearly on the side of the Arabs and against Israel, but that would risk the wrath of the USA, Japan's mentor and its most vital export market. The Cabinet was in disarray. Masayoshi Ohira, the firmly pro-American Foreign Minister, spoke out implying that Japan could not change its policy suddenly in response to such pressure. 'Japan,' he said, 'cannot survive without the trust of other nations.' He would have to eat his words later. Kakuei Tanaka was more independent and determined to do whatever might be necessary. But it was not clear how far Japan could go without injuring its vital ties with the USA.

The government was slow to react with practical steps to calm the business community and the public. Some ministers hoped that the threat would pass and allowed themselves to believe the Saudi Arabian Ambassador to Japan who said he 'hoped that Japan would not be inconvenienced'. But on 4 November the Arab oil-producing countries hardened their position, announcing an overall 25 per cent production cut. Japanese oil companies in the Gulf were told their quotas were being reduced at once. The 'seven sisters', the Western oil majors that provided three-quarters of Japan's purchases, announced that they were giving first priority to the United States, and that Japan should expect sharp cutbacks in supply. Many feared that Japan's assets in the Middle East would be nationalised. The Arab leaders who had always previously treated Japan gently suddenly turned hard-headed. Saudi Arabia's oil minister, Sheikh Ahmed Zaki Yamani, hinted that Japan might have to break off diplomatic ties with Israel altogether if it was to avoid a cut-off in oil from the Arab world. Fears fed on rumours, and the government began drawing up plans for controlling energy consumption and reining in price rises.

In the meantime the country's much-vaunted internal discipline broke down. Manufacturers and wholesalers hoarded goods in order to raise market prices. Shoppers saw items on the shelves dwindling and began buying up whatever they could lay their hands on. In Osaka there were scenes of panic in the shops, as ordinary household goods like soap, toilet paper and detergent became scarce and the prices were regularly marked up. An elderly woman suffered a broken leg when she was trampled underfoot during a stampede of 200 shoppers racing for delivery of toilet rolls. Soon the scramble spread to other cities. Japan's oil companies behaved in much the same way as the frightened shoppers, looking only to their own interests. They hoarded their supplies and forced through a series of price increases for propane gas, kerosene and petrol even before the supply cuts had happened. During November those fuels were in short supply and so were salt, soy sauce and sugar. The year-on-year increase in wholesale prices reached 20 per cent by the end of October and the consumer-price index was up 30 per cent by the end of the year.

Diplomatically, Japan was isolated. On 18 November the Arabs gave 'friendly status' to the European Community states – except the Netherlands, which took a strong pro-Israeli stance – but Japan was still out in the cold. The government was confused by the quick pace of events and its decision-making machinery was painfully slow. Ever since the war Japan had followed in America's diplomatic footsteps, and described its diplomacy as based on 'separation of political and economic issues'. Now here was a political issue that was bound to put Japan on the wrong side of the USA. Henry Kissinger visited Tokyo in mid-November and had a frosty meeting with Prime Minister Tanaka, during which he urged the Japanese Premier not to bow to Arab pressures. Tanaka asked for an assurance that if necessary the USA would guarantee Japan's supply of oil. The reply was negative.

Japan's frantic search for a compromise resulted in a new statement of its old Middle East policy, including a demand for Israel's withdrawal from all the occupied territories and support for the Palestinians' right to self-determination, but also 'respect for all countries in the region'. The new ingredient was that Japan also spoke of the possible need to 'reconsider' its ties with Israel. This was a hint of what the government was in fact actively planning: to place an effective freeze on its economic ties with Israel, while committing itself to develop the Arab economies. The USA said it 'deeply regretted' the Japanese decision, but Japan was duly rewarded by the Arab league with a temporary suspension of the threatened quota cut. Tanaka promptly decided to send the Deputy Prime Minister, Takeo Miki, to the Middle East states in December. Miki took with him the promise of a major programme of Japanese assistance to the Arab belligerents, including government credits for Egypt to widen the Suez Canal. In a speech he declared roundly: 'Justice is on the side of the Arabs.' On Christmas Day the Arab nations let Japan off the hook: the country was exempted from any specific cuts in its imports. It had managed to get itself on the 'friendly countries' list without being forced to cut its official links with Israel.

Still, the crisis for Japan's economy was only just beginning. Crude oil prices were rising by the week and supplies were still subject to the political whims of the main producing countries. Gulf crude prices quadrupled, from $2.70 before the crisis to $11.65 on 1 January 1974. Japan had closed most of its coal mines during the 1960s and had no means of making up the expected shortfall from domestic energy sources. As chance would have it, the winter of 1973 was also an exceptionally cold one in Japan.

Eiji Yamagata and his forty-man staff in the Natural Resources Agency had front-line responsibility for saving the situation. His staff was immediately doubled with reinforcements from inside his ministry. They tried to get extra oil from other sources of supply, especially from Mexico. They worked through the night to draw up a national energy-saving plan. Yamagata allowed himself several hours' break to go home each night while most of the others could only snatch some rest under blankets on the office floor. At 8.30 in the morning their boss would come in to find them sleeping on the floor 'like a row of tuna fish'. The pace was so unrelenting that after some weeks, Yamagata says, 'two people went crazy because of lack of sleep.... They were taken off to hospital and given morphine injections to prevent their brain cells from dying.' Even so, as the boss, Yamagata could not authorise any time off for Japan's mandarins, on whom the whole nation was depending. Relief came only with the news of the reprieve from the Arabs at the year's end: Yamagata saw that as a *kamikaze* ('divine wind') which saved his country from disaster.

On 16 November the government announced its programme for saving energy. It included a 10 per cent cut in oil supplies to all the major industries, including steel, cars and shipbuilding. The prices of a wide range of goods would be controlled by law, and some would be rationed. The large-scale construction projects in the Prime Minister's own 'Building a New Japan' scheme were put on hold. Petrol stations were ordered to close at weekends, and cinemas and other places of entertainment had to shut early. Tokyo's frenetic pace visibly slowed down. The busy bar-life of the Ginza and Roppongi was suddenly subdued. Many of the spectacular neon displays were turned off – although for months a skyscraper in Shinjuku kept its lights blazing through the night with a sign in Japanese characters reading: 'SAVE ENERGY'.

Television came to an end at midnight. Lifts and hot water in public buildings were stopped, the heating was turned down to a regulation 20°C and linen towels were removed from lavatories, never to be

115

replaced. Some schools had to postpone their year-end exams because they could not get hold of paper on which to print the questions. Taxis formed long queues outside the petrol stations for their lique-fied natural gas (LNG) fuel, and when it ran out they went on strike. MITI took it upon itself to order out emergency LNG and petrol supplies to damp down the public displays of annoyance. It tried to do the same to shore up the most glaring goods shortages in the cities. For several months MITI acted in effect as quartermaster to the nation.

At the height of the uncertainty, on 23 November 1973, the Finance Minister, Kiichi Aichi, died. Tanaka swallowed his pride and called on his arch political rival, Takeo Fukuda, to take the job. Fukuda had been a high-flying official in the Finance Ministry and a diplomat in London before going into politics. He had served three times before as Finance Minister, and if anyone knew how to manage the economy in a crisis, it was he.

There was one major problem: Fukuda, who had been beaten by Tanaka in the race for the LDP presidency in part because of the latter's 'New Japan' policy, had taken a stand publicly denouncing the plan as spendthrift and irresponsible. Now he insisted that the whole programme must be put on hold. At a press conference on taking up his new post, he announced an across-the-board review of the government's high-spending policies and a freeze on planned tax cuts. 'Our new economic policy must be to hold a sword in each hand – one against inflation and the other against an "oil recession".' He told the nation to expect six months of hardship: that meant higher interest rates and deep cuts in government and consumer spending. 'If every-one pulls together,' Fukuda said, 'inflation will fall below 15 per cent in 1974.' In January 1974, wholesale price increases peaked at nearly 70 per cent above the previous year, but then fell steadily. Fukuda's prediction came true in the first quarter of 1975.

In the short term Japan faced a financial crisis: it needed new reserve funds quickly or it would not be able to settle its mounting bills for food and basic raw materials. The yen had come under heavy selling pressure, as many international investors had concluded that Japan would not be able to afford all the oil it needed. The yen fell in value from a rate of 254 to the dollar in July to 300 at the end of the year and this made matters much worse since oil and other resources would become even dearer in yen as the currency weakened. Masao Fujioka, then head of the government's Export–Import Bank, was charged with finding a billion dollars to tide Japan over its foreign-exchange shortage. Later, he told the story like this:

Friends of Japan, not only American but also Europeans, felt after the oil shock that Japan was after all a weak country. [Dozens] of financiers visited me, advising that Japan should borrow money from them: and I politely declined their offers every time, and flew to an OPEC country to do it myself. After this was leaked to the newspapers the exchange rate of the yen went up five yen in two days ... and the crisis was over.

That OPEC country was Saudi Arabia, and Fujioka's loan agreement was the start of a long-term economic understanding between the world's largest oil exporter and the world's foremost oil-importing country.

To curb inflation, the discount rate charged by the Bank of Japan to the commercial banks was raised in the autumn of 1973 to 9 per cent, compared to 4.25 per cent in April. Manufacturing industry was hit hard by the high interest rates and soaring costs. Electric power supplies to every factory were cut back as announced. The prices of raw materials rose by 7 per cent in November alone, and by an annual rate of 30 per cent in the second half of 1973. The first quarter of 1974 was the worst period of recession in Japan's post-war history: manufacturing output fell by 19 per cent compared with the previous quarter. In 1974 as a whole, industrial output fell by 9 per cent and the post-war economy marked its first negative growth ever (of 0.2 per cent). Company profits fell on average more than 80 per cent; the textile, car and electronics industries recorded their sharpest downturns since the war; about a third of publicly listed firms went into the red.

As production in every major industry slowed down, the big firms began laying off employees on hourly or daily contracts. In steel, chemicals and other high-energy-using industries, companies also saved costs by forming their own transport and other support subsidiaries. Textile firms were among the worst affected: one of the largest, the Toyo Spinning Company, shed 3000 employees, and across the country textile mills closed down. In most industries, management took voluntary pay cuts. Men who had always worked in factories were trained instead to work in accounting or sales. Across Japanese industry, more than 400 000 people were laid off for several months or more. Thanks to the unwritten rules of their employment, few of these people were actually taken off their companies' pay-rolls so they did not appear in the official unemployment figure, which rose to 1.1 million, very nearly its highest level since the 1950s.

Japan's big companies put the squeeze on the subcontracted firms which by custom supplied up to half or more of the parts used in car-making and other industrial sectors. Bankruptcies reached a post-war peak of 11 000 in 1974 and every week the press reported the suicide of another businessman who could not cope. Most of the smaller firms had no redress whatever, as their contracts were short-term or based only on trust. MITI took steps to support some small and medium-sized firms in key sectors with subsidised loan schemes, considerably below commercial rates.

Michizo Masuda exemplified the stoicism of many small businessmen at the time. He was the factory manager of Okada Bankin, a family-owned firm making metal stampings and other parts for the bigger electrical companies. The firm employed only twenty people and it was one of Masuda's tasks to visit major clients to secure orders. Through the autumn of 1973 and spring of 1974 new orders gradually tailed off until the day came the next spring when they dried up completely.

'After the regular morning meeting,' Masuda recalls, 'I made the usual rounds determined to get fresh orders; but at each of the places I called I was told, "Sorry, we don't need anything from you now. Please come back another time."' After several days of making the rounds, Masuda had exhausted all the possibilities. It was the cherry-blossom season, and he found himself one early afternoon with nowhere to go, yet unable to go back to the factory empty-handed.

> I *had* to get some new orders, both for the other workers and for my family's sake. I parked my car by the roadside and kept watching the cherry blossoms falling to the ground in a drift of pink petals. I stayed there for hours so that I could go straight home and avoid facing the others at the factory.

In the case of Okada Bankin, Michizo Masuda and some of the younger employees spoke out against the attitude of passive resignation shown at first by the two senior executives, and persuaded them to search actively for new sources of business. To Masuda's mind, it was the tradition of *gaman*, endurance in the face of all adversity, a virtue associated with the centuries of Japan's rural poverty, which kept his own company and the nation as a whole going. Employee–company loyalty, the unwillingness of even small companies and workshops to lay off staff, and flexible work practices each played a part in the way Japanese industry struggled back to its feet within about eighteen months.

The hardship made the public unusually critical of the methods of big business, and Japan's oil companies quickly fell foul of the general mood. Under the prompting of MITI, the major firms in the oil-refining and distributing business formed a cartel within a few days of the OAPEC announcement of cuts, ostensibly to hold down the price and supply of fuel. The price of kerosene, the fuel most commonly used in domestic heating, rose from 300 to 450 yen per 18-litre can within a few weeks of the Middle East War. There was strong public criticism of the way that MITI's action led to some vendors' *raising* their prices to the level recommended by MITI – 380 yen – and then charging arbitrary surcharges on top. The press made much of the disclosure of a secret internal memo inside one oil firm, General Sekiyu, which described the oil crisis as 'a golden chance to make profits'.

Japan's Fair Trade Commission had earned the reputation of being a drowsy watchdog. The commission had been set up under the Occupation but had been virtually neutered by its supervising ministry, MITI, in the following twenty years. It had no powers to impose fines and limited powers even to investigate abuses. Several important industries, including transport and agriculture, were outside its remit altogether, and the government permitted an estimated 1000 legal cartels to exist in the early 1970s. But when the impact of the oil crisis was at its peak, the beast woke up. Its officials raided the offices of thirteen oil firms and the Petroleum Association, the key government advisory panel. The commission determined that the oil cartel was illegal and had acted against the law to restrict production, leading to higher prices. Later the commission took twelve oil companies and the association, as well as seventeen executives, to court. In 1980 the oil cartel was ruled illegal.

The Fair Trade Commission's president, Toshihide Takahashi, was a former Finance Ministry official who made the case into a crusade. The oil-industry indictments, he said, should serve as a warning to other industries. In their wake an attempt was made to widen the commission's ambit and strengthen its powers to break illegal cartels, but the proposed bill was much watered down before it became law in 1977. The balance of advantage remained with businesses. A group of housewives were successful in getting a lower court to uphold their complaint about high kerosene prices in the 'oil shock' period; a number of firms selling kerosene were ordered to pay compensation for their 'unreasonably high' prices, fixed through a cartel. The corporate defendants had the last word, however. They appealed against that verdict and eventually, in 1989, had it reversed.

Several other cases of hoarding and price-fixing, of detergent and other mundane goods, also came to light. The low point for Japan's captains of industry came in February 1974, when twenty-three of them including the chief executives of leading oil companies, trading and electronics firms, were summoned to the Diet and had to submit to hostile questioning by politicians of all parties about their firm's alleged profiteering at the public's expense. Some humbly apologised for having, as they put it, 'caused trouble' to the whole society. Others

119

defended their own firms against all allegations of unfair play. Shame was perhaps the most effective means of bringing those businesses to book. However, Japanese consumers were afterwards forced to go on paying in excess of world prices for manufactured goods made in Japan, as well as for food and other materials imported from overseas.

By mid-1974 Japanese industry was able to find the oil it needed for its scaled-down production targets, although at ever higher prices. The main danger to the economy came from inflation, which was up by 29 per cent during the year. After the first few months of corporate indiscipline and misbehaviour, the big firms were prevailed on to hold price rises down as far as possible. Administrative guidance backed up the government's legal powers in this area. But the government was losing the battle to hold down wage rises. The labour unions were determined to win the annual confrontation with management over pay, known as the spring wage offensive, by getting an average pay increase higher than the inflation rate. This was the theme of the large-scale rallies which took place during the spring offensive between March and May of 1974. Psychologically the unions had a strong case because of the bad publicity heaped on large corporations, not only over price-fixing but also over neglect of pollution control and large windfall profits from stock and land speculation. The average wage increase for workers in large firms in 1974 was 33 per cent.

Takeo Fukuda kept the squeeze on the rest of the economy. He intended to catch up with labour the next time round, and so he did: in 1975 he persuaded the steelworkers, traditionally the trendsetters in wage claims, to moderate their demands, and that year the average was held down to 11 per cent, only just over the annual inflation rate of 9.6 per cent.

The contrast between Japan's strong recovery from the oil shock within two years and the sluggish response of other leading industrialised countries is striking. The Japanese economy, after a slight dip in 1974, grew by 3.2 per cent in 1975, 5.9 per cent in 1976 and by around 6 per cent for the rest of the decade; while the USA and EC economies grew barely 2 per cent a year from 1973 to 1980. When Takeo Fukuda as Prime Minister attended the Western economic summit in Bonn in 1978, he faced strong calls from the other leaders for Japan, as well as West Germany, to act as an 'engine of growth' to help pull the world economy back on to its feet. Given that Japan had suffered more directly than any other country from the oil crisis, Fukuda had no false modesty about the achievement, and was cock-a-hoop in the knowledge that the Japanese economy was 'soaring as high as Mount Fuji'.

Fukuda's account of how this was done is simple and terse:

> The first thing we did, after returning to a state of normality, was to invest in saving energy and then in labour-saving methods and modernisation. So while the rest of the world was in turmoil and unable to invest, Japan was making new investments across the board. That's how we overtook other countries and picked ourselves up after the oil shock.

Higher interest rates forced firms to save costs and cut output until their productivity improved. They also squeezed profits so that wage increases were held down, and that in turn discouraged consumer spending. By 1975 the government borrowed one quarter of its own budget in the form of national bonds to pump into the economy. The next year, bond issues rose to 30 per cent of the government's income. It was not until the late 1980s that the government was able to stop making new borrowings simply to service that long-term debt.

As for Tanaka's 'New Japan' plan, hardly any of it was carried out in the three years after its publication in 1972. Thereafter the brakes were lifted and each year during the drawing up of the national budget there was intense haggling by the various regional and business interest groups which sought to have funds earmarked for the plan. As of 1990 five of the twelve planned bullet-train lines envisaged are running; one of the three new bridges is in use; the Seikan tunnel underneath the Tsugaru Strait between Hokkaido and Honshu was triumphantly opened in 1988, but the money was not there for the planned bullet-train line. Parts of Kakuei Tanaka's dreams have been realised, although many years late. His vision of a decentralised Japan remains an impossibility, with Tokyo thoroughly dominating the nation's commercial and political life.

The government's major task was to secure energy supplies and hold down Japan's absolute level of energy consumption, while keeping up a steady rate of growth, and this was entrusted to MITI. In the early 1970s Japan's energy demand was growing at an annual rate of 10 per cent, twice the world average, and it appeared that by the end of that decade the country would account for fully 20 per cent of all the world's consumption. In fact, over the next ten years, while the GNP grew by 30 per cent, Japan's energy consumption grew only slightly overall, and oil consumption fell by one-tenth. Whereas before the oil crisis Japanese power stations had relied on oil for 71 per cent of their output, by 1989 this had shrunk to only 34 per cent.

This remarkable husbanding of scarce resources was achieved, first, by a determined campaign to conserve energy. MITI was given special powers to allocate electric power to industry and to enforce cutbacks in consumption. The ministry also moved quickly, using 'administrative guidance', to question individual firms about their insulation levels and other techniques for energy conservation, imposing uniformly strict standards on the larger companies. MITI also pressed the heavy energy-users to lessen their dependence on imported oil. The steel firms converted their blast furnaces to rely on coke alone, and by 1980 they were able to do without oil almost completely. During the 1970s liquefied natural gas took the place of oil as the main fuel in electric power generation. At the same time MITI and its Natural Resources Agency set about boosting the output of hydro-electric and nuclear power, as well as solar power and energy from other alternative sources.

Japan's nuclear-energy programme, which had started in the 1950s using US-designed light-water reactors, was speeded up as a matter of urgency. By 1982 there were twenty-four nuclear reactors, accounting for 30 per cent of electricity needs: Japan was then the world's third biggest producer of nuclear energy, behind the USA and France but ahead of the USSR – although since then the Soviet Union has overtaken Japan again. The government also resolved to complete the nuclear-fuel cycle in order to reduce dependency on imported uranium (from Britain and France) and plutonium (from the USA). Uranium-enrichment plants were built, and an experimental fast-breeder reactor was put through its paces at Tokai-mura, north of Tokyo. In 1987 the advisory Committee on Atomic Energy released a plan to increase the share taken by nuclear power in Japan's power output to 60 per cent by 2030.

The growing reliance on nuclear energy was strongly resisted by many groups for both environmental and political reasons. In 1974 the government suffered a public-relations disaster when Japan's first nuclear-powered ship, the *Mutsu*, made its first test voyage from its home port of Ominato (formerly Mutsu) on the northern tip of Tohoku: its reactor was found to have leaked minute amounts of radioactivity into the sea. Local fishermen, claiming that there was a risk that their scallop-fishing grounds would be contaminated, successfully campaigned to have the ship mothballed for the next fifteen years. In 1978 radioactive water leaked from a pipe at a nuclear-power plant in Fukui prefecture, on the Sea of Japan coast, and dozens of workers used mops to clear it away. The authorities attempted to cover up this incident, arousing much anger among local people and anti-nuclear campaigners when the truth came to light. Some scientists also criticised the government's plans to store low-level nuclear waste in drums underground, in a marshy district of the Sea of Japan coast, and argued that because of the risk of major earthquakes the whole nuclear-power programme was fraught with risk. However, Japan has so far had a fairly good overall record of safety in nuclear energy.

In spite of the achievements, Japan is destined to rely on oil from the traditional sources of supply in the Middle East for the bulk of its primary energy needs, and the goal of stabilising that supply required careful diplomacy. In the autumn of 1973 Japan resolved to forge a special relationship with the Arab nations as a group. Takeo Miki's visit to the Gulf in December of that year was followed by another by the MITI minister Yasuhiro Nakasone, to Iran and Iraq in January 1974. In return for pledges of official aid and soft loans for various industrial plants, he secured a promise from Iraq to provide long-term oil supplies. Iran was promised a massive petrochemical complex, to be funded by mixed government and Mitsui Trading Company credits. (The project later became a prime target of the Iraqi air force during the Gulf War.) Japan also earmarked large-scale funds for telecommunications and other infrastructure projects in Algeria, Morocco, Jordan and Sudan. In disregard of American objections, the government pressed ahead on its own initiative in recognising the Palestinians' right to self-determination. In 1977 Japan approved the setting up of a permanent office of the Palestinian Liberation Organisation in Tokyo. Such moves were carefully calculated and cost Japan nothing, but gave it the necessary credentials to be counted as consistently pro-Arab.

While trying to wean industry as far as possible off oil, MITI also set about spreading Japan's risks. By the time of the Iranian revolution and a second oil crisis in 1979, Japan's oil from the troubled Middle East was substantially reduced, although it still accounted for some two thirds of Japan's total oil imports. The role of the international oil companies had also been scaled down in favour of more direct contracts with Japanese firms. So when Iran drastically cut its oil exports, Japan was not thrown into confusion. OAPEC oil prices rose in June 1979 from $14.50 to $18, and then again in October to $23.50, but in Japan this time there was no hoarding and no panic. The country endured a year of 8 per cent inflation and no growth before picking up momentum again.

The high-profile courtship of Arab interests meant, however, that Japan, already married to the USA in terms of its foreign policy, was open to the charge of unfaithfulness. Washington became heavily preoccupied with its hostage crisis after Iranian 'students' stormed the American Embassy in Tehran and took sixty-seven people hostage; but Japanese commercial interests continued with business as usual. The conspicuous efforts of Japanese oil companies to buy up Iranian crude on the spot market at a time when the USA was seeking to isolate Iran led to an outcry from some American politicians. The Speaker of the House of Representatives, 'Tip' O'Neill, fulminated against 'treachery' from the same country that had carried out the sneak attack on Pearl Harbor. But the criticism died down when the Japanese government ordered the oil firms to desist.

Japan has kept up its careful planning for maximum risk avoidance since the two 'oil shocks'. Indonesia overtook Saudi Arabia to become Japan's largest supplier of energy. Japan also took the precaution of more than doubling its emergency oil stocks to 140 days' supply.

Just as, in the summer of 1974, the measures to contain the effects of the oil crisis were showing signs of working, another kind of shock ran through the Japanese body politic: unanswered allegations of grand-scale corruption on the part of the Prime Minister. Kakuei Tanaka, who took over from Eisaku Sato as Premier in 1972, was unlike most of his LDP predecessors, who rose through the ranks of the national bureaucracy before entering politics. He was a self-made man, full of native cunning and a brilliant organiser. His gravelly voice and colloquial manner of speaking appealed to many ordinary people. He was a modern man, untrammelled by the past; hence he was able to grasp the popular mood – for example, in hurrying along the pace of Japan's rapprochement with China with the same slogan as that employed by the military in the 1930s: 'Don't miss the bus to China.' Some of the other LDP bosses were deeply committed, personally and through their own financial interests, to supporting Chiang Kai-shek's nationalist government in Taiwan.

Tanaka amassed a large personal fortune through wartime contracts and his own construction business, which he used crudely to win political influence on a scale never before seen in Japan. His financial excesses led to the coining of a new term, *kinken seiji* – 'money-power politics'. He had been charged with bribery early on in his political career, in 1948, one year after he was first elected to the Lower House of the Diet. At that time he had already been appointed Vice-minister of Justice and was recognised as the most powerful political figure in his region – Niigata, on the Sea of Japan. Tanaka was accused of taking bribes from local coal-mine owners in return for his help in opposing plans to run down the mines and turn them over to public ownership. He was found guilty in the lower court but later acquitted by a higher court.

To the Japanese public Tanaka's accession to power in 1972 was nothing less than a sensation. He was photographed in the garden of his opulent Tokyo home wearing a traditional kimono and wooden clogs. Hundreds of petitioners, from powerful political leaders to groups from the countryside, would regularly queue up for the sake of a few moments in his presence. His level of popular support reached a record high of 62 per cent. The nation as a whole was proud of now having a Prime Minister who came from a poor rural background. It was often cited as proof that Japan was less élitist than many Western countries.

Tanaka was ruthless in demanding loyalty from all those who associated with him. In Japan, since before the war, relations between public figures and the press have been regulated by a framework of reporters, or *kisha* clubs, through which selected groups of reporters cover every ministry or prominent public office. Only major news organisations are allowed to be represented in the clubs covering central government agencies, the most important of which is attached to the Prime Minister's office. The system ensures journalistic access to government leaders, but customarily also guarantees politicians a friendly press. Tanaka took no chance on that loyalty, and on a trip out of Tokyo soon after he came to office he reportedly threatened the accompanying members of the *kisha* club assigned to cover his every movement that if any of them wrote critically about him he would see to it that they lost their jobs. One of the reporters present apparently leaked the Prime Minister's words to a weekly magazine, *Shukan Gendai* . Tanaka was quoted as saying: 'It is easy to stop a story in the newspapers. I won't telephone the mass media as [Prime Minister] Sato used to do. It's already arranged to stop it.' The threat was entirely plausible. Japanese newspaper companies have frequently discouraged their reporters from going out on a limb, however extraordinary the story, when the reputations of important vested interests are at stake. Anyone sacked from a major daily paper would expect to become an outcast from his own profession.

Tanaka had ways of exerting pressure on Japan's 'establishment' press, meaning the national and regional newspapers that were full members of the Newspaper Publishers' and Editors' Association. The Association subscribed to the idea of 'responsible journalism', and individual reporters exercised self-censorship, not writing what they knew about corrupt goings-on in their daily articles. However, the irreverent periodical magazines and daily scandal-sheets were not put off. A freelance journalist, Takashi Tachibana, wrote a series of damning articles entitled 'Kakuei Tanaka: His Money and His Men' in the most influential of Japan's numerous socio-political magazines, the monthly *Bungei Shunju*. They alleged in graphic detail that the Prime Minister and his close associates had brow-beaten industrialists to give vast sums in campaign donations, invented dummy organisations to launder the money, used it to bribe politicians and others to help win the LDP leadership for Tanaka, and failed to report the earnings to the tax authorities. The articles were well documented from already published materials, including the LDP's own financial reports, and they alleged that in one year, 1973, Tanaka had bought stock worth $425 million, although his declared income was only $260,000.

The articles were an anatomical study of Japanese-style institutionalised corruption. They described the LDP's various fundraising bodies and showed how they functioned as almost bottomless wells of cash. They painted a picture of a torrent of money, going from big firms and industrial and professional associations like those of the car and electrical-machine industries and the country's doctors into the ruling party coffers. Tachibana claimed that billions of yen were dispensed by the Tanaka machine from massive funds raised from big companies in return for contracts or favours. Tachibana alleged, too, that many of the donations were in the form of 'backdoor funds' which were flowing into the hands of individual top politicians without being accounted for at all.

Japanese newspaper-readers were not surprised by the revelations, only surprised that any publication had printed them. The articles showed that Tanaka was simply more adept at practising the dubious money-raising techniques of the ruling party than any of his rivals or predecessors. This was illustrated in the Diet by an independent opposition member, Yukio Aoshima, who asked the Prime Minister about reports that 'dirty money' had been distributed to LDP members during the 1972 party leadership election:

> Supporters are induced with cash-filled knapsacks and so factions are expanded. The one who succeeds in enlarging his supporting faction the most becomes the President of the LDP. Doesn't this mean that he's buying the seat of Prime Minister with the money he has collected from his support groups. Doesn't it mean that *you* are buying the premiership?

The *Bungei Shunju* articles were the talk of Tokyo, but for about two weeks after they began to appear nothing much happened. The Japanese political establishment had no mechanisms for the LDP to investigate or answer the allegations of its own accord. No one in the party was prepared to cast a stone against their leader, but neither would anyone come to his defence. At length the *Washington Post* and other American newspapers published reports of the confusion and scandal in Japan. That was the signal for the leading Japanese papers, the *Asahi*, *Mainichi* and *Yomiuri*, to write factual accounts of the American press coverage, and so the issue moved from the zone of embarrassed silence into the public sphere. On 22 October Tanaka appeared at the Foreign Correspondents' Club of Japan before a gathering of Western journalists, who asked about the published allegations so persistently that Tanaka stormed out of the gathering. That was a fatal mistake. The illusion of propriety and dignity had been broken. By November Tanaka's popular support had sunk to only 12 per cent. On 26 November, on the advice from his own close associates, he resigned. The case had more to do with Tanaka's losing the trust and support of the nation than it did with the letter of the law. The public prosecutors turned a blind eye to the allegations of bribes for favours, and only much later did the tax authorities demand from Tanaka the payment of taxes of his large undeclared income.

The ignominious end of Tanaka's reign left the ruling LDP in complete disarray. Its five main factions were quarrelling openly about the party's misfortunes. The public mood appeared to be deeply critical. The so-called progressive opposition parties – Socialist, Communist and Democratic Socialist – separately or in alliance held control of Tokyo, Yokohama, Nagoya, Kyoto and Osaka. Various citizens' movements backed by the opposition were attacking the government's record on pollution problems. Welfare demands were growing just as the Japanese economy met its first recession coupled with hyper-inflation since the Occupation years. The LDP bosses rejected the idea of holding a general election, or of electing their own new leader in an open vote of MPs as the party rules would have allowed. Instead, a cabal of party elders conferred and hit on a compromise choice to succeed Tanaka: Takeo Miki, the head of a minor faction of the party.

Miki himself had one outstanding merit for the party's purposes: he had the reputation of being untouched by the venal excesses of Tanaka and other senior party figures. His elevation to the party presidency (without any contest) and to the premiership (by a majority vote of all MPs in the Diet) was meant to show the Japanese public that the party was turning over a new leaf. Miki had first been elected to the Diet in 1937 and criticised the military government throughout the war years. After the war he became leader of a reform-minded conservative grouping, the National Co-operative Party, which had a tradition of non-conformity and was always at the edge of LDP affairs, even after it was subsumed into the party in 1955.

On becoming Premier, Miki used this rare moment in the party's life to push through a set of fundamental reforms to try to halt the LDP's slide towards institutionalised corruption. He tried to force through the dissolution of the party factions, on the grounds that the conventional concentration of power and money around several godfather-like figures – the faction leaders – inevitably created a cast of politics dictated by money not by ideas. The press took up the general cry that the factions were 'the root of all evil'. Miki led the way in announcing the dissolution of his own faction. All the other faction bosses, including Tanaka himself, were obliged to follow suit, with fulsome expressions of contrition for past practices. But the action turned out to be a sham. All the old factions were immediately reconstituted in the form of 'policy study groups' which carved up privileges and allocated funds to their own members in the old familiar way.

In 1976, fresh trouble swept over the Liberal Democrat bosses, this time from across the Pacific. In February of that year senior executives of the Lockheed Aircraft Corporation gave testimony before a US Senate panel in Washington about the firm's lobbying activities in Japan, aimed at selling Lockheed TriStar jets to a commercial Japanese airline, All Nippon Airways (ANA). In 1972, Prime Minister Tanaka had made a promise to President Nixon that, in order to ease trade tensions, Japan would buy 'wide-bodied civil aircraft' from the United States. Tanaka was known later to have met Lockheed executives and others concerned; shortly afterwards ANA suddenly announced that it was dropping plans to buy short-haul jets from McDonnell Douglas Corporation and was instead to buy wide-bodied TriStars from Lockheed. Evidence came to light that Lockheed had employed middlemen to hand out some $12 million in bribes, some of it to Japanese government officials and political leaders. Depositions obtained by the Japanese authorities said Lockheed's agents had passed over the money in wooden crates and taken receipts describing it variously as 'peanuts', 'pieces' or 'units'.

On 27 July 1976 Japanese state prosecutors ordered the arrest of Kakuei Tanaka on bribery charges. The ex-Prime Minister was seen on national television being taken away from his home, handcuffed, to a police detention centre. It appeared to be a kind of revolution for Japan. Tanaka was released on bail on 17 August pending his trial. The prosecutor's charges were that the Lockheed Corporation had used several routes to funnel bribes to public figures, including to the Prime Minister himself. The money was said to have gone directly to ANA, through a trading firm, Marubeni, and through Yoshio Kodama, the right-wing activist during the war years who had a network of close links both with *yakuza* (gangsters) and with top politicians, including Kakuei Tanaka.

The long-drawn-out court case disclosed, among other details, that at a secret rendezvous on a street near the British Embassy Tanaka's private secretary, who was also his chauffeur, had taken delivery of several suitcases stuffed with 10 000 yen notes. Altogether Tanaka was alleged to have received 500 million yen, the equivalent then of $2 million in bribes; the ex-Premier was no longer available for public comment, but his associates spoke freely to reporters off the record. Tanaka was quoted as being beside himself with rage over the charge. One account had him demanding rhetorically, 'How dare they arrest me over such a trifling sum?!'

The period from July to December 1976 was like an extended carnival for politics in Japan. Miki himself was like a conjurer, producing rabbits out of his hat, announcing new plans for reforms at regular intervals. The changes included the setting of legal limits for the first time on cash donations to politicians and parties, a new provision for electing the LDP party leader by a grassroots party vote, and the beefing up of the Anti-Monopoly Law mentioned above. The other faction bosses in the party were seriously alarmed at the trend of events. In June six LDP Dietmen had split from the party to distance themselves from the scandals and formed a breakaway conservative party, the New Liberal Club. There seemed to them to be no end in sight to the party's humiliation under Miki's leadership.

At the end of the year the Diet's full four-year term was almost up and the Prime Minister had to call a general election. Miki went into the campaign with a relatively high public support rate of 35 per cent for his leadership; still, the Lockheed affair combined with the continuing troubles of the economy led to the LDP's losing its overall parliamentary majority for the first time since its formation. All the other factions within the party were itching to dump Takeo Miki, and this was an ideal reason to do so. According to Japanese thinking, the man who presides over a loss of face for his organisation must go, even though the fault may not be his personally. Miki went quietly, giving way to his near contemporary, Takeo Fukuda. The new Premier restored the usual order of things in Japan, with the focus of public attention relentlessly fixed on the health of the economy.

The open season on criticising the ruling party ended nearly as suddenly as it had begun. Some Japanese called the Lockheed affair 'Japan's Watergate', as it led to the disgrace of a former Japanese leader in the wake of the Watergate affair which forced the resignation of President Nixon in 1974. However, the two cases demonstrated the contrast between the political dynamics of the two countries as much as they showed the similarities. Nixon, though pardoned, was stripped of real influence within American politics. Tanaka, on the other hand, even though he faced criminal charges, remained the single most dominant figure in Japanese politics for another ten years. The effect of his backstage influence was to weaken each successive leader who followed him: each of the next four lasted a mere two years in office.

Those leaders were obliged constantly to look over their shoulders and to shore up temporary alliances within the LDP. As a result, particular policies came to matter less and less in the party's internal debates. The focus of political activity turned to the mundane process of working out a consensus among several jealous party factions, with money and influence regularly easing the way.

Even after losing the premiership and being criminally charged, Tanaka retained his parliamentary seat, as Japanese law permits. The opposition parties sought persistently to have him ousted, but were helpless against the LDP's superior numbers. He still controlled by far the largest single LDP faction, comprising more than 120 out of the party's total of just under 400 Dietmen in both houses of parliament. As a result, his faction was able to pick up the most lucrative and powerful Cabinet posts. That in turn gave its members a strong grip on industrial and business lobbies. The process was self-fulfilling, and after his arrest the factions' ranks swelled with more recruits. His faction remained so active and well-organised that it became known as the *Tanaka gundan*, the Tanaka 'army', and each successive LDP premier needed its support to be effective. Tanaka was given a new nickname by the press: 'the Shadow Shogun'.

In the countryside most ordinary Japanese had no understanding of politics, except as a mechanism which did or did not bring them material benefits. Tanaka's constituency of Niigata had a history of poverty and neglect. People there regarded Tanaka quite simply as a local hero. They knew him affectionately by the diminutive 'Kaku-san' (*san* being a general honorific term, approximating to 'Mister'). Thousands of people joined the numerous and overlapping Tanaka support groups or *koenkai*, and poured scorn on the court case as no more than a vindictive attempt by his political rivals to bring him down. Each time there was a general election – in 1976, 1979, 1980 and 1983 (shortly after he was found guilty in the Tokyo District Court) – Tanaka won handsome victories in Niigata. Each time, his supporters claimed the vote had given him *misogi*, purification, at the hands of the voters. *Misogi* is a Shinto religious concept, and Shinto is a forgiving religion with no firm ethical framework of right and wrong. By appealing to this aspect of Japanese custom and native religious faith, Tanaka, like others who remained in politics while fighting court cases, evaded or lessened the censure from public opinion. The hierarchical structure of the Liberal Democrats' factions further discouraged internal criticism of the party bosses.

In practice the contract that Kakuei Tanaka had offered his constituents had been amply fulfilled: the bullet-train line and roads he had promised them were in place. They gave their votes in return. A grateful community also erected a statue of Tanaka at Urasa, a modest-sized town which has enjoyed the benefits of being a stop on the Joetsu bullet-train line. Each year during the New Year holiday hundreds of powerful figures, including Cabinet ministers and presidents of large companies, paid courtesy visits on the 'Shadow Shogun' at his Tokyo home.

When in 1983 Tanaka was found guilty of the bribery charges, his appeal went up to the Supreme Court, but by 1990 its justices had still not passed their judgement. Takayuki Sato, the parliamentary Vice-Minister for Transport, told reporters while the trial was in progress that it was a waste of time. Tanaka did not even bother to appeal against his suspended jail sentence. The lesson of the whole affair appears to be that in Japan corruption can pay, since none of those found guilty of bribery has had to serve a jail sentence, and several of the politicians found guilty have continued successful careers.

Takeo Fukuda, who succeeded Takeo Miki in 1976, was shackled by Tanaka's hostility and was able to survive only until 1978 before being supplanted by a Tanaka ally, Masayoshi Ohira. Ohira made a crusade out of trying to institute a significant addition to government revenues in the form of a new sales tax, but failed to square the voting public or the myriad interest groups in his party to the idea. In elections in September the LDP put up just as dismal a showing as in the 1976 election, and retained its majority in the Lower House only with the assistance of a motley group of conservative independents. In May of the following year the split between the Tanaka-led and Fukuda-led forces burst into the open. The opposition tabled a motion of no confidence in the government, a move which the LDP should have been able to defeat; but Fukuda, taking indirect revenge at last on his old foe, led members of his own and the Miki faction in abstaining, and the motion passed. During the ensuing campaign, Ohira died of heart failure and the resulting sympathy vote returned the LDP to power with 284 Diet seats out of 511, a solid majority of 28 seats.

At this point the LDP ran out of strong candidates for the top job. All the faction leaders had already had their turn. The party's internal dynamics won out over considerations of leadership ability and the LDP appointed Zenko Suzuki, the dull and plodding heir to the Ohira faction. Suzuki was unable to conceal the fact that he was out of his depth in handling high affairs of state. His worst moment came when in May 1981 he visited Washington: there he signed a joint communiqué which referred explicitly for the first time to the 'alliance relationship' between the USA and Japan. The Americans saw this as an important step forward in defining Japan's place in world affairs; but only a few hours later, in briefing Japanese reporters on the flight home, Suzuki asserted that there was 'no military alliance' with the USA. His Foreign Minister, Masayoshi Ito, resigned to take the rap, but confidence in Suzuki at home was shaken and in Washington it was badly undermined. At the end of his first two-year term, Suzuki opted to retire and take up the unstressful post of 'party elder'. His place was taken by perhaps the nation's most ambitious and purposeful politician, Yasuhiro Nakasone. The story of his five eventful years in office is told in Chapter 6.

In retrospect, the political reforms of Takeo Miki's brief two years failed to change the underlying pattern of Japanese public life. The public thrilled to the disclosures of the Lockheed affair, but in general elections most people continued to vote on local issues, and for personalities rather than for policies. The press was tamed and had no regular opportunity to challenge the power-holders. Soon after Miki was replaced, the factions began openly to operate as laundries for fabulous sums of money. The LDP's vote-winning machine went on functioning as well as ever. The new limits on political fund-giving were easily circumvented, and in the countryside politicians were still expected to act the part of the rich uncle to allcomers – attending weddings and funerals, and leaving cash gifts as tokens of 'goodwill'. They would be re-elected only if they continued the custom of using their influence to get favours done for their constituents – such as intervening to make sure their children got into the right school – and above all to divert central government money into their constituency.

In this way the politics of patronage, both at the local and the national level, grew more deep-rooted as time passed. As for the opposition parties, each represented a distinct segment of society, and they were deeply divided among themselves. The Socialist Party, the largest in the opposition camp, was weak in the countryside, which returned about half of all parliamentary seats, and so had to content itself between 1960 and 1980 with at most 130 out of the 511 total seats. The Socialists clung to their old Marxist-influenced platform and continued to promise that if elected they would scrap the US–Japan Security Treaty and abolish the Self-Defence Forces. That was a recipe for electoral disaster, and the menu was not changed despite a string of defeats in this period. The Democratic Socialists appealed to a similar constituency as that of the LDP, but professed to have a keener social conscience. The Communists were seen as 'clean' of money corruption and they maintained strong support among people on low incomes, but they were shunned by the majority of voters as well as by the other opposition parties because of their ideology. The

Komeito ('Clean Government Party'), an offshoot of a neo-Buddhist organisation, Soka Gakkai ('Value-Creating Society'), gained the allegiance of several million voters, mostly city-dwellers with lowly jobs; but, like the Communists, they provoked antipathy among other groups. The Soka Gakkai's somewhat suspect popular image was strengthened when in 1969 its followers used intimidation to prevent the publication of a book critical of the movement. In elections, the four main opposition groups always split the anti-LDP vote, allowing the Liberal Democrats to win.

Having almost given up hope of achieving power, the opposition parties resorted to frequent boycotts of parliamentary business. In the give-and-take world of Japanese politics this sometimes made the ruling party compromise on minor points of legislation or policy. However, the LDP in turn, playing to the gallery of Japanese public opinion, was able then to charge its opponents with obstructing the necessary work of parliament. Diet business grew increasingly remote from the public. Japan was becoming a country where important decisions in the nation's life were made with little reference to the national legislature. Those decisions were taken elsewhere: among gatherings of the ruling élites in the high-class restaurants of Tokyo's Akasaka district; in the ministry conference rooms of Kasumigaseki, Japan's Whitehall; or in closed sessions of LDP Dietmen, divided according to the industries which they were paid large sums to represent. Bills coming before the Diet were all drafted by civil servants. Civil servants also answered questions on behalf of ministers on the floor of the committee chambers. Politicians had little to do except mediate among various conflicting interest groups within society, and they regularly took large sums of money as their reward.

Still, the LDP was able to present itself as the party which ensured that Japan remained prosperous and non-communist, and which fostered Japanese traditions. It had become the natural party of government. The tight stricture of the patronage system prevented the appearance of many reformers within the party. Ambitious men who aspired to high office would automatically do so through the LDP. Most LDP seats were run almost as fiefdoms. Politicians, when they retired, generally sought to hand over their domain to their son, or to another protégé. All LDP Dietmen insisted on being respectfully addresses as *sensei* (literally 'teacher'). Without the benefit of the network of loyalty and money of the appropriate *sensei*, few people could hope to be selected, let alone to win.

In this climate, cynicism abounded in public life. As the then Justice Minister, Akira Hatano, remarked in 1983 after the Tanaka verdict, 'Looking for honesty in politicians is like asking for fish in the greengrocer's.' The Japanese themselves collectively recognised that the value system underlying the nation's politics was lacking in integrity. Even some of those in the midst of it openly deplored the practices of the Liberal Democratic Party. One outspoken LDP party Dietman, former novelist Shintaro Ishihara, reacted to Kakuei Tanaka's resignation in 1974 by saying that the disgraced Prime Minister represented 'a symbol of the ruin and confusion in Japanese affairs, at home and abroad'. Ishihara also deplored the absence of ethical sense among the Japanese, asking aloud if it was not 'a nation without morality'.

The opposition parties decried what they called 'structural corruption' and put it down to the Liberal Democrats' complacency after remaining in power without a break for two decades and more. Others, though, denounced the Socialists and some other opposition groups (but not the Communist Party, which stayed aloof) for allegedly accepting regular cash gifts and privileges from the government party. It was widely reported that Tanaka had made lavish gifts not only to politicians and civil servants on his own side but to dozens of opposition Diet members as well. His critics accused him of corrupting not just his own party but the whole of the Japanese body politic. In reality Tanaka was only the foremost practitioner of the Japanese art of politics.

On paper Japan had a structure of government similar to that of Britain or Canada, with a prime minister as head of government presiding over a Cabinet making up the executive branch of government; that in turn was circumscribed by other constitutional powers, notably the legislature and the courts. In practice Japan's decision-making system was based on an indigenous hierarchy of authority with elements reminiscent of the pre-war period. The courts regularly passed judgements taking into account the 'interests of the state' rather then neutrally interpreting the law. In several cases citizens demanded that public elections be ruled unlawful because of a more than three to one bias in favour of the value of votes to elected seats in country areas (which tend to return ruling-party Diet members) compared with the cities. On each occasion the argument of the plaintiffs was upheld but no redress was given. The domestic political system set enormous store on reaching consensus rather than allowing the executive to take decisions and responsibility for the results. The Cabinet therefore had much less room for independent decisions than its counterparts in other democratic political systems. Japanese prime ministers and their Cabinets were bound, on domestic and foreign-policy matters equally, to follow certain ordained steps before announcing any significant decision. Custom demanded this and custom ruled.

Decisions on foreign policy were often fudged and came late, and Japan had difficulty in framing a response to events elsewhere based on anything broader than its own economic self-interest. As a consequence, in the 1970s Japan's diplomacy at various times was criticised in the West and the East alike as unprincipled and self-serving. The response to the OAPEC ultimatum on policy towards Israel was one example: one foreign observer deplored the manner of Japan's sudden shift to the Arab side, saying that the country had moved 'from disdainful indifference to sycophantic solicitude'.

Another instance was Japan's half-hearted attempt to mediate for peace between Iran and Iraq during the 1980–8 Gulf War. The Foreign Ministry made much of the fact that Japan was the only member of the 'Western Bloc' to maintain friendly ties with both Iran and Iraq throughout the war. However, a reluctance to scuttle any commercial interests with either of the belligerents reduced Japan's role to that of go-between, constantly calling on both sides for restraint and sometimes carrying messages from the USA to Baghdad and Tehran. Japan never earned the stature to propose an original peace formula of its own. Its ties with Iran were explicitly reinforced by the government and business together in the form of the most expensive single overseas plant investment Japan had made anywhere, the petrochemical complex at Bandar Khomeini. The Mitsui executive in charge of the project was a retired MITI Vice-minister. In 1979, when the scheme looked like becoming a multi-billion dollar disaster for Mitsui, the government stepped in and turned it into a 'national project'. Japanese reports said this was done in return for very large election-fund donations by Mitsui to the LDP in general elections in the same year.

The issue that above all concerned the outside world in Japan's resurgence was also the one that gave rise to the most confusion: rearmament. This emerged gradually as a defined Japanese national goal during the 1970s, thanks both to strong American pressure and to the lessening of Chinese objections. The post-war Prime Minister, Yoshida, and his successors had believed in Japan's rearmament, but they did not wish to pursue it at the expense of the more urgent goals of economic recovery and industrial strength. To the conservative politicians who ran Japan from 1948 onwards, the important aim was the achievement of genuine national independence – and to them that meant two things: the removal of the 'no-war' clause in the constitution and adequate defence capability. However, they recognised that any sudden move to improve the size or quality of the Self-Defence Forces would provoke an outcry abroad. On one side, from 1950 onwards the USA was publicly urging Japan to build up its army – partly spurred on by Congressional feeling that Japan was getting 'a free ride' on America's back in the area of defence. On the other side, China and other Asian countries vehemently opposed Japan's rearmament.

Japan therefore plied a middle course, heeding American demands, but without seeming to take the initiative. A large factor in deciding this 'no offence meant' stance was public disapproval of things military. Public opinion supported the Self-Defence Forces but was against Japan's having becoming a conspicuous military power and consistently opposed higher defence spending. In particular, the great majority of Japanese wanted the country to have nothing to do with nuclear arms: this sentiment was dubbed the 'nuclear allergy'. In 1971 Eisaku Sato announced that Japan would follow three 'non-nuclear principles', of not possessing, manufacturing or allowing the introduction into Japan of nuclear arms; he was rewarded with the Nobel Peace Prize in 1974. Thereafter the opposition parties and organised left seized every opportunity to show that the principles were being violated, as it was common knowledge that many US warships carried nuclear missiles, depth charges and other weapons as a matter of routine, and they made regular port calls to Japan. Also, in 1973 the American Yokosuka naval base near Tokyo was made the 'home port' of the aircraft-carrier USS *Midway*.

In 1974 a retired officer of the US Seventh Fleet, Rear-Admiral Larocque, caused a storm of controversy in Japan when he publicly made clear that US ships had always carried their nuclear arms with them into Japanese ports. Even then, when challenged in the Diet, the Japanese government preferred to hide behind the old, ambiguous formula: that the USA is bound by the terms of the US–Japan Security Treaty to advise Japan in case nuclear arms are to be brought into Japanese territory, and since there had been no such communication, it was assumed no nuclear weapons had been brought in. It was a flimsy fig-leaf. Edwin Reischauer, who had been US Ambassador to Tokyo in the early 1960s, crisply explained the matter, writing that

> The Japanese government had been too timid to explain the validity of the American interpretation that the ban on the 'introduction' of nuclear weapons did not apply to American warships, resorting instead to evasive statements about its complete confidence that the United States would live up to its agreements.

Still, the 1970s saw less hesitancy over defence matters. Takeo Miki summed up Japan's defence policy as being like 'a timid porcupine': the bristles should be sharp and tough enough to put off an intruder, but the animal is not the aggressive type. Miki was a politician of rare independence of mind among his contemporaries, who had absorbed the liberal thinking of Franklin Roosevelt before Pearl Harbor and stood out in his own country against the rush to war. In 1976 his government produced a Basic Defence Outline, by which Japan would have enough military strength to repel 'a small-scale invasion'. It was the first time that Japan's defence goals had been formally spelled out and it was the start of a ten-year process of transformation for the Self-Defence Forces in which they ceased to be a toy-town army and became a credible fighting force.

In the same year, 1976, the annual defence white paper for the first time identified the Soviet Union as a 'potential threat' to Japan's security. The following year a Soviet fighter pilot defected to Japan, flying without being challenged through Japanese air-defence detection systems. The inadequacy of Japan's early-warning system was exposed. Japanese officers bewailed the fact that their forces had only enough ammunition to fight for a few days in case of need. It was pointed out that, according to Japanese law, if an enemy were to invade Japan, Self-Defence Force tanks would be obliged to stop at every traffic light they came to. Gradually these loopholes were closed. An emergency law was passed, explicitly authorising local commanders to engage an enemy on Japanese territory without the permission of the Cabinet in full session. The three services for the first time pooled their authority in a joint staff command structure. The first combined exercises between the American and Japanese navies took place in the Sea of Japan, amid sporadic protests. By 1982 the goals were more ambitious: the government gave in to persistent American pressure and publicly set a target for Japan to develop the capability to defend the sea-lanes leading to the country from 1000 miles south in the Pacific.

At the same time, Miki used his brief spell in office to create a framework to contain Japan's military growth. His Cabinet passed a resolution in 1976 limiting spending on defence to 1 per cent of Japan's GNP; that rule was maintained until the late 1980s. He also reaffirmed Eisaku Sato's non-nuclear principles. Finally, the government decided to ban the export of weapons from Japan to three categories of states: hostile, communist, or engaged in a war. That ban was not entirely effective. Much equipment, such as radar and vehicles, falls into the ambiguous category, recognised by international arms-monitoring agencies, of 'dual' military and civilian use. Still, the fact remains that in large part thanks to the policy against arms-export, Japan did not enter the world 'arms bazaar' in a serious way.

These various measures amounted in effect to a series of tripwires designed to stop Japan from ever drifting back towards the belligerency and breakdown of democratic forms that occurred in the 1930s. The policy was faithfully maintained by successive Japanese leaders in the period up to 1982. It could well be described as a remarkable recognition on their part that the nation collectively still could not trust itself to follow the path of peaceful development without formal constraints.

The question of whether or not post-war Japan could be trusted by other nations went a lot deeper than the number of its battle tanks or the quality of its military radar. At its heart was the issue of responsibility for the war. If Japan could not find it in its conscience to abjure the invasion of China and other Asian countries, then the world must be ready in case it sought to have a second try at imposing its will by force.

Suspicions of Japanese 'revisionism' concerning the Pacific War gradually increased in other parts of Asia with a series of what were taken to be signs that Japanese government leaders were either sealing off the past or deliberately seeking to whitewash it. Emperor Hirohito, as the wartime head of state, was in a position as far as the rest of the world was concerned to resolve these doubts once and for all, but he studiously avoided any remarks which could be construed as accepting blame on the part of Imperial Japan or himself. The Imperial Household Agency jealously shielded the Emperor's immunity from occasions where he could be quoted speaking about the war or about current political affairs, citing the constitutional constraint against his playing any independent political role. The Emperor's lukewarm phrases, drafted for him by palace officials for delivery on rare public occasions, did little to allay the suspicions directed both at him personally and at successive Japanese post-war heads of governments.

In 1971 Hirohito made his first overseas visit since the war, to Denmark, the Netherlands, Belgium, France, Britain, Switzerland and West Germany. In London he rode beside Queen Elizabeth II down the Mall to Buckingham Palace. In his speech at the banquet in his honour he avoided all mention of the war, prompting a sharp protest from the *Guardian* newspaper. In an editorial the paper commented that Emperor Hirohito was the same man in whose name many Allied prisoners of war had died of maltreatment, and 'Official protocol must not stand in the way of recognition of the truth'. The tour was counted a success overall, but it was partly marred by angry demonstrations against the visit in the Netherlands as well as in Britain. In 1975, before his state visit to the United States, Hirohito spoke of Japan's war against the Allies as 'that deeply regrettable war'. Asked whether he felt personally responsible for permitting Japan to wage war against the Allies, he replied cryptically that he could not answer because, as he put it, 'I am not well versed in the usage of words.'

The issue of Japan's attitude to the war flared up at regular intervals from the mid-1970s onwards because of the bitter 'textbook dispute'. The central government kept for itself the power to determine the content of all classroom teaching. Despite fierce opposition from the main teachers' union, in the 1950s the Education Ministry instituted a system of supervising and in some cases censoring the history books used in Japan's schools. In many cases ministry officials used this power to tone down or remove references to Japanese army atrocities and acts of aggression in the Second World War. In a celebrated case, Professor Saburo Ienaga, a historian, challenged the legality of this system after he had received requests from ministry officials asking him to doctor his descriptions of the wartime actions of the Japanese army. He refused, but other scholars bowed to similar pressure. After a court battle lasting two decades, Professor Ienaga lost the main court case, arguing that the screening was in breach of the constitution.

The issue flared up again in 1982 when China, North Korea, South Korea and other Asian governments voiced objections to new examples of the policy of officially vetting school textbooks. The Japanese government backed down under a barrage of fierce criticism, but officials made clear that it was done under duress: government spokesmen continued to denounce what they saw as interference in Japan's internal affairs, and the episode brought a series of overt threats by right-wing fanatics against groups of teachers and others who took the side of Japan's critics. The government barely satisfied the outside world. It appeared also to be trying to mollify the right-wing activists who regularly besieged the Foreign Ministry in Tokyo with vans blaring out demands and martial music.

In spite of these ambiguities, Japan made steady headway in winning economic security and stable relations with most countries. The Security Treaty with the USA remained the fulcrum of its foreign relations, although 'omnidirectional diplomacy' served as a formula to sanction Japan's own policy towards the Arab nations and the Third World in general. Only once did America's actions cause serious strain with the Japanese government – when, in 1979, Tokyo learned after the event that the USA had mounted a commando expedition to free the American hostages in Iran. The attempt ended in fiasco, with the US helicopters crash-landing in the desert. Through the 1970s Japan gradually showed itself acting in concert with America's other principal allies: it joined in Western sanctions against the Soviet Union, in protest at the Soviet invasion of Afghanistan in 1979 and again after the clampdown on Solidarity in Poland in 1981.

Japan's own initiatives were limited to making overtures in the Asia–Pacific region aimed at advancing the country's economic security without alarming other governments. Hence Takeo Fukuda sought to forge a twin policy in south-east Asia, creating a $1 billion economic aid fund for projects in the non-communist states of ASEAN (the Association of South-East Asian Nations, made up of Thailand, Malaysia, Singapore, Indonesia and the Philippines), while maintaining good relations with communist Vietnam, Cambodia and Laos. Masayoshi Ohira put his weight behind a vaguely defined 'Pacific basin' which reminded some critics of the wartime 'Co-Prosperity Sphere' and never took concrete shape. By the early 1980s Zenko Suzuki was advancing the merits for Japan of what was called 'comprehensive security'. By this way of thinking, Japan recognised that military protection alone could not guarantee its security. In addition, the country must have security for its raw materials and markets, underpinned by consistently good relations with other states. In the end none of the grand-sounding diplomatic slogans of the decade altered the overall thrust of Japanese foreign relations, which was to be able to trade to advantage with everyone while remaining under the protection of the USA.

As the 1970s drew to a close, Japan remained an unsolved riddle. It behaved submissively in international councils, yet was poised to challenge the West's supremacy by economic means. It had the world's fourth most costly conventional army, but that was maintained in the name of self-defence. The country's post-war purposes were unclear, but its ever-growing wealth was unmistakably increasing its status in the world at large. Still, living out its new identity as a good world citizen, Japan was exporting manufactured goods, not ideology or revolution. Throughout the 1970s opinion polls showed that the foreign nation that the Japanese most admired was neutral, uncontroversial, mercantile Switzerland.

▪ 5 ▪

Targets

OVERTAKING THE WEST

ON a June day in 1982 two employees of Hitachi, the giant Japanese electronics firm, drove to an office in Santa Clara, California. They had looked forward to this as the moment when the trade secrets of IBM's latest computer series would be handed over in return for half a million dollars. The IBM man they had been dealing with was waiting for them, with the piles of documents, just as they hoped, resting on a table. Kenji Hayashi, a senior engineer in Hitachi's computer department, looked over the papers and triumphantly tore the blue IBM logo off one of the boxes they were lying in, pasting it on to his own notebook. At that moment two FBI agents burst in. One said: 'It's all over.' The two Japanese were under arrest, caught in a trap laid jointly by the federal investigators and IBM.

The case came to be known as 'Japscam'. It was the most dramatic 'sting' operation ever mounted to uncover industrial espionage between two supposedly friendly trading nations. The case had begun when Hitachi, in its eagerness to get hold of crucial IBM designs, had confidentially requested a computer consultant in Silicon Valley to supply details of the new software. The consultant, Maxwell Paley, was a former head of IBM's Advanced Computing Systems laboratory: he had tipped off his one-time employers that Hitachi were on the trail of their 'crown jewels', and IBM had turned the case over to the Federal Bureau of Information. Hitachi's first instinct was to go on the attack, and the company charged that 'IBM's goal was not a law-enforcement goal ... it was instead anti-competitive economic benefit for itself.' However, after much soul-searching and a shower of bad publicity in the world's press, Hitachi pleaded guilty in an American federal court to attempting to steal IBM property. The company and the two employees involved were fined. Nobody went to jail, but as a result of out-of-court negotiations Hitachi was obliged to pay IBM $300 million in compensation, and had to modify a range of its own machines to replace software which it had functionally replicated from that of IBM.

IBM had achieved its purpose: to make an example out of one Japanese firm that was prepared to break American laws to get hold of its closely guarded secrets. In the fiercely competitive computer marketplace, understanding and copying the designs used by IBM, the undisputed frontrunner, was essential to rivals whose machines had to be 'plug-compatible' – designed to operate with IBM equipment. Several of the leading Japanese firms, including Hitachi and Fujitsu, were in that predicament. They resented the way IBM had always used its dominant market position to bind much of the industry to its software standards. In Japan, Hitachi was seen as more sinned against than sinning. There the press treated it as a case of Us versus Them – the Japanese being made into scapegoats by a hostile world. Most articles focused not on the transgressions of Hitachi but on the anti-Japan conspiracy between the FBI and the world's dominant computer company.

The Hitachi affair was one skirmish in a long-drawn-out battle for the world lead in computers, in which half a dozen Japanese firms tried to catch up with IBM and then take the lead in the world computer industry. The Japanese were second to none in making computer hardware, using advanced manufacturing skills; but in the early 1980s they lagged behind the USA and European firms in terms of the software programmes to make efficient use of computers in business, science and other applications. Soon after Hitachi was thwarted by the 'sting' in California, Japan's Ministry of International Trade and Industry tried another tactic. It drafted a law which would have forced IBM, and all foreign computer firms, to register their software in Tokyo and to license it to Japanese firms. The senior American trade negotiator at the time, Clyde Prestowitz, described this as 'a declaration of war on the US computer industry'. The bill was only narrowly blocked from being made into law by internal rivalries between MITI and the Japanese Ministry of Posts and Tele-communications, as well as frantic lobbying by the American officials involved.

The Japanese were not alone in thinking that computers and com-munications would make possible a 'third industrial revolution', to succeed the English industrial revolution and the American assembly-line revolution exemplified by Henry Ford. However, no other government had as well-formed an idea as Japan about what the future would be like in 'the information age'; and no other industry was as closely and lovingly fostered as electronics.

The transistor had revolutionised electronic products once already. As more and more transistors came to be packed on to integrated circuits, the industry advanced with dizzying speed. Japanese government officials and industrialists realised that semiconductors, especially memory chips, were the key to the whole electronics industry. The government formulated policies aimed at building up the Japanese industry from scratch and preventing it from being overrun by America. Later, the goal was to replace IBM as the driving force in the world computer business. In 1960 America seemed to hold all the cards, as its firms owned patents to existing computer designs, and IBM had an overwhelming market share in Japan, as indeed it had everywhere. But Japan was not daunted.

To foster their infant industry the Japanese built a fortress against the American giant. In 1960 IBM formally applied to begin manufacturing in Japan, and the deputy head of MITI's Heavy Machineries Bureau, Shigeru Sahashi, laid down tough terms: 'We will take every measure possible to obstruct the success of your business', he declared, 'unless you license IBM patents to Japanese firms and charge them no more than a 5 per cent royalty.' IBM felt it had no choice but to agree to the terms. It released its technical know-how in exchange for securing a strong market position in Japan as the domestic industry grew. But as a Japanese company, IBM Japan had to accept the government's guidelines for conducting its business. They involved giving priority to domestic Japanese competitors through the awarding of public-sector computer contracts as well as 'guidance' to private corporate customers to buy Japanese. It took until 1983 for the Japanese leader, Fujitsu, to displace IBM as the biggest-selling computer firm in Japan. In 1986, NEC (Nippon Electric Company) pushed IBM into third place.

Texas Instruments, a leading American maker of integrated circuits, had a similar experience. The firm applied in 1964 to produce its own products in Japan, but when it was met with similarly punitive conditions it turned them down and refused to license its technology in Japan. Later it was allowed to form a fifty–fifty subsidiary with Sony in exchange for licensing its technology, but like IBM it had to accept fixed limits on its production until domestic firms were better able to compete. Robert Galvin, the chairman of Motorola since 1976, saw it as blatantly unfair. He remembers how in the 1950s President Dwight Eisenhower himself encouraged US firms to transfer their technology and trade with Japan in order to help its recovery:

At the same time, we asked what *our* opportunities were and we were told quite clearly that we were not allowed to invest in Japan – and that really there wasn't much opportunity to sell your product because 'we don't need it'. When we did try to sell we were faced with a very large number of tariff barriers originally, and then non-tariff barriers and barriers based on custom.

The USA was confident in its technology lead, and almost entirely open to the approaches of visitors from Japan. At the Bell Laboratories in America the basic research for the first transistor was sold to allcomers without discrimination, and Sony was among the first buyers. During the 1950s and 1960s the US electronics industry sold the bulk of its expertise to Japan for a total sum estimated at less than $10 billion. Mark Shepherd, chairman of Texas Instruments, blames the attitude of American company executives, and says that for the sake of short-term cash they 'sold their birthright to the Japanese at a very low cost.' He watched the process being repeated in a range of industries:

> In the early days, the Japanese would visit you as companies *en masse* and as a result they would find technologies that they wanted, whether it be semiconductors or television or telecommunications or whatever, and then they would proceed to make proposals to the companies that had that technology. Unfortunately a large percentage of them chose to get a short-term profit for far too low a price.

The Japanese naturally saw the situation quite differently. For Kenichi Ohmae, head of the McKinsey consultancy firm's Tokyo office, the important thing was that in the early 1970s IBM, GE, RCA, Texas Instruments and other American firms were still a great deal bigger than their Japanese counterparts:

> Throughout our history we always learned about the gigantic Western corporations, the wealth they had accumulated, the technological lead which they had, and so we took Western strength for granted: we often compared ourselves to an ant trying to fight an elephant!

Takuma Yamamoto, who worked his way up to become president of Fujitsu, remembers the days in the mid-1950s when his firm woke up to the need to carve out a place within the computer marketplace. IBM was then thirty times bigger than Fujitsu: it was far ahead of all rivals in terms of automation, technological research and investment funds. 'They seemed so far ahead,' Yamamoto says. 'It was really a case of Gulliver and the little people. But I did not think it impossible for us to close the gap and catch up.'

Michiyuki Uenohara, who later became research director of NEC, spent much of his early career as a researcher at the Bell Laboratories. He returned home in 1967 to find that 'people who were making computers in Japan had no faith in the Japanese semiconductor chips: they imported most of the chips they used from America.' Uenohara devoted his energies to building up his company's computer-chip production, because he felt that unless Japan had the capacity to produce its own chips, Japanese industry itself would not expand. He says frankly that his aim was to gain the competitive edge for his company in making chips: 'Rather than contribute to the development of world technology as a whole,' he says, 'I was convinced that it was more important to advance IC [integrated circuit] technology and mass-produce, in order to offer cheap yet good-quality products to a large number of people.'

By the 1960s the difference in approach on the opposite sides of the Pacific was obvious. The American electronics firms were geared up to make large-scale and capital goods: mainframe computers, and equipment for the Pentagon and the NASA space programme. They had much less interest in the high-volume production of consumer goods, such as radios, TVs and hi-fi sets. Meanwhile, Japanese firms concentrated their energies on that fast-growing world market. The Americans were taken aback at the single-mindedness of the Japanese commercial instinct, but the bafflement was mutual. Michiyuki Uenohara stressed to his American friends, 'If you turn your backs on mass-produced goods, then to some extent at least you will lose your technological capacity too.'

The arrival in the early 1970s of large-scale integrated circuits, or LSIs, was an important leap forward for the whole industry. LSIs were known as 'third-generation' devices, after transistors and ICs, and they made possible a new degree of precision and miniaturisation. With their appearance the contest between the USA and Japan grew still more intense, with Siemens of West Germany and several other European firms holding on to a small share of the world market.

In the USA, IBM made easily the largest number of semiconductors, but it used virtually all of them in-house. Other American semiconductor-makers were 'merchant firms', selling their products in the market. A host of American smaller firms specialised only in software, or in producing custom-made ICs. In Japan the chip-makers were all firms with tens of thousands of employees which also made finished products. NEC and Fujitsu were the largest; they each made a wide range of products, including consumer electronic goods, mainframe computers and capital telecommunications equipment. Firms like those had a strong incentive to produce the vital ingredients for all their products – the chips. Even so, NEC wavered over making large-scale investments until in 1972 MITI came up with an overall plan for the Japanese industry: the ministry organised the major Japanese firms in a 'national project' to develop LSIs with government sponsorship.

The Japanese firms were still obliged to buy in most of their semiconductors from America, but they began to complain that the chips were too prone to breakdown. Uenohara says that NEC's early computer models, using imported chips, were fine when tested in the laboratory, but that in the Japanese rainy season, a month of high humidity and rainfall in early summer, a host of complaints came in from customers. 'It took us a lot of time and effort trying to locate the origins of the trouble,' he says, 'but finally we realised that the problems lay in the unreliability of imported chips: they weren't up to the Japanese high standards.' That, he says, was the spur that drove NEC to produce its own chips in large quantities. The company quickly became Japan's number one producer.

Mark Shepherd of Texas Instruments, like others in the American industry, disputes the claim that American chips were unreliable, believing it was no more than an excuse for a buy-Japanese policy. 'They went in our computers', he says, 'and they worked fine.' Shepherd insists that the Japanese were having the same problem in supplying the US manufacturers; the difference was that the Japanese took a decision as a matter of policy not to go on buying American chips unless there was no way they could buy them within Japan. The *keiretsu* system was regarded with suspicion: a common view from outside was that Japanese firms wanted to make their own computer chips; failing that they would buy from within their own *keiretsu* group; only as a last resort would they buy from abroad. One senior Fujitsu executive, Taiyo Kobayashi, made no bones about how valuable MITI's support was. 'Before we even knew whether our products would work or not,' he said, 'MITI was actively lobbying the carmakers and steel companies to start using domestically made computers.' Universities in Japan, as in other countries, could count on receiving hefty 'academic discounts' from domestic firms, giving them a strong incentive not to buy from abroad.

The American firms stayed ahead in making the most sophisticated semiconductor products, including micro-processors, but the large Japanese firms established an unmatched reputation for quality in producing the most common types of memory chips. The semiconductors that came out of Japanese plants went into the whole range of household products in which the Japanese firms excelled. There was fierce rivalry among them to achieve ever higher production yields and to eliminate faults. Japanese firms borrowed the American ideas of aiming for quality control and 'zero defects', and far outdid their former masters. In 1979 the US computer firm Hewlett Packard published its own finding: that Japanese-made chips were only one-fifth as likely to fail as American-made products. The improvements resulted in consumer electronic goods becoming more reliable than ever before.

IBM's market dominance meant that other firms' products had to be compatible with its standards, and they risked being outflanked each time IBM brought out a new application. The problem for those rivals was eased when in the early 1970s other American firms launched a series of computers and peripherals which were plug-compatible. The dependent status was a problem, too, for European computer-makers, but it was Japan that made the running in the attempt to prevent IBM from dictating standards to the whole industry. Mark Shepherd of Texas Instruments acknowledges that up until the early 1970s IBM's domination was so strong that without protection the Japanese competition would probably have been driven out of the race. Still, he does not condone the methods they used: 'The way they go about doing the job', he says, 'is to close their markets, in effect, to other people: and that's not right.' Shepherd recalls that on a trip to Japan as chairman of the US Electronic Industries Association his Japanese counterpart said to him, 'We've been nurturing this rose, and you're trying to crush it.' Shepherd replied with equal directness: 'That's right!' The tough-talking of the Americans only confirmed their Japanese opposite numbers in the wisdom of their chosen strategy.

In the early 1970s Japan was faced with strong demands for the opening up of its computer market. It responded with a phased, three-year programme of tariff reductions and an easing of investment restrictions, designed to buy time for domestic firms. The government wanted to leave nothing to chance. It sponsored a computer-rental agency, JECC (Japan Electronic Computer Company) to acquaint user firms with Japanese-made mainframe computers and to forestall any urge on their part to buy foreign ones.

It was certain that the next thing would be a 'super-chip', using very large-scale integration (VLSI) to produce a 64k RAM (Random Access Memory) semiconductor – one that can store 64 000 bits of information. Computer costs would come down sharply and their speed and memory would be greatly increased. The worldwide computer industry was shaken up when it emerged that IBM was expecting to make VLSIs by the end of the 1970s. The Japanese were especially alarmed, knowing that their technology still lagged well behind. Michi-

147

yuki Uenohara of NEC says that at that time he feared 'if the Americans were able to develop a VLSI computer, it would mean the end of the Japanese semiconductor business.' MITI, acting as the eyes and ears of the Japanese industry, decided that the only way Japan could compete was by a systematic pooling of the resources of the country's major firms; and so Japan's VLSI research programme was born.

The idea was partly that of the private firms themselves. They went to MITI for funds to support the research they each thought they needed. MITI lent 29 billion yen, or about $100 million, but imposed one key condition: that the work must be done by the companies acting as a consortium, and that the resulting technology must be shared. MITI invited the five leading computer firms – Fujitsu, NEC, Hitachi, Toshiba and Mitsubishi Electric – to join in. In 1976 researchers from the five firms began the work, some of it in a central laboratory, some farmed out to the individual companies. The aim was to develop Japanese VLSI technology within four years and use it to beat the Americans into second place around the world.

The programme excited strong suspicion in the minds of the American companies directly in competition, including Texas Instruments, Motorola, Intel, and the many specialist firms in Silicon Valley. Some in those firms feared that the exercise could lead to a technology blockade, with the Japanese government patenting the research results in such a way that others could not access them. Moreover, many were convinced that once the Japanese acquired the skills they needed to make a new level of computer, all non-Japanese would be squeezed out from selling that type of product in the Japanese market. Robert Galvin said that was only to be expected, and that is how it worked out: 'Every time they had acquired a capacity and a competence to produce a given class of chips, the market closed down for those same opportunities for us.' The Americans knew full well that such a grouping of private firms for a common commercial end would not be legal in the USA.

Michiyuki Uenohara took the closest interest in the VLSI project. He believed the young researchers were doing work ten years ahead of its time. 'It gave me great pleasure', he said, 'to see them aiming at technological developments that would outstrip IBM and put us as the world's number one.' Uenohara was aware of strong complaints from his American associates that the whole thing was unfair, but he put them down to sour grapes: 'I felt that the Americans wanted government aid just like the Japanese VLSI was receiving and *that* was what they didn't like.' Yamamoto of Fujitsu believes that Western disapproval of Japanese collaboration in the VLSI project is misplaced: 'It is undoubtedly true that a number of Japanese industrial firms collaborated, but more important was the sense of competition which took us forward. That is what we see as the essential element in the story.'

At the beginning all involved in the work were uneasy. The individual researchers came from firms that were fierce rivals in the marketplace. They worried that their own technological know-how might leak out to their competitors, so hardly any useful work was done. But after about a year the people involved had formed a common sense of purpose, and the parent companies wanted the project to succeed. The programme was completed on schedule by the end of 1979, and rival firms in the West were astonished when the next year the first Japanese-made 64k-RAM chips appeared on the market. From the start Japan began to outpace by far the USA and Europe in marketing them in large volume, and by 1982 they had taken two-thirds of the world market for 64k-RAMs, the lifeblood of the semiconductor industry.

The Japanese research was not for outside consumption. When Western visitors were shown round, they were kept away from the production lines. The Americans were incensed that the same people who had been given ready access to America's publicly funded research, and to the technical discoveries of companies, were now not reciprocating. Fears of a 'patent cartel' aimed at keeping the technology secrets locked up for years proved unfounded; but the anger increased when the Japanese firms began flooding the world markets with their new products at what rivals judged to be unreasonably low prices. Robert Galvin admired the discipline of his Japanese rivals and the technical excellence of the products. His objection was: 'They marketed them at predatory prices, prices that were under their costs and lower than what they were allowing for their sales prices in their home market: dumping, in other words.' Again, the Japanese firms used a quite different logic. NEC, Fujitsu, Hitachi and the other makers were each part of a 'vertically integrated' company system in which the semiconductor division supplied the various product divisions as a matter of course, achieving high volumes quickly and so keeping unit costs down. If semiconductor production made losses, they could generally be offset by profits from consumer goods, machine tools or other product divisions.

As the pressure grew for more and speedy investment, Japanese electronic firms made full use of their relatively cheap and plentiful credit lines. Low rates of interest and the lack of pressure from shareholders for dividends allowed the Japanese firms to invest most of their after-tax profits in new plant. NEC, Fujitsu and the others were able to borrow freely from the commercial banks for their new investments, relying on bank borrowing for up to 80 per cent of the needed capital. That strategy was approved by the financial authorities; shareholders by custom had little if any chance to question the policy. Interest rates for industrial borrowers were considerably lower than for private borrowers; ordinary Japanese people did not use credit cards and were not allowed even a small overdraft from their bank. Direct government loans were modest, and all those for the VLSI project proper were eventually paid back. American firms, by contrast, were bound by shareholders' interests to restrict borrowing to 20 per cent of their equity value. Japanese firms remained in the vanguard of development of subsequent generations of VLSIs, including 256k and 1-megabit D-RAM chips.

Semiconductors were to be the subject of a fierce political row across the Pacific in the late 1980s. By then the race was on for a 'fifth-generation' computer and Japan's traditional weakness in software was being tested; but the impact of its successful catch-up effort in the high-volume chip market altered the whole industrial balance of power in Japan's favour. Mark Shepherd is blunt in his assessment that Japan set out deliberately to crush its rivals: 'If the Japanese can drive competitors out by whatever tactic necessary, that leaves a gigantic share for them in the future. The Japanese moved with immense aggressiveness in this area.' Japanese businessmen involved saw it as only natural for the government to help its own side.

The oil crisis, which wrought havoc with Japan's industry in 1973 and 1974, provided a strong spur for the country's rush to high technology. Semiconductors were hailed as 'the crude oil of the 1980s'. In the first months of the oil crisis MITI reworked its own policy paper for the 1970s, written in 1971 under the title *Basic Direction of the New International Trade and Industry Policy: A Vision for the 1970s*. This had sketched out a conceptual framework for a major shift in the pattern of Japan's economic activity: there would be lower levels of growth, less direct government involvement in industry, and a conscious move away from old heavy-industry sectors into new ones such as electronics and industrial robots, which were described as 'knowledge-intensive'. Japan was to move from general industrial goods to high technology as the mainspring of its wealth and well-being. With disarming simplicity Naohiro Amaya, the MITI official who wrote the original 'Vision', says that, since Japan has very poor resources under the ground, 'We thought the most abundant resources in Japan are our own brains, so' – pointing at his own head – 'we have to develop our resources in this small box, instead of the resources underground.' Amaya's declaration of Japan's need for self-sufficiency is essentially the same as that made a century ago by the men of Meiji,

■ *13* Empty shelves after shoppers besieged supermarkets following the first oil crisis of 1973.

■ *14* Tokyo businessmen read about the arrest of ex-Prime Minister Tanaka on 27 July 1976.

■ *Opposite 15* Prime Minister Nakasone between President Reagan and Mrs Thatcher during the Williamsburg Summit of 1983.

■ *16* Another scandal: former Prime Minister Nakasone testifies in the Diet over his alleged role in Recruit Affair, May 1989.

■ *17* The Diet in full session, November 1987.

■ *Top 18* Honda employees discuss the day's tasks and problems with their section leader before starting work.

■ *Above 19* Assembly-line production of motor cycles at the Honda factory.

■ *Opposite above 20* Boom days on the floor of the Tokyo Stock Exchange.

■ *Opposite below 21* Electric city: a schoolboy in traditional uniform shops for calculators in the Akihabara district of Tokyo.

■ *22* Left-wing protests against the celebrations for the eighty-fifth birthday of Emperor Hirohito and the imminent arrival in Tokyo of President Reagan, April 1986.

■ *23* Japanese warships celebrate the thirtieth anniversary of the creation of the Self-Defence Forces, 1984.

■ *Overleaf 24* Self-Defence Force troops parade in front of Prime Minister Kaifu (front row, third from left), March 1990.

faced with what they saw as the military and industrial challenges of the West.

As in the years of high growth, the government worked hand in glove with industry to formulate a complex of plans to change the country's 'industrial structure'. Japan had to adapt to new circumstances, especially the high cost of raw materials, and the challenge from the newly industrialising nations like South Korea and Taiwan. The plans were a logical extension of the policy of the first twenty post-war years for creating a world-beating set of basic industries. The explicit aim now was to be a model of an efficient and 'advanced' economy, drawing strength from high-technology manufacturing and from so-called 'clean' jobs of all kinds, in research, finance and the service industries. The plans were drawn up in close consultation between civil servants and industry representatives. The key deliberative body was the Industrial Structure Council, made up of government officials, industrialists and bankers. The council had thirty sub-committees and commanded much respect.

During the 1970s Japan came under increasingly heavy fire from other countries over the government's role in directing industry, and officials played down the extent to which they intervened in the mechanisms of the market. In reality, to achieve its goal the Japanese government used the full range of its formal and informal powers: the law, subsidies, incentives and the long-established practice of 'administrative guidance' (*gyosei shido*), meaning official directives based not on laws but on the supposedly voluntary co-operation of various interested parties. Administrative guidance has been widely exercised throughout the post-war years: for example, the Bank of Japan's direct influence over the business of commercial banks, and MITI's setting of output and price targets in the steel and petrochemical industries are in this category. After the oil crisis the Japanese government, in consultation with business leaders, set targets in a wide range of industries for production, energy saving and automation.

The list of sweeping new laws enacted in the 1970s gives an indication of how the government took the power to manage the environment for the various sectors of industry. They have unwieldy titles: in the case of electronics the Provisional Measures Law for the Promotion of Specified Electronic and Machine Industries was the first. It was enacted in 1957 to upgrade Japan's technology, and specifically included funds and tax incentives for exports. An update of the same law in 1971 set out measures designed to let Japan catch up with the West in technologies where it still lagged behind. It helped Japanese firms to upgrade their production of high-capacity TV tubes; the Japan Development Bank provided funds for commercialising video cassette recorders (VCRs). A further update in 1978 aimed to bring Japan's computer industry up to par with America's.

The oil crisis gave rise to the 1973 Law for Adjusting Petroleum Supply and Demand, regulating the supply of oil to particular sectors of industry. In 1974 the Law on Temporary Measures for Stabilisation of the National Life fixed the prices of many products and sought to assure their distribution. In 1978 a Depressed Industries Law paved the way for the creation of recession cartels, and led to cutbacks in uncompetitive sectors such as aluminium. Each one of these laws was drafted by specialist civil servants and passed without detailed debate in the Diet. Politicians, even those of the ruling LDP, had little to do with thinking them up or implementing them. Although MITI officials liked to say that their days of real power were over, bureaucratic power still quietly reigned.

The industry which first made a strong showing among the chosen 'knowledge-intensive' industries was consumer electronics. Japanese firms had already in the 1960s topped the world league for output of colour television sets and audio products. The star among them was the home video cassette recorder. VCR manufacture depends heavily on production skills, especially the human skills of trained line-workers. Japan's high levels of discipline and training paid off hand-somely, and productivity rose sharply. An American firm, Ampex, produced the first commercial VCR, but it decided to focus on the professional market. That meant that prices would remain high, machines bulky and potential sales severely limited. Sony pioneered the development of home-use VCRs in its own Beta format. Its main rival, the Matsushita group, developed the VHS format, and stole a march on Sony by marketing tapes which could record for much longer than one hour: the 'battle of the formats' was won, people in the industry said, because American football fans in the USA could set Matsushita's machines to record a whole game, while Sony's smaller tapes could not. By investing many times more than Sony both in production and marketing, the VHS camp won the contest decisively. In Europe Philips put its own format on the market, but it could not keep pace in price or production volume with its Japanese rivals.

The man in charge of Matsushita Electric's VCR division in the 1970s, Akio Tanii, was typical of the breed of engineer–managers who rose to the top of Japanese manufacturing firms, and he became the company's president in 1986. He is enthusiastic when he explains how chips allowed highly automated factories to produce millions of components of extremely good quality. They revolutionised the manufacture of VCRs by enabling the parts in them to be fewer, smaller and much more precise. The most sophisticated parts of all are the playback and recording heads. The cylinder head rotates 1800 times a minute over the moving video tape. The shape of the head has to be absolutely symmetrical to avoid any oscillation, and the end has a very narrow magnetic belt, only 19 microns (millionths of a metre) across. The heads make up a large part of the value of the whole product, and throughout the 1980s, when South Korean and other Asian rivals started to make ever larger numbers of home VCRs for export, Japanese firms were still supplying the heads.

As with transistors and with video technology, so with robots in industry. The Americans got to the starting line well ahead of the rest of the field, but the Japanese changed the character of the race. Joseph Engelberger, one of the fathers of the industry, noted that when the Japanese came across robotics they 'jumped right in, ran with it, and didn't agonise'. When Engelberger – as head of Unimation, a leading American firm – gave a lecture on robotics in Tokyo in 1967 he was astonished to find himself the centre of attention for 700 eager Japanese engineers and executives. In the USA his theme had never attracted such interest. Two years later a Japanese company, Kawasaki Heavy Industries, produced the first Japanese robot under licence from Unimation, and Nissan's first spot-welding robot, a Kawasaki–Unimate, was introduced on to one of its assembly lines. Kawasaki is one of the country's biggest conglomerates, making not only motorcycles and trains but ships, planes and industrial machinery. It set out at once to improve on the original models, with the aim of improving its own productivity, as well as selling to the motor industry.

Robots fitted exactly into MITI's and the leading business groups' plans for automation and for increasing Japan's international competitiveness. As in the case of computers, the government put up funds for a robot-leasing company to encourage their use in smaller firms, and gave other incentives. Many Japanese organisations were already obsessed with the idea of 'flexible manufacturing systems', producing relatively small runs of different lines to meet the demand. Robots proved to be an important part of the solution. Fanuc, an affiliate of the computer firm Fujitsu, was at the head of a group of a dozen large firms that started making robots. By the mid-1980s Japan had about a quarter of a million industrial robots in service, well over half the world total. In a reversal of the original roles, Unimation began to make Kawasaki-designed models to sell under its own name. In the 1980s several Japanese firms built unmanned factories, in which machines make cars and calculators, while their masters sleep.

The robots were aptly named 'steel-collar workers'. The advantages to employers were obvious: they were never sick, they did not ask for wage rises, and after the first years of trial and error they made far fewer mistakes than blue-collar workers. Above all, they took the place of people in performing simple, repetitive tasks, and hastened the integration of production lines. As the robot population in Japan swelled, they directly replaced workers in many cases, yet there were few labour disputes over the issue. To employers, the company union structure, in which full-time employees are effectively guaranteed a job in return for loyalty and flexible work practices, paid off handsomely. In-house unions were not inclined to protest to save a few jobs when the arrival of robots often gave the prospect of more profits and higher wages for all the employees of a company. Unions called for high safety standards and guarantees against lay-offs, but in practice overall employment levels never dropped appreciably as a result of new technology in the workplace. In 1965 the official estimates said that Japan was short of 1.8 million workers, and during most of the 1970s the leading firms, especially in the car industry, remained short of skilled labour. Official figures for the unemployed remained low, at around the 1 million mark, even in the recession that followed the oil crisis.

Japan has kept strict immigration controls ever since it regained independence in 1952, and the option of hiring large numbers of foreign workers was never seriously considered. There was no great demand from industry to change the immigration rules, and a good deal of prejudice existed against the Koreans and Chinese who constituted long-established minorities in Japan. In practice robots generally replaced people in 'dirty' jobs, such as painting and welding; and the higher productivity often created new jobs in sales, marketing and other divisions of large firms. Nissan's union was a model of how the enterprise unions worked closely with management in installing robots on the production lines. In its plants the robots were often affectionately given girls' names, and were treated as part of the team, although they did *not* have to join the company union.

With the car industry Japan rewrote the basic lessons of mass production. In 1950 the Japanese made a total of 1600 cars; in 1980 they made 11 million – more than the USA. It was a shock for Detroit and a triumph for Toyota, Nissan and the other Japanese makers. It was also a landmark in industrial history, and demonstrated Japan's strengths in mass production: the effective management of money, men and machines.

Before the war Toyota and Nissan, the former a family firm of loom-makers, had turned out some passenger cars as well as lorries for army use, basing their designs respectively on those of Ford and Chrysler, and Austin of England. After the war it seemed likely that the car industry would not be revived at all. When independence came in 1952 the companies wanted to get into cars, but they met strong opposition from the Bank of Japan's governor, Naoto Ichimada, who had an important say in the allocation of sparse funds. His view was clear: 'The attempt to foster a car industry in Japan is futile. This is the age of the international division of labour. Since America can produce cheap, high-quality cars, shouldn't we depend on them?' MITI was adamant that the answer was 'no'. The officers of Japan's 'economic high command' believed that a car industry would stimulate others and raise Japan's level of research. They had their way.

MITI decided that the home motor industry needed three things: money, technology and protection; and it became a top priority for the ministry to provide these. Technology could be had by friendly tie-ups with Western companies, and in the early 1950s four Japanese firms signed technical agreements with Western companies: Nissan with Austin, Isuzu with Rootes, Hino with Renault and Shin–Mitsubishi Heavy Industries with Willys-Overland. The government banks were induced to provide the initial investment funds for the favoured firms. Protection was thrown up in the form of tariffs and quotas against imports, and limits on foreign direct investment.

Nissan's founder, Gisuke Ayukawa, was among the industrialists purged in the Occupation for his group's role in the military development of Manchuria; but his ambition was carried on by others. At MITI's urging, the company at first relied on its old partner, Austin, importing all the parts from Britain to assemble the A40 in Japan. Nissan's chief of production, Sadamichi Sasaki, was used to the frantic manual grind of Japan's wartime factories. He could hardly believe his eyes on seeing a network of moving conveyor belts when he went to England to visit Austin's Longbridge plant. 'I'd never seen anything like it,' he recalls. 'Parts would come all the way out from the casting bay on the conveyor belt, and were carried on another conveyor to the machine works. It was all automatic: I was amazed.' On the other hand, he was shocked to see that at ten in the morning the British workers stopped and the production line was halted while they took a ten-minute tea break. At Nissan's plants rest periods were staggered so that the production line kept moving.

After coming through the major strike of 1953, Nissan set about making cars based on its own designs, and in 1958 tested its first all-Japanese Datsun model in the Round-Australia Road Rally. The other competitors scorned the new entry, but it won. The impact in Japan was electrifying. It was as though the whole nation had won the competition. The press greeted it as a portent of Japan's reawakening

155

pride after years of self-denigration. Nissan had recovered a large part of the prestige it had enjoyed in the war years as the centrepiece of a group of more than seventy companies spanning a wide range of industries. Now Nissan was a key member of the major Fuyo business group, based on the Fuji Bank.

Toyota chose a different route, relying on its own development from the start. It described its tactic as 'look and learn'. During the war Toyota, like Nissan, had made lorries for the army. Only a few days after Japan's surrender the company's then chairman, Keiichi Toyoda, gathered his employees together and told them: 'We *must* overtake the Americans within three years, or that will be the end of the Japanese motor industry.' His aim proved far too ambitious, but the contest was to be a long one. One of his sons, Eiji Toyoda, himself spent three months at Ford's headquarters in Detroit studying techniques of production. He was deeply impressed at the advanced assembly line and the scale of production, but he thought, 'Ford is doing nothing that Toyota couldn't do.'

At its complex of factories near Nagoya, Toyota became a byword for high productivity based on unremitting hard work. The company had the reputation of being a 'provincial' enterprise, without the polish of the big firms of Tokyo and Osaka, but that only seemed to make its management more determined to beat the opposition, at home and abroad. In 1959 Toyota built its Motomachi plant, one of the largest and best-equipped car plants in the world, close to its headquarters. It hired thousands of raw recruits from the countryside and housed them in its company dormitories.

The workers lived in fear of Taiichi Ono, the head of the machine shop, who had survived the bombing of one of Toyota's factories. He seemed to his juniors like a man with a special mission. His contribution to Toyota's production technology was copied later by much of Japanese industry: the 'just in time' method. Ono recognised that demand, not supply, should determine the rate of production. By carefully regulating the large stocks of parts that cluttered the floors or filled warehouses of existing factories, Toyota could save money and greatly increase efficiency.

Ono reorganised the factories so that parts were made and brought to the assembly line only in the quantity that was needed. In Japanese the system was called *kanban*, meaning 'ticket number', after the tickets that the workers exchanged for supplies and components each time they were required on the assembly line. It meant imposing the strictest conditions of quality and delivery time on the parts manufacturers who provide most of the components that go into Toyota cars. One worker, Shigeru Osawa, recalls that

If Ono found a pile of ten or a dozen doors or bumpers stacked together in one place, he would kick it with his boot as he walked past and say, 'Don't make extra ones like that, just stick to making what's needed, *when* it's needed, okay?'

The regime also meant that more precision and concentration was needed on the part of Toyota's own workers. Before, they had been required to operate only one machine in the machine shop or engine factories. In time they had to manage several. There was strong resistance from workers, who resented the intense pressures the system brought. Akio Terada was one of the assembly-workers whose place was at the end of the line. The pace was so hard that he began to have nightmares about his work:

> I would dream that I couldn't keep pace with the speed of the line, so the parts would be coming down towards me and I couldn't cope; but just as they were about to fall off the end of the line I'd wake up and cry out.

Seasonal workers, on lower pay rates than full employees, suffered the harshest workload, but there was no shortage of schoolleavers or graduates eager to work for Japan's top manufacturing firm. Toyota's output increased ten times in a decade, from 150 000 vehicles in 1960 to 1.5 million in 1970, and in that year Japan's total production topped 5 million.

MITI's policies for the car industry could not have worked without calculated protectionism. During and right after the Occupation, foreign car makes were unopposed in the Japanese market in price and quality. To help the home industry MITI imposed a 40 per cent tariff on all imported vehicles, cutting the proportion of imports (including commercial vehicles) from two-fifths in 1951 to less than 10 per cent in 1955. In 1960, when other countries began to insist that Japan must remove its protective barriers, MITI side-stepped the issue. It removed import quotas on large cars and three-wheelers, neither of which had significant sales in Japan. At the same time it not only kept a high tariff on smaller models, but expanded the category of 'small' cars to all vehicles up to 2000cc, so extending protection to the 1800cc models, into which Japanese firms were moving. The growing clamour from overseas led to Japan's cutting its tariffs on finished cars and then removing them altogether in the 1970s. By then, though, Japanese cars had a reputation for reliability and good value. Foreign makes were kept to a share of around 1 per cent of the Japanese market between 1960 and 1980. MITI also relied on more questionable means to keep competition out. When imported cars arrived at Japanese ports, customs officials had instructions to inspect each vehicle separately, instead of allowing a sample to be inspected and the rest of a shipment to come in all at once, as was the practice in other countries. That meant long delays.

These irksome regulations torpedoed the early efforts of several leading European firms to get a real foothold in Japan. British Leyland (incorporating Austin), like many others, suffered from having to follow local regulations and deal through a single importing and distributing agent. In the mid-1970s Western firms met with another setback when Japan announced new exhaust-emission standards. Japanese firms had taken part in the deliberations to set the standards and were ready with engines adapted with catalytic converters in time for their introduction. The change gave MITI officials a bargaining card in the increasingly harsh trade talks. They announced that they would generously give foreign makes a 'grace period' of three years to adapt their cars to Japanese standards. Still, to conform would mean expensive redesigning of engines and most European and American car firms were not ready to make that investment or effort.

Although MITI could help domestic firms to expand, the ministry was far less successful when it came to trying to make them merge for the sake of economies of scale. In the 1960s MITI tried to re-organise the ten Japanese motor companies to this end. Toyota bought a stake in a truck and van manufacturer, Hino Motors, and Nissan swallowed Prince Motors, but all the rest strongly resisted being subsumed in others. MITI clashed head-on with one of the most vigorous and successful entrepreneurs in the country, Soichiro Honda. Honda had been a complete newcomer to the motor industry after the war but he had native talents as an engineer. He claimed to have made the first ever Japanese motorcycle soon after the war by strapping a 50cc engine to a pedal-bike. Indeed the Honda Cub swiftly established itself as a favourite in many parts of Asia: one analyst calls it simply 'the most important bike ever'. Soichiro Honda built his firm up into the biggest motorcycle-maker in Japan, and in the world. In 1963 he resolved to start making cars as well, aiming to compete with the giants, Toyota and Nissan, using the best technology.

Honda went to MITI and was advised to drop his idea. MITI officials were used to having their own way and most Japanese industrialists would have given up at that point, but Honda was determined. 'In those days,' he recalls, 'the officials controlled virtually everything and they were very narrow-minded, but I thought I was free to make whatever I wanted, so I said to them: "We're not at war now, you know! Why shouldn't I go ahead?"' He did and, despite MITI's opposition, Honda Motors quickly established itself among the major producers. In 1972 it produced the Honda Civic, which, with its

European-inspired front-wheel drive and 'clean' engine, was judged to be technologically well ahead of its rivals. Manufacturers in the West were at a loss to know how to emulate the performance of a car with a 1200cc engine which could do 70 miles to the gallon.

The 'oil shock' hit all Japan's car firms hard. As petrol prices soared, production had to be drastically cut. One firm, Mazda, had to be rescued by a group of banks. But in the USA Japan got an unexpected bonus when the federal government published a report saying that the Datsun was the most fuel-efficient car on the road. Detroit had paid little attention to the small- and medium-sized-car market, believing that Americans would always be willing to pay for large cars with luxurious interiors and the latest extras, to enjoy driving on the inter-state freeways. General Motors and Ford were producing gas-guzzlers, and sales of small imported cars, of which Volkswagen had traditionally been the most successful, soared. Now Japanese firms overtook the competition from Europe. In 1976 Japan exported 3.7 million cars, or half its total production – more than a million of them to the USA. It was time for the rest of the world to go to Japan to learn about fuel-efficient engines, flexible production, the 'just in time' system, quality control and peaceful labour relations.

In 1980, after American manufacturers started laying off workers and closing plants, Japan took the number-one place in the world car-making league. American car-workers vented their feelings by taking sledge-hammers to Toyotas, but that could not change the economic facts of life. With strong pressures appearing in the West to keep Japanese cars out and protect local industries, Japan accepted a series of bilateral deals to limit its exports: 2200 units in the case of Italy, 3 per cent of the French market, 11 per cent of the market in the UK. In the USA political pressures grew to the point where only a quota would satisfy Congress and the domestic motor lobby. In 1981 Japan was induced to accept 'voluntary' restraint of 1.68 million units on its exports to the USA. The age of managed trade had truly arrived.

To get round the walls of tariffs and quotas, Japan began to follow the path of previous world powers: taking its capital abroad. Japanese firms began planning a series of investments, mostly in North America, Europe and South-east Asia, in order to keep on expanding their share of those markets.

What began in the 1970s as a trickle became in the 1980s the greatest outflow of direct investment capital the world has ever seen. In electronics, Sony led the way in 1972 with the first Japanese TV assembly plant in San Diego, California; all the other major names followed suit. Sony was first in the UK, too, with its TV plant at Bridgend in Wales, which started up in 1974. Honda became the first

Japanese car firm to put down roots in the USA, when it opened a car plant in Ohio in 1982. It was followed by all the other major producers. Sometimes there was resistance, from unions or local people; but the Japanese brought jobs, and their track record in employment proved on the whole to be a good one. They chose the UK as the beachhead for their fast-growing local production in Europe. In 1984 the British government welcomed Nissan's decision to build a plant on a greenfield site at Sunderland in north-east England, with financial support and promises of a new industrial partnership between the two nations. Five years later Toyota announced that it was building a plant outside the Midlands city of Derby, and Honda increased the production of its own cars from Rover Group's Longbridge factory. By 1986 12 per cent of Japanese car firms' output was being made in factories abroad. In the same year Japan overtook the UK as the country with the largest amount of assets of all kinds around the world.

MITI's 'Vision' helped to spread the idea in the public mind that the old 'sunset' or 'smokestack' industries, especially steelmaking in the older mills, aluminium refining and cotton textiles, were doomed to decline and that Japan would not lose much when they did. For several years MITI relied on 'administrative guidance' to encourage the firms to slim themselves down. The industries continued to turn in poor results and struggled with excess capacity. In 1978 a number of industries were officially designated 'depressed', and MITI enforced the scrapping of whole plants, financed the shift into other areas of business and secured special treatment for the redundant workers to learn other skills. It formed a number of new cartels to fix output levels and prices during the slimming-down process. Significantly, MITI negotiated directly with the firms concerned the details of what products would be phased out and by whom. There was no escape from this embrace. MITI was 'being cruel only to be kind'.

Shipbuilding was hurt as deeply as any industry by the sudden cost rises of the oil crisis, and a sharp worldwide fall-off in orders for supertankers made things worse again. But in the long run the industry pulled through. In 1974, when the Japanese firms had completed most of their backlog of orders, it accounted for more than half the world production. Two years later half the shipbuilding berths were lying empty and the leading firms, Mitsubishi Heavy Industries and Ishikawajima-Harima Heavy Industries, suffered badly. South Korean firms, led by Hyundai, won new contracts. The major Japanese firms got together to form a temporary cartel under the umbrella of the Transport Ministry, and agreed on a carefully staged plan for all of them to phase out capacity. In this period the government guaranteed prices and provided funds to help scrap the unwanted stock. By the end of the decade the Japanese firms were back in profit. They fought off the challenge of Taiwan and Korea to recapture the lead in the rejuvenated market for high-grade ships, mostly leaving the lower end of the market to the newcomers.

Protectionism at home was an integral part of Japan's overall industrial policy up to the early 1970s. Thereafter, in response to constant and sometimes acute pressure from abroad, the formal and informal barriers were gradually brought down, but in many cases only after the market was seen as impenetrably secure. In 1973, anxious to be regarded as a good member of the international trading club, the Japanese government declared that the country's markets were now completely liberalised. At that time its industrial tariff levels were lower than those of most other developed countries, but Japan also kept quantitative import controls in more than twenty industries, including computers, food and some consumer goods. The rules on investment from abroad remained harsh and off-putting. Foreign firms were still in practice barred from owning Japanese concerns; and the age of the non-tariff barrier was at its height.

Japan's labyrinth of rules were administered as if by feudal right by the various ministries, with MITI, Agriculture, Construction, Health and Welfare, and others competing for influence in exchange for guidance through the jungle of red tape that they had created. The detailed industrial standards and certification procedures discouraged many foreign firms from trying to enter. Those that did try needed big money, long-term commitment and a trusted Japanese partner to stand any chance of success. The country's employment practices – especially jobs for life and obligation to pay twice-yearly bonuses – made Japan an unappetising prospect; other business customs, such as lavish gift-giving and entertainment of clients, required a drastic change of behaviour on the part of foreign businessmen in Tokyo. Not all had the capacity to adapt. Frequently the head offices of North American and European firms lacked the patience and investment funds to build up a viable operation in Japan.

In 1982 Japanese trade officials solemnly told Western negotiators that Japan had no special non-tariff barriers standing in the way of other countries' exports. When details were given about the complaints, though, the Japanese government was stampeded into a fresh round of reductions in its industrial tariffs and other steps, such as improving customs procedures and the distribution system, aimed at easing the import of foreign goods. That was the first of seven repetitive and increasingly suspect Japanese 'market-opening packages' spread over the next three years.

MITI's 'Vision' of the 1970s was, in effect, a blueprint for a major new export surge. It encouraged the growth of industries in which world demand was expected to expand, which were capital-intensive, required skilled labour and could be classified as 'clean' not dirty. Each of these sectors was in fact also suitable for exports. When Japan recovered before its main industrial rivals from the effects of expensive oil, corporations were urged to invest in new generations of products with more 'value added' and so with a wider profit margin. In Japanese business culture it was chic to say that 'large, bulky, long and heavy' were out; 'small, compact, short and light' were in.

Kenichi Ohmae of McKinsey in Tokyo was then advising many Japanese firms bent on increasing their exports. The equation, he remarks, was simple: 'In Japan, the market is a hundred million. In the rest of the world, it could be a billion!' Japan was coming from behind, and Ohmae says there was no feeling of guilt for the effect the onslaught began to have on other countries' industries.

The pathfinders in Japan's expansion into foreign markets were a special breed of companies, the *sogo shosha* or general trading companies. They had formed the core of the pre-war *zaibatsu* and masterminded the gathering-in of industrial raw materials during the period of Japan's heavy-industry growth. In the 1970s, they came into their own again. The largest, Mitsui and Co., Mitsubishi Corporation and Sumitomo Corporation, had offices everywhere that mattered in the Americas, Western Europe and Asia. Mitsui alone has maintained more than 150 offices worldwide, acting as a vast intelligence-gathering network on behalf of its clients, mostly manufacturing firms. Japanese embassies were often obliged to rely on the superior information of commercial firms on economic and political trends abroad.

The *sogo shosha* acted as all-in-one consultants, merchant bankers, buyers, sellers, public-relations officers and travel agents. They negotiated the sale of Western technology to the Japanese plastics industry. They sold Japanese goods to store chains in the USA. They set up copper mines in South America and shipped the produce to Japan. They built Japanese lumber mills in Indonesia and imported fashion designs from Italy. Often, they owned a large stake in the manufacturing ventures they set up. After the oil crisis, they negotiated long-term direct deals with oil-producing countries and took over from the specialist oil firms the main role in importing crude oil to Japan. The big trading companies kept up their own prestige 'think-tanks' in Tokyo, staging conferences and cultivating powerful friends. They recruited newcomers only from among the graduates of Japan's best universities. They kept on the right side of Japan's most important power-brokers, the LDP politicians and élite bureaucrats. To the politicians they handed over millions of dollars in donations; the top bureaucrats they hired as highly paid advisers.

In the aftermath of the dollar shock and the oil shock in the early 1970s, Japan reaped the harvest not only of a new co-ordinated and rational plan for the whole economy, but also of the careful investment and protection of the previous decades. The policy of 'picking winners', or as MITI preferred to call it of 'helping infant industries', led to unmatched economies of scale. By 1971 Japan had twelve modern integrated steelworks, while the United States had only two, which were also older. In 1975 a new integrated steelworks was built on a man-made island: ore and coal were off-loaded at one end and turned into steel products, which were loaded straight on to bulk-carriers bound for foreign markets.

The trade war spluttered and seethed throughout the 1970s. As Japanese domestic investment rose in each sector, exports of those goods went up in absolute terms and as a percentage of Japan's output; and in each case the export surge was followed by complaints and attempts to impose controls on the part of Japan's major trade partners. The aim was generally to protect specific industrial sectors: thus the USA forced Japan to accept quotas in turn on its exports of TV sets, steel and cars. But calls from the floor of Congress for 'punitive tariffs' or boycotts on Japanese goods foundered because of opposition from consumer groups and the unwillingness of successive presidents to be branded as taking the world down the road to protectionism.

The Europeans were also provoked into active protest, but they, too, spoke with many different voices. In 1972 an EC commissioner, Ralf Dahrendorf, voiced the frustration of trade negotiators at the time, saying that 'Protectionism is traditional in Japan'. In 1975 EC officials were incensed to find that the value of Japan's exports to the Community stood at almost exactly double those of the Community's the other way. Japan's bilateral surplus widened from $3 billion in that year to nearly $17 billion in 1980. Japan's period of fastest productivity improvement came at a time when the Community was suffering from declining competitiveness and internal wrangling. 'Euro-pessimism' had set in.

The bulk of the deficit with Japan could be accounted for by five 'problem sectors': steel, cars, ships, home electronics and ballbearings. The real issue was that while Japan's share of the EC market in these industries had reached as much as 25 per cent, European firms reported that their efforts at selling the same goods in Japan had met with little but disappointment. In one year, 1976, Japan exported 400 000 cars to the EC while the Europeans sent only 25 000 to Japan. Customs procedures and problems in setting up dealer networks hindered the growth of the European exports. Punitively high taxes on wines and liquor limited Bordeaux wines, Scotch whisky and Bourbon to the luxury end of the Japanese market and therefore to modest sales. Pharmaceutical and telecommunications firms were kept at bay because the EC's own testing procedures were not accepted by the Japanese ministries concerned, and tests had to be carried out all over again. Often foreign firms complained that the standards and certification procedures were not even readily available for them to view.

Matters came to a head when a mission of senior Japanese industrialists, under the umbrella of the Keidanren, toured Europe in the autumn of 1976. The mission's leader was the man nicknamed 'Japan's business prime minister', Toshio Doko, who had pioneered the growth of IHI shipbuilding. In each port of call – London, Paris, Brussels and Bonn – the Doko delegation met blistering criticism of the trade surplus and of the barriers standing in the way of exporting to Japan. As a direct result of the tour, Japan extended its export restraint to cover all five of the problem areas identified by the Europeans. At about the same time, loud complaints were being voiced in the USA on similar issues, and from 1976 on both sets of negotiators rounded on Japan demanding concessions which sometimes overlapped and sometimes seemed to give an advantage to one side – usually the Americans, who had much more power to harm Japan if they were ever to cut off their markets to Japanese goods. Progress was painfully slow.

France then sought to give Japan a taste of its own medicine: Japanese electronics firms were told late in 1982 that all their shipments of VCRs to France must be sent to the small port of Poitiers, 150 miles from Paris, where a handful of ill-equipped customs men took many weeks to process their import papers. The scenes were like those from a comic opera. The ploy reflected the wish of some in France to ensure that a European standard video recorder, the Philips V2000, would stay in competition with the Japanese. The attempt failed. More than that, though, it was a device to pressurise Japan into making more concessions over a range of disputed issues.

The EC Commission, acting for the nine member states of the Community, began to flesh out a legal case that Japan's market structures themselves were the root cause of the country's 'unfair trade practices'. The plan was to take Japan to the international trade body, the General Agreement on Tariffs and Trade, arguing that the whole structure of Japan's economy and trade contradicted the principles of free trade. The target was not only the government's overt support for industry, but also the *keiretsu* system which keeps Japanese firms

164

immune from takeover. That, it was alleged, enabled them to 'target' particular industries and produce goods in very large volumes regardless of profitability over long periods. The Japanese showed acute embarrassment and pleaded with the Europeans to desist. The whole GATT framework was in crisis, with negotiated restrictions on all sides and a series of suits being prepared by member states against one another.

As it happened, an alternative strategy presented itself. The EC offered to drop the GATT case if Japan would agree to a three-year period of general restraint and close monitoring covering, among other industrial sectors, cars, VCRs, machine tools and ballbearings. Japan agreed, and a publicity photograph of the negotiators taken at the time suggests one reason why: it shows two large and fleshy Europeans, well over six feet tall – Wilhelm Haferkamp and Viscount Davignon, both senior members of the EC Commission – straddling the diminutive figure of Sousuke Uno, then the Japanese Minister of International Trade and Industry. Japan was cornered, and took the line of least resistance.

Japanese firms derived great advantages from being part of the *keiretsu* system, through which whole product lines could be conceived, developed, made and sold by people in a range of allied companies who saw themselves as working for the same goal. In essence, Japanese firms came to regard their highest goal as increasing market share, in Japan and in the export market; by contrast most company executives in the West remained preoccupied with the quarterly and annual balance sheet. During the 1970s and 1980s as the balance sheet of economic power shifted away from America and Europe towards Japan, there was little room for doubt which approach was working for a broad range of industries. Some critics, both inside and outside Japan, said that in effect the *zaibatsu* were back. In the newer industries a number of innovative companies such as Honda and Sony have prospered without strong dependence on one of the traditional groups, but major firms generally preserve cross-holdings of shares for the sake of 'mutual benefit'. The Fair Trade Commission has had no mandate to break up the friendly collusion between companies that has become ingrained in Japan's business world.

At the same time, the close co-operation between private firms and government officials became a way of life. The two sides acquired the habit of meeting regularly in the various industry committees sponsored by MITI to make Japan more competitive. Also, each year scores of the most senior bureaucrats who had reached retirement age performed their 'descent from heaven', moving smoothly into the board rooms of the major corporations. There, both their knowledge and their influence over their former subordinates have often been crucial in determining administrative decisions. Businessmen and the mandarins were in turn closely tied to the LDP politicians, whose say-so was necessary for laws to be passed. International economists debated how to define the Japanese-style economic system: they called it variously a 'developmental state', a 'plan rational state' and 'corporate capitalism'. All were agreed that a special feature of Japan's political economy was the way the government moulded the society and economy to specific goals. None the less, some continued to maintain that Japan's was a free market economy – only one which was more efficient than others.

In 1979 a Harvard Professor, Ezra Vogel, wrote in *Japan as No. 1* that the USA should look to and learn from Japan as 'the world's most competitive economic power'. In July 1980, *The Times* of London wrote in an editorial that Japan should be regarded as 'the world's leading industrialised nation'. Japanese consumer electronics firms did not need two years' lead time to develop a new model line. Their 'turnaround time' for translating an idea for satisfying a consumer need into a new product was often as short as six months. Every six months Sony, Matsushita, Sanyo and other firms would astonish buyers at the Chicago Electronics Fair with new features on old products, or with completely new products.

Above all, Japan rejected the idea of the international division of labour. Japanese government officials and businessmen wanted to avoid being dependent on the outside world in all major lines of finished goods. The USA made the most advanced satellites and aircraft in the world, but the Japanese government had a policy of buying only satellites made in Japan. Under strong internal pressure, Japan made most of its military aircraft under licence from American or European firms within Japan. Its spending on commercial research and development was at a level close to that of the United States. It had its own growing space programme, with plans to go into the market launching commercial satellites for other countries by the 1990s.

At the same time, in some ways Japanese society presented a sinister picture to the outside world: it appeared secretive, exclusive, uncaring of human values. Japan seemed intent on fulfilling its own ambitions at the expense of its competitors, and of the environment everywhere its industries settled. To some, Japan seemed a place where the collective will ruled supreme; where children were deprived of time to play in order to make them into more perfect material for the great industrial campaign; and where no power or authority could stand in the way of ever more economic expansion. Japan was constantly pressed to be more 'altruistic' by giving more foreign aid; yet even its official aid programme was criticised for being used to promote the country's commercial interests. In 1975 Japan devoted only 0.2 per cent of its GNP to overseas aid, much less than most other developed countries; its composition was overwhelmingly of 'soft' loans, which critics elsewhere saw as a form of export subsidy.

At the end of the 1970s Japan represented a puzzle to the world's other leading powers. It had without doubt become a country that mattered on the world stage, yet its purposes appeared unclear, and its presence in world trade was intrusive. In 1975, when Western leaders gathered at Rambouillet in France for the first of the annual economic summits, Japan was invited – a recognition that its consent was absolutely needed if international economic measures were to work. The Japanese were clearly essential to preserving peace in Asia; and they increasingly held the power to determine the health of other economies through their country's trade, aid and investment. At the same time, there were serious strains, sometimes unspoken, in Japan's dealings with the other nations represented at the summits. They arose partly from natural conflicts of economic interest, but partly also from the fact that Japan did not belong to the same political and diplomatic tradition as its partners. Japan was the odd man out in the industrialised world, not only by race but also by political and trade philosophy.

In 1952 the USA had welcomed Masaru Ibuka of Sony when he joined the queue for American transistor designs. Thirty years later, in 1982, industrial spies from Hitachi were caught trying to steal computer secrets from IBM, and the battle-lines of the economic contest were laid bare. The political and military alliance was still something of great value to both sides, but it was distorted by the fierce contest between them for economic and industrial leadership. The USA, and the West as a whole, was starting to be haunted by fears that Japan was not only taking its markets by storm, but was also beginning to usurp the West's control over its own future.

In the early 1980s a Japanese economist was attending a symposium on the world in the twenty-first century. He predicted that Japan would be the research laboratory of the world and the rest of Asia the factory, while the USA would be the granary. 'And what about Europe?' asked one of the Europeans present. 'Ah yes,' the Japanese speaker said, 'Europe will be Japan's boutique.' The story may be apocryphal, but as the stream of Japanese shoppers became more visible on Oxford Street, the Via Veneto and Fifth Avenue, the time had already come for the Japanese, the world's new rich, to start buying up some of the most prestigious shops and buildings of the West's commercial capitals.

6

Breaking the Taboos

THE NAKASONE YEARS

'Japan is not like anywhere else.... Receiving a cultural impetus from China, Japan endowed it with its own subtle and special forms, blending it into a heritage that has made Japanese society more like a family than a state.'

That was the conclusion of Dr Henry Kissinger after many years of dealing with the Japanese government; and the thought was mirrored by other negotiators as Japan's presence on the world stage grew more influential. Kissinger, who served President Nixon as National Security Adviser from 1969 to 1973 and was then Secretary of State for three years under Presidents Nixon and Ford, was infuriated by Japan's evasiveness during the textile dispute of the late 1960s; but he also appreciated that the Japanese Prime Minister of the day, Eisaku Sato, was not a leader in the Western sense. Rather, in the Japanese tradition, he had the role of master of the consensus. In his *Memoirs*, Kissinger defined the difference in philosophies, saying that whereas the West has developed a system of government based on a concept of legal or constitutional authority, 'Japan relies on consensus.... High office in Japan does not entitle the holder to issue orders; it gives the privilege of taking the lead in persuasion.'

Kissinger had the task in 1973, at the time of the first oil crisis, of trying to dissuade the Japanese from shifting to a pro-Arab policy in the Middle East. He did not succeed in that attempt, but he savoured the delicacy of the Japanese way of saying 'no'. 'Only amateurs would seek to pressure an individual Japanese minister,' Kissinger concluded. 'Even when he yields out of politeness, he cannot carry out his promise.' The accomplished international power-broker took it upon himself to award the title of modern Machiavellians to the Japanese; writing of their decision to follow Arab dictates towards Israel in 1973,

169

he said, 'they claimed neither justice nor wisdom for their course of action. It reflected necessity and was thus beyond debate.'

One might have expected Japanese officials to argue against such criticisms, but they rarely did. Japan's foremost goal in the post-war era has been to adapt to the global framework which others have made, and to avoid confrontation in diplomacy at almost any cost. As the conviction grew among its trade partners that Tokyo was not serious about opening its markets and redressing the trade balance, the complaints grew more strident. Japan's so-called 'omnidirectional diplomacy' was criticised as no more than a front for the pursuit of economic advantage. Washington's confidence was badly undermined by Premier Zenko Suzuki's *faux pas* in 1982, denying that the US–Japan Security Treaty represented a 'military alliance'. In that year the American Ambassador to Tokyo, Mike Mansfield, described US–Japan relations as only just 'short of an explosion'. The European Community was growing hostile over trade: it had concluded that Japan was not playing by the normal rules between states, because it was bent on making practically all the high-technology goods it needed for itself.

In Asia, virtually every country looked keenly to Japan for economic assistance and investment; but at the same time much of the region nursed a deep-seated sense of suspicion and mistrust of the Japanese. The Chinese, South Koreans and Filipinos, among others, were troubled by Japan's perennial trade surpluses, and at the neo-colonial relationship which they implied. In 1982 the ghosts of the war returned to undermine Japan's ties with China and other Asian countries: the Japanese government was exposed to the glare of international publicity for its system of censoring school textbooks dealing with the war. Under a long-standing system of 'vetting' textbooks, officials were pressing scholars to delete the phrase 'Japanese aggression' and instead to refer to the army's 'advance' into China. The 1937 Rape of Nanking and other atrocities committed by the Japanese army were glossed over, and made to sound as though they were provoked by unreasonable resistance on the part of the Chinese. In Peking the Chinese Communist Party Chairman, Hu Yaobang, declared that some forces in Japan were attempting to revive Japanese militarism by suppressing the facts about past Japanese aggression against China and other Asian countries.

At home, Japan faced another major problem which successive governments had allowed to get worse: a huge public-sector debt. This had burgeoned over the years since the mid-1970s as the government regularly gave in to Western pressure to stimulate its home economy by more government spending. The policy had served to keep the

Japanese economy growing at a steady pace, but failed to turn Japan into 'an engine of the world economy', since the extra public spending had led to very little measurable increase in imports. The scale of deficit-covering national bonds grew to the point, in 1982, where their aggregate value reached double that of the government's annual spending budget. In September of that year the Suzuki government declared 'a state of economic emergency' because of the burgeoning public debt. With its pork-barrel methods, of favouring special-interest groups and the entire agricultural sector, the government was by its own admission endangering the wealth that the nation had earned by more than three decades of thrift.

There was one Japanese politician above all who paraded his ambition to tackle these issues: he was Yasuhiro Nakasone, a self-proclaimed nationalist. The 1980s in Japan turned out to be his decade. He was Prime Minister from November 1982 until November 1987, and in that time he took Japan decisively into the Western camp. He also championed the drive to sweep away the legacy of Japan's centuries of close bureaucratic controls, and to convert it into a more open, pluralistic society.

Nakasone stood out from his political colleagues first of all by his appearance: taller than the Japanese average and self-possessed, he made a point of appearing in public dressed in well-tailored Western suits, with designer silk ties. In a country where, as a much-used Japanese proverb says, 'the nail that sticks out gets hammered down', Nakasone infuriated his staider colleagues and rivals with his naked ambition and self-confidence. By character and political conviction, in office he was determined to clarify Japan's role in world affairs. He had long coveted the job of leading Japan, rather than just presiding over the government as other prime ministers had done. He set out to win policy making control into his own hands, away from the unelected bureaucrats.

Reminiscing in the summer of 1990 on his time in office, Nakasone recalled that in 1982, when he became Prime Minister, Japan was facing crises both in its foreign relations and in its internal affairs. He saw the necessity of shaking up the whole structure of modern (post-Meiji Restoration) Japanese government. Nakasone even framed the problem in terms somewhat similar to those used by Henry Kissinger, although from a different perspective. He saw an urgent need to rid Japan of the traditions of bureaucratic and autocratic government which had served to steer the economy in the post-war years:

I was carrying out a kind of 'improvement' of Japan's government structure. For 110 years, ever since the Meiji Restoration, Japan had been striving to catch up with America and Britain. In the 1970s we *did* catch up. Beyond that point the [state's] regulations only stand in the way of the growth of the economy. If government officials have too much power, the private sector of the economy will not grow. We had to change the system, which had been in place ever since the Meiji period, of centralised control, complicated regulations, and too much government involvement in decision-making. We had to look to Japan's next stage of economic expansion through the power of the private sector, carry out government reform, and have an 'open door' policy.

The rhetoric may sound familiar enough in the West, but for Japan it was new.

Nakasone coined simple slogans to convey his ambitious goals: in a keynote policy speech to the Diet in January 1983 he pledged to work 'to make Japan open to, accepted by and respected by the rest of the world'. This was what the outside world wanted to hear; the message was popular, too, among most Japanese, even if some of his policies were not.

On 6 August 1945, the day the atom bomb fell on Hiroshima, Yasuhiro Nakasone saw the mushroom cloud in the distance from his naval billet. He was then a twenty-seven-year-old Lieutenant-Commander in the Imperial Navy. In late August 1945, he returned to Tokyo. He remembered that moment much later: 'I stood vacantly amid the ruins of Tokyo, after discarding my officer's short sword and removing the epaulettes of my uniform. As I looked around me, I swore to resurrect my homeland from the ashes of defeat.'

Nakasone was the son of a wealthy timber merchant. More importantly, he was one of Japan's 'best and brightest' – a graduate from the law faculty of Tokyo Imperial University (renamed plain Tokyo University after the war). This élite has long dominated the senior posts in government ministries and important official councils; they make up a cohesive ruling group. Their dominance is at least as pervasive as that of Oxford and Cambridge University graduates in the British civil service. A brief period spent as a young career official in the powerful Naimusho, the Home Affairs Ministry, before the war initiated Nakasone into Japan's traditions of power-broking, and he made valuable connections at the top of the security apparatus which were to serve him well in later years.

In the second post-war general election, in 1947, he entered politics. It was also the first national election for Kakuei Tanaka; but while in the 'snow country' of Niigata Tanaka was proclaiming how he would build bridges and roads to end the region's backwardness, Nakasone based his appeal on a revival of patriotism. He campaigned for a seat in his home district of Gumma prefecture, a short way north of Tokyo; and at a time when most were carefully hiding their old symbols of Imperial Japan from public view, Nakasone rode a bicycle with a Rising Sun flag fluttering from the handlebars. He won a seat on an unashamedly nationalist platform.

From the early years of his political career, Nakasone set out to undo the three principal 'taboos' of post-war Japan, all of which were facets of the way that the country had been obliged to accept the shame and guilt of its part in the war. The first was the constraint on its armed forces: the Self-Defence Forces had grown to be 250 000 strong by the 1980s, but they were a bastard army, because the post-war constitution banned the maintenance of all 'land, sea and air forces'. The second was the broad legacy of the war: Nakasone wanted to revive the proud symbols of Japanese patriotism, including respect for the Emperor. The third taboo was the constitution itself. The plan to amend it, and so to restore fully the nation's sovereignty, was a basic aim of successive Japanese governments, but no one leader had dared to grasp that nettle.

Once in the Diet, Nakasone took every opportunity to attack the cautious line of Prime Minister Yoshida and other conservatives of the older generation. He ostentatiously wore a black tie in 'mourning' for Japan's loss of independence. 'I attacked the Yoshida government in order to make General MacArthur aware of certain things', he says.

> I thought Yoshida's policy was based only on *economism*, and was making the Japanese nation lose all sense of independence and self-respect.... I said that unless Japan defended itself, America would not come to our aid. No such country existed anywhere else in the world; so I argued that we must maintain a minimum level of armed forces to defend ourselves – but Yoshida rejected that. I attacked Yoshida on the matters of Japanese identity and moral values, and got the message through to the public, too.

Nakasone's strength of feeling on this subject is a commentary on the complex mix of policies Yoshida pursued: to many contemporary observers and scholars, Yoshida appeared as an arch-conservative; but with regard to the question of rearmament he was extremely cautious – hence the strong criticism of those, like Yasuhiro Nakasone, who advocated an independent stand for Japan in spite of the political constraints of the post-war period.

Nakasone was outspoken in attacking the Occupation's educational and social reforms, and chafed at the seven-year delay before Japan could regain its independence. In 1951 he delivered a personal manifesto to General MacArthur, advocating the signing of a mutual security pact on equal terms and the speedy withdrawal of American servicemen from Japanese soil. With this he earned his spurs as a young leader of the political right wing. Soon Nakasone founded the Seiranjuku ('Blue Storm School') with a group of other nationalist-minded LDP Diet members whose radical goals included amending the American-inspired constitution.

Nakasone was cut from a different cloth than most of his LDP colleagues. His political hero was John F. Kennedy; he admired America's presidential system of government and wanted Japan to have something similar. If the country's leadership were to be decided by a popular vote, he hoped that he himself might win it.

In reality the power centres inside the LDP were the factions – collections of national politicians united loosely by political outlook but more importantly by their allegiance to a single 'boss' figure. Inside the LDP the only politicians who could become candidates for the party leadership were those who already headed sizeable factions of their own. Nakasone was a rising star among the *toha*, the career politicians, and a sworn foe of the *kanryoha*, the ex-bureaucrat politicians. He joined the faction of Ichiro Kono, one of the LDP's founding members, and loudly criticised the Prime Minister, Eisaku Sato – a former bureaucrat – for his cautious handling of the nation's affairs. In 1967, after Kono died, Nakasone inherited most of his factional following and confounded observers by quickly mending his fences with Sato. Nakasone himself says that his motive was to support the government in its drive to have Okinawa returned; in any case, he was rewarded by the Prime Minister with two successive senior Cabinet jobs, first as Transport Minister and later as head of the Defence Agency. In the defence post, he advocated both a highly controversial course of increasing Japan's defence spending to 3 per cent of GNP, and Japan's possession of tactical nuclear weapons.

As a faction boss, Yasuhiro Nakasone became one of the select group of power-brokers inside the LDP. Thanks to the hierarchical organisation of the party, the choice of successive leaders was (as it still is) made by the faction leaders. On occasions when there was a contest for the top job, it was decided through a vote by rank and file members of the Diet. Even then it was by no means a free vote: faction members were strictly obliged to vote according to the instructions of their own boss or risk being cut off from their lifeline of funds and status. In 1972, when Sato retired, the leadership contest was an open one, and Nakasone's influence was decisive. Sato's heir apparent was the mandarin-style Takeo Fukuda, but Kakuei Tanaka, the 'computerised bulldozer', mustered just enough Diet members' votes to win – thanks to the support of the Nakasone faction. Nakasone won the damaging nickname of 'the Weathervane' for swapping sides.

Tanaka made Nakasone his International Trade and Industry Minister. In that capacity he played a central part in the management of the oil crisis and revelled in the responsibility it brought him. Later, though, when the Lockheed bribery scandal surfaced, Nakasone suffered some political damage from having been a key member of the Tanaka Cabinet. Nakasone was put through the ordeal of giving evidence before the Diet about his role in the case, but he was never charged in connection with the affair.

The whiff of scandal did not seriously harm his career. From 1974 to 1976 he served as the LDP's Secretary-general, the best position for tapping the funds of big business and forging political alliances. The Liberal Democratic Party was at that time riven by a deep split between Takeo Fukuda and Kakuei Tanaka: the conflict was dubbed the 'Kaku–Fuku war'. The reasons for the split had little or nothing to do with policy matters, and everything to do with power politics and personality. The pro-Tanaka group remained powerful in spite of the fact that Tanaka himself was the foremost defendant in the Lockheed-related trials. His faction remained easily the largest, and he became the 'kingmaker' of the Ohira and Suzuki Cabinets. The same factor enabled him to claim plum ministerial and party posts for his henchmen at each of the regular Cabinet reshuffles.

In 1980 Nakasone had another chance to serve in a senior ministerial post, under Zenko Suzuki, whose only known policy expertise was in the fishing industry. By then the consensus among the top group of decision-makers in the LDP and the bureaucracy was in favour of sizeable cuts in government spending, with the aim of reducing the bloated public-sector deficit. This meant paring the budget of government departments and making a range of public-sector organisations more efficient. Nakasone was given the apparently thankless task of overseeing 'administrative reform', as this was called. He managed to turn it to his own advantage, though, spearheading the drive to hold down government spending to zero growth in successive years for the health of the economy.

When, in 1982, Zenko Suzuki suddenly announced that he would not seek re-election as the LDP president, the stage was set for a fresh power struggle. The Tanaka faction still felt obliged to stay out of the fray, since its leader was technically in disgrace; instead Tanaka himself threw his weight behind Nakasone's candidacy. Against him was an alliance of the Fukuda forces, whose strongest candidate was a veteran figure, Toshio Komoto, the owner of a large shipping company and a former Economic Planning Minister. Two others threw their hats in the ring, which meant under party rules that there had to be a 'primary' election among the party's rank and file, followed by a run-off in which the party's Diet members would make the final choice.

The 'primary' idea had been devised by Takeo Miki, the 'Mr Clean' of Japanese politics, in the mid-1970s. It was intended to prevent a repeat of the open venality of earlier elections – in particular the 1972 leadership contest, when Tanaka won the seat of power after bankrolling hundreds of Dietmen into supporting him, and the money-driven Upper House elections of 1974. Unfortunately for that idealistic principle, the party rank and file proved, if anything, easier to buy up – literally – than the national politicians. LDP membership swelled greatly in the weeks before the 'primary', with the bulk of the new membership fees being paid for not by the individuals concerned but by the factions of the candidates or of their backers.

According to the usual 'rules of the game', Nakasone would have been destined to lose: his own faction was only the fourth largest in size. But he was saved by his alliance with Kakuei Tanaka. This 'primary' was a contest of money and influence which suited Tanaka's special talents perfectly. Nakasone's forceful speaking skills also helped his candidacy. He polled an overwhelming 58 per cent of the votes cast, compared with only 27 per cent for Komoto, with the two others trailing far behind. After that the party caucus vote was a mere formality. Nakasone was in as party head, and was confirmed as Prime Minister in a Diet vote. At the age of sixty-four he duly became Japan's Premier.

Every post-war Japanese Prime Minister has aspired to some personal triumph in foreign policy. Yoshida established the relationship with the USA as the cornerstone of Japanese diplomacy, while Hatoyama broke the Cold War ice with Moscow, normalising the two countries' diplomatic relations; Kishi renegotiated the Security Treaty with the Americans; Sato won back Okinawa; Tanaka established formal relations with China. Nakasone's aims were both specific and broadly ambitious: to set the ties with Washington on a solid foundation by insisting on Japan's equal role in the alliance, and at the same time to raise his country's influence around the world. He sneered at the popular concept of Japan as merely a trading nation.

His all-embracing slogan was to achieve 'a final settlement of post-war politics' – *sengo seiji no sokessan*. The phrase could be interpreted in many ways, but at the least it meant Japan's stepping out from the shadow of the war and ending its sometimes craven dependence on the USA. Nakasone wished to confront the consequences of the Allied Occupation, drawing up a balance sheet of which parts of the legacy should be kept and which discarded, and dismantling the cumbersome network of controls and regulations that had been built up by the government since the end of the war. From his very first days in office Nakasone administered a shock to the system.

As his first overseas exercise in summit diplomacy, he flew to Seoul for talks with the military strongman there, General Chun Doo Hwan. The relationship with Japan's nearest neighbour, South Korea, had been fraught with tension – and on the Korean side with resentment – even after the two governments started their post-war dialogue in 1965. Japan had not been forgiven for its long and brutal occupation of Korea. Nakasone improved the climate at a stroke by pledging $4 billion in official economic aid to South Korea. There was a controversial note to this, as it was widely rumoured that part of the money would be spent on the South Korean military – hardly an appropriate target for funds from 'peace-loving' Japan. But the gesture went down well among the ruling military and bureaucratic élite in Seoul. Nakasone also persuaded the South Koreans to award a lucrative subway contract to Japanese business, instead of to a British firm: an evening of relaxed drinking with President Chun helped to smooth that deal.

Personal diplomacy was Nakasone's strong suit. He prepared painstakingly for his first talks with President Ronald Reagan in January 1983. He sent Toshikazu Kase, a diplomat who had been present at Japan's wartime surrender, to the USA in advance; Kase reported back that 'the US had lost patience with the Suzuki Cabinet, and could not trust it.' Nakasone set a completely new tone, speaking of the two nations having 'a common destiny', promising a new accord on the exchange of military technology, and pledging that Japan would play its full part with the USA in containing Soviet military forces in the Far East. In an interview with the *Washington Post*, he went further. He was quoted as saying that in the event of war Japan was ready to act as 'an unsinkable aircraft-carrier' to defend the Pacific against Soviet air power. Elaborating on Japan's proper role, he spoke of a second target: 'to keep complete control of the four straits that go through the Japanese islands, to prevent the passage of Soviet submarines'; and a third: 'to secure and maintain the ocean lines of communication.'

At home in Tokyo these remarks caused acute alarm. Japan's goal of defending its own sea-lanes of communication for 1000 miles to the south towards Taiwan and Indonesia had been agreed in Zenko Suzuki's time. But the rest was new. The opposition parties lashed out at Nakasone as 'a dangerous militarist', though such verbal attacks had little impact because of the opposition's endemic weakness in the

Diet. The press comment was perhaps more important in forming public opinion: much of it was vitriolic. Some writers pointed out that the last so-called 'unsinkable aircraft-carrier' in Japanese history was the battleship *Yamato*, once the pride of the Imperial Navy, now resting at the bottom of the Pacific Ocean.

In vain did government spokesmen seek to explain that the Prime Minister's words had been 'a big aircraft-carrier' not 'an unsinkable aircraft-carrier'. The *Mainichi Shimbun*, a national daily, wrote that Nakasone 'has talked too much', and objected that the Prime Minister had made a series of pledges without the proper national debate. The Soviet media chimed in: the official news agency, Tass, asked rhetorically if Japan realised that 'the authors of such plans make Japan a likely target for a response strike? For such a densely populated, island country as Japan, this could spell a national disaster more serious than the one that befell it 37 years ago [at Hiroshima and Nagasaki]'.

On the other hand, American reactions were very favourable. Ronald Reagan spoke warmly of Yasuhiro Nakasone as his 'friend'. The White House press corps was advised that the two leaders had agreed to address one another henceforth using their first names: the 'Ron–Yasu' relationship was born. The American Ambassador to Tokyo, Mike Mansfield, said of Nakasone: 'He's a new type of Japanese leader: he tries to lead!' Several Asian countries expressed concern about Nakasone's intentions; but in May 1983 he visited Singapore, Malaysia, Indonesia and Thailand; in each port of call he reiterated that Japan would not become a military threat to the region again. Singapore's Prime Minister, Lee Kuan Yew, spoke approvingly of Mr Nakasone's foreign and defence policies, and Nakasone returned to Tokyo to report to his Cabinet colleagues that there was no strong antipathy in the region to Japan's gradual rearmament. The first-name relationship between Nakasone and Reagan only added fuel to the fire by implying that Prime Minister and President had secured a special understanding which might involve a greater strategic role in Asia for Japan.

The furore over Nakasone's Washington trip, a mere seven weeks into his term of office, set the tone for much of what followed over the next five years. Japan's energetic Prime Minister repeatedly broke the rules of his country's usually staid and inward-looking politics by trying to be active rather than reactive. On his return from Washington he sought to advance the political goal closest to his heart: he attended a regular convention of the Liberal Democratic Party at which a resolution was adopted calling for more urgent efforts to win public support for a revision of the constitution. The leader of the Japan Socialist Party promptly warned: 'the new government will be the

most reactionary and militaristic of the post-war era'. Soon afterwards
Nakasone bowed to a concerted campaign against any LDP attempt
to revise the constitution: he announced that no such attempt would
be made during his term of office as Prime Minister. Speaking in 1990,
he said:

> I think it is right to keep the question of the country's constitution con-
> stantly under review as time goes on. But if you ask, 'Is there an urgent
> need to amend the constitution *now*? – the answer is 'No.' It would lead to
> a wasteful social upheaval. Still, I must say there are certain articles in the
> constitution which should be revised, and we should keep the matter under
> study.

Nakasone describes his first year in office as an exercise in crisis
management:

> When I took power I thought we faced a critical situation both in our
> international relations and internally. Our relations with America were
> damaged by the argument over interpretations of the Anpo [US–Japan
> Security] Treaty, and America was extremely annoyed.... Internally I
> sought to open up Japan in a basic sense by pursuing the ideal of 'small
> government' and pressing on with administrative reform. I knew we had
> to cut down the number of officials, cut back their powers, and advance
> the business of deregulation. I saw the need for sweeping reforms, covering
> many fields from education to government finance, and I pushed ahead
> with policies in each of these areas.

Nakasone devised his own way of bypassing the slow and usually
conservative consensus-forming process that had become a strong
feature of Japan's way of government in the post-war years. In tackling
one issue after another he set up informal advisory panels, answerable
to himself, to come up with the specific proposals. He made use of
many policy-thinkers outside his own staff – men like Ryuzo Sejima,
a wartime army strategist in China who became a senior adviser to the
big trading company C. Itoh, as well as some of the sharpest brains in
Japan's universities. Sometimes he drew on the think-tanks of Japan's
most successful business institutions, such as the Nomura Research
Institute and Dentsu Advertising Agency, for new ideas and approaches. At a later stage he would form an official committee to look at
the same topic, with economists, journalists and academics as
members. Their recommendations would generally help to build a
consensus for what the Prime Minister intended, before the matter
reached the policy committees of the Liberal Democratic Party or the
floor of the Diet. Nakasone was often attacked for acting like an

American president, or for ignoring the Diet. He retorted that 'the ways of previous prime ministers were old-fashioned.'

Japan had sheltered under America's wing for so long in the foreign and defence areas that its voice barely counted in the strategic equation; nor did those of the Philippines or South Korea. All three were loyal allies of Washington and provided important bases for US forces. For each of them 'consultations' with the US Defense Department were mostly a one-way process: the Americans took the decisions. Nakasone's government was worried that Japan might lose out from the current round of arms-control talks on intermediate-range nuclear forces (INF). The Soviet Union had deployed SS-20 missiles with a range of around 3500 kilometres in forward positions, from which they could hit anywhere in Western Europe; in Asia they could easily reach Japan, and at maximum range they could even strike the US Subic Bay naval base in the Philippines. In Europe America's policy was one of 'peace through strength'. A controversial decision had been taken to deploy US Cruise and Pershing II medium-range missiles in Western Europe. The policy was aimed at pressurising the Soviets to sign a treaty removing that category of weapons from the European theatre. No concrete plans were laid, however, for banning SS-20s from Asia, and the Soviet Union announced its intention to withdraw the weapons from the European theatre and redeploy them in the Far East.

Nakasone set his sights on the annual seven-nation economic summit. It was due to be held in the former colonial settlement of Williamsburg, Virginia, in June 1983. At the previous two summits Japan had been on the fringes of the discussion, except over the contentious issue of trade. Prime Minister Suzuki had looked distinctly uncomfortable in the company of the other leaders. During one of the early summit sessions at Williamsburg, Nakasone had his chance to speak on East–West relations. He spoke out vigorously on the issue of the INF, underlining the fact that SS-20s were mobile, so it would be meaningless to ban them from Europe without also removing those kept east of the Urals. He spoke eloquently of how Japan was determined to play its part as a 'full member of the Western camp'; and he proposed that an extra line should be added to the seven leaders' joint statement, saying that 'the security of the West is indivisible.' Nakasone had his way in the discussions, and Ronald Reagan and Margaret Thatcher, among others, spoke highly of his contribution. It was the first time that Japan had explicitly played a part with the leading Western nations on such a sensitive security issue. Now Japan not only claimed to be 'a member of the West': it was publicly accepted as such.

In Japan the mass media gave full play to the Prime Minister's summit '*coup*'. Most of all, though, audiences at home were astonished when they saw the photo line-up of the world leaders: instead of the Japanese representative being relegated to the end of the line and looking uncomfortably from side to side, Mr Nakasone was standing proudly between President Reagan and Mrs Thatcher, near the centre. The impact was extraordinary. Commentators in Japan dwelt on this fact as though by itself it signified a realignment of Japan's place in the world order. Nakasone's popularity among the voters went on rising.

From that time on, Japanese officials seized every chance to press home the message that an INF treaty should cover Asia as well as Europe. The government in Tokyo welcomed an American decision to start deploying nuclear-capable Tomohawk Cruise missiles on US naval ships in the Pacific from 1984. By contrast with past cases of American military reinforcement in and around Japan, there was only muted protest from left-wing and other peace groups. Official insecurity on the INF issue gave way to confidence. When the INF treaty was signed in 1984 it met the wishes of Japan, providing as it did for the phasing out of all land-based medium-range weapons, while leaving sea-based systems aside.

Japanese public opinion was against any marked expansion of Japan's defence effort; but Nakasone used all the authority of his office to shake off the old 'allergy' towards the subject. Events unfolded in favour of that attempt. On 1 September 1983, radio monitors were working routinely at the secret listening post at Wakkanai, on the northern tip of Hokkaido island. They were tuned in to the frequencies used by Soviet fighter pilots, and before dawn on that day they picked up a highly unusual exchange: Soviet fighter planes were scrambled from a base on Sakhalin island to intercept a plane flying over it from the east. The aircraft was headed directly for Vladivostok, headquarters of the Soviet Union's Pacific fleet. One of the Soviet pilots attempted to challenge the pilot of the mystery plane, but received no response. His orders were to shoot, so he flew close, fired two heat-seeking missiles into the side of the plane and reported back that 'the target has been destroyed.' At Wakkanai, the larger, westward-flying plane dropped suddenly off the radar screen.

Within hours it became inescapably clear that the Soviet pilot had shot down a Boeing 747 airliner of Korean Air Lines which was carrying 269 passengers and crew, including an American Congressman, right-winger Lawrence McDonald. President Reagan and Secretary of State George Shultz expressed their outrage and extracted maximum propaganda value against Moscow from the incident. The

Soviet side accused the Americans and South Koreans of using the KAL plane to spy on military installations. Others suggested that it might have been sent over Sakhalin deliberately to test Soviet air defences. Korean Air Lines said the plane's pilot had flown off course into Soviet air space by mistake. Nobody from the plane lived to give evidence, and the flight recorder of the Jumbo jet was never retrieved from the seabed.

The KAL incident starkly underlined the strategic importance and high tension between the superpowers in the north-west Pacific. There the interests of the US, the Soviet Union and China all converged. Some 50 000 US forces were based in South Korea to guard against a repeat of the North Korean invasion of 1950. A similar number of American forces were based in Japan, and American naval ships were calling ever more frequently at Japanese ports in order to stay ahead of the growing strength of the Vladivostok fleet. Above all, the Soviet Union was using the Sea of Okhotsk, to the north of Japan, as a sanctuary for its strategic submarines, whose missiles were trained on targets in the continental USA.

In Washington's eyes, Japan acquitted itself well as an ally in this international incident. Within Japan, the public was made vividly aware of the 'Soviet threat' referred to in Japanese government defence white papers. The following month that message was reinforced when a time-bomb explosion in Burma killed seventeen members of a South Korean government delegation, and agents of communist North Korea were found to be responsible. Nakasone resolved to keep on increasing defence spending, while holding down welfare and other general expenditure to zero growth, or less, each year. From 1983 onwards the Prime Minister led the way in proposing that the government should reverse the 1976 decision to limit defence spending to within 1 per cent of GNP. Polls at the time showed a clear majority of opinion against such a change, and it was also fiercely resisted by the opposition parties and some areas of the press; nevertheless, Nakasone achieved his aim in 1986. The government adjusted the old '1 per cent rule' and announced that in future military spending would be limited to '*about* 1 per cent' of the government spending budget.

To some, it seemed that on this issue the mountain had laboured to give forth a mouse, but psychologically the change mattered. In the Nakasone years the Defence Agency started to procure more advanced weapons and defence systems than before, including new anti-ship and anti-aircraft missiles and very long-distance ('Over-the-Horizon') radar. The sea-lane defence programme went ahead quickly, using anti-submarine patrol planes, and so did joint sea and air exercises aimed at making American and Japanese forces 'interoperable'. The lowering of public resistance to military matters enabled the Nakasone government to press ahead with the introduction of US F-16 jets to American bases, and, in 1986, to sign an accord allowing Japanese firms to take part in research for the Strategic Defence Initiative, popularly known as 'Star Wars'.

Nakasone's strategy for putting Japan on the world's political and diplomatic map included inviting world leaders to visit Tokyo. A feast of high-level diplomacy lasted throughout the autumn of 1983. President Reagan visited in November, and flattered his hosts by describing US–Japan relations, in a phrase often used by Ambassador Mansfield, as 'the most important bilateral relationship in the world, bar none'. Nakasone, who was being expertly advised by Japan's top public-relations firm, Dentsu, invited Ronald and Nancy Reagan to his private villa just outside Tokyo where he performed the tea ceremony for them amid carefully controlled publicity. Chancellor Kohl of West Germany spoke admiringly of Japan's achievements in industry and nation-building. The Chinese Communist Party Secretary-General, Hu Yaobang, became the first government representative from China to meet Emperor Hirohito – a potent symbol of reconciliation, thirty-eight years after the end of the war. Hu spoke of China's relations with Japan being based on 'mutual trust'. Nakasone made the most of the occasion to confirm that Japan would go ahead with a programme of low-interest government loans for Chinese public-works projects.

The high-level diplomacy was an outstanding box-office attraction for the Nakasone administration: the Japanese public was impressed; the Foreign Ministry felt gratified; even the press, which was largely hostile to the new Prime Minister, approved. But in the midst of it all a new hazard emerged in Nakasone's path: on 12 October the Lockheed trial reached a climax with the judgement of the Tokyo District Court concerning the charges facing Kakuei Tanaka, of having taken bribes from the Lockheed aircraft firm in return for ensuring the sale of its planes in Japan. It was the most celebrated and probably the most important of a score of political bribery cases in post-war Japan. The case had already dragged on for seven years, since Tanaka's arrest in 1976. The Japanese courts reckon without the idea that a modicum of speed is necessary to the administration of justice: difficult political cases usually drag on for many years. The issue was not so much whether Tanaka would be found guilty, since legal experts agreed that the prosecution's case against him was overwhelmingly strong; it was the impact of the outcome on the power balance among Japan's ruling

183

élite, and in particular whether Yasuhiro Nakasone would survive or be overturned.

The verdict on former Prime Minister Tanaka was guilty: the sentence, four years' imprisonment. Tanaka himself was in the dock when the judges pronounced the sentence, and his lawyers at once lodged an appeal to the High Court. He remained a free man, and waved in his customary way to the crowds waiting outside the court-house. He also remained a member of the Diet – there was nothing in Japan's statutes to prevent it. His supporters made plain that Tanaka would continue to fight to prove his innocence, and would remain at the head of the 'Tanaka faction' of the Liberal Democratic Party, even though he had resigned his party membership.

Diet members on all sides treated the situation as a constitutional crisis. The opposition demanded Tanaka's resignation from national politics and boycotted all Diet proceedings, effectively bringing them to a halt. Nakasone prevaricated. Many LDP politicians would pri-vately have like to see Tanaka bow out of public life, but his own faction members were fiercely loyal, and the other faction leaders were wary of presenting the LDP's enemies with such an obvious free shot. The public mood was a mixture of genuine indignation, deep-seated cynicism and complete indifference. Within the political world, the situation demanded some kind of denouement. Some observers saw Kakuei Tanaka as an 'over-mighty subject', trampling on the accepted political rules of his day by the crude exercise of influence based on money.

On television news programmes and in the editorial columns of the press, public figures and journalists discussed the impasse with great relish. There was much gloating over the LDP's embarrassment, but no killer instinct on the part either of influential commentators or of ordinary members of the public. The phrase on everyone's lips was *kejime o tsukeru*: literally, to 'draw a line', or 'put a stop' (to a scandal). The issue was, how was the LDP to achieve such a desired end to a sordid affair? The vagueness of the Japanese formulation of that pol-itical problem is a measure of the lack of clear standards of behaviour in Japanese public life. A preference for compromise over clear-cut solutions permeates the fabric of party and national politics. The one solution which might have brought a tidy end to the affair – Tanaka's resignation from the Diet – was in practice ruled out by the reality that Tanaka still wielded significant control over the executive and legislative sides of the government. What was called for on the part of Prime Minister Nakasone, for his own self-preservation, was a piece of political theatre.

The stage chosen for the action was a private room in a luxury

Tokyo hotel. Appearances required that Nakasone should at least go through the motions of scolding Tanaka, and of seeking to persuade him to resign his Diet seat. Accordingly a meeting was arranged between the two men at the Hotel Okura, a favourite gathering-place of politicians. Afterwards Nakasone would not divulge any details of the conversation; he declined to respond to the intense public interest over whether or not he had urged Tanaka to resign his Diet seat.

The occasion was a triumph for political cynicism, and a humiliation for the press in its role as would-be watchdog of the establishment. It was altogether an unsatisfactory denouement, but Japan's collective political leadership, made up of the faction chieftains, the Cabinet and elders of the conservative camp, let it pass; so it passed. The common interpretation of what had really happened was contained in an article in the *Japan Economic Journal*. Writing of the closeness of Nakasone and Tanaka, a senior staff writer commented:

> It is any politician's guess that those two have discussed the issues of Diet dissolution, the general election, and how to handle politics afterwards. Presumably, in the talks, Nakasone got some assurance from Tanaka that the Tanaka faction would support his administration even after the general election.

In his 1990 interview for the BBC, Nakasone was still unwilling to reveal what transpired on that occasion; but he said: 'I expressed my feelings to Mr Tanaka in a friendly way; I discussed things with him as a friend, and as his contemporary.' Nakasone adds that the verdict against Tanaka was another 'crisis' for his administration:

> The opposition parties submitted a resolution in the Diet for Mr Tanaka to resign his parliamentary seat, but I protected Tanaka. The issue, I believed, was one of the ethics of our politicians, and it had to be settled according to individual conscience. Also the voters would determine the result. It would have been wrong to have a decision forced through by the action of the opposition parties, or anyone else. The ties between the Diet member and his constituents were paramount: that is what I believed, and I was severely criticised by some people for that.

The Diet impasse and accumulated sense of public expectation made it unavoidable for the Prime Minister to dissolve the Diet and call a general election in December 1983. The 'Tanaka problem' was a major theme, but the results showed that in Japan, as popular wisdom has it, 'all politics is local politics'. Tanaka himself was triumphantly elected in his Niigata constituency once again. Also re-elected was one of the other Lockheed trial convicts, the former Vice-Minister for Transport, Takayuki Sato, and several so-called 'grey officials' – senior

LDP politicians who were implicated but not charged in the Lockheed affair. The press and opposition parties bewailed the way that the LDP was able to make a mockery of parliamentary democracy, but to no effect. Tanaka and the 'grey officials' claimed that they had received 'the blessing of the voters', and public opinion was powerless to stop the conclusion: that money could buy power – or even, perhaps, immunity from the law.

The LDP as a whole lost heavily, sliding from 286 seats in the 1980 election to only 259, including a number of 'unofficial' LDP candidates who took the party whip after their election. That gave the party a bare majority of two seats in the 511-seat chamber. The LDP quickly forged a parliamentary alliance with the splinter group, the New Liberal Club, who had nineteen Diet members. The deal involved one Cabinet post being awarded to a New Liberal Club representative – who thus became the first Cabinet minister from outside the LDP since 1955 – but the crisis was over. Nakasone still felt the need to distance himself from Tanaka, so he made speeches blaming the election result on 'public mistrust of politics', while continuing to reap the benefits of Tanaka's support.

For five years Nakasone was unchallenged in power, largely thanks to Kakuei Tanaka, who made sure that no one else from inside his faction put himself forward as a rival. The other potential contenders might have mounted a challenge, but for the fact that they were not the acknowledged leaders of their own factions: Shintaro Abe was overshadowed by his faction boss Takeo Fukuda, and Kiichi Miyazawa stayed junior to Zenko Suzuki within the Suzuki faction. Noboru Takeshita was in the most delicate predicament of all among the so-called 'new leaders'. He was the heir apparent to the Tanaka faction, but was closely watched by Tanaka and his closest allies to prevent him from either trying to take it over or quitting to form his own faction. Takeshita's ambitions were patently clear, but under the prevailing rules of the Japanese political game he could not openly challenge his mentor.

The two men played a long-drawn-out game of strategy and tactics – a real-world version of the board game *go*, which Japanese *samurai* generals used to sharpen their mental stamina. In 1985 Takeshita made a preliminary move, forming what he called a 'policy-study group' (the prototype of a faction) *within* the Tanaka faction, but it was promptly denounced by other senior faction figures who were clearly speaking for the 'Shadow Shogun' himself, and Takeshita meekly disbanded it.

It was not until Kakuei Tanaka suffered a serious stroke in 1986 that Takeshita finally made his move. He formed a policy group called Keiseikai (Foundation of Policy Society) and when the dust had settled, Takeshita had become the formal head of a 113-member faction, while a much smaller group of former Tanaka faction men formed a splinter group.

Meanwhile Nakasone used a policy of 'divide and rule' to great effect through the Prime Minister's power of appointment to Cabinet and party posts. It is normal practice for aspiring party leaders to change their jobs frequently within the government and party hierarchy, the better to cultivate their power bases in each of the essential areas. These areas would include, in roughly descending order of importance, the posts of LDP Secretary-General (party paymaster), Finance Minister (government paymaster), MITI Minister (for links to industry) and Foreign Minister (for prestige). Other positions, such as head of the Policy Affairs Council or of the all-purpose General Affairs Council in the LDP, and Chief Cabinet Secretary (senior government spokesman), are also important stepping-stones: the factions vie fiercely to fill those posts with their own people. Nakasone effectively froze the political *go* board for four years in a row. He made Shintaro Abe his Foreign Minister from 1982 to 1986, and Noboru Takeshita Finance Minister throughout the same period.

Japanese politics had not enjoyed such relative internal stability since the days of Eisaku Sato before 1972, and it left the way open for Yasuhiro Nakasone to push forward with his 'final settlement of postwar politics'. In pursuit of this goal he had accepted an initial setback over constitutional revision but in practice won the contest on military spending; his other broad goal, the 'restoration of the nation's pride', had no conclusive result: indeed it is still going on.

Nakasone picked one highly symbolic target in order, as he hoped, to restore an open sense of national pride among the Japanese. On 15 August 1985, on the fortieth anniversary of the surrender, he went to the Yasukuni Shinto shrine close to the Imperial Palace. Wearing formal morning dress, he strode under the *torii* (shrine gate) and up to the main prayer hall, an all-wooden building of classical simplicity and open contours. There he bowed his head in the customary Shinto style of prayer. Afterwards the Prime Minister made clear that he had visited Yasukuni in his official capacity, not only as a private individual.

The Yasukuni shrine, meaning 'Shrine for the Tranquil Rule of the Country' is an especially sacred place for followers of the native Japanese religion of Shinto, the 'way of the gods'. It enshrines the souls of Japan's war dead: those from the Sino-Japanese War of 1894–5, the Russo-Japanese War of 1904–5, and the souls of 2.5 million Japanese who died for their country during the 'Great Pacific War' of

1937–45. The shrine grounds and museum are filled with relics from these conflicts: artillery pieces, suicide torpedo shells and a fighter plane. In 1979 friends of the Japanese Association of Families of the War Dead secretly disinterred the ashes of the seven 'Class A' war criminals hanged after the war, including those of General Hideki Tojo, and had them moved to the Yasukuni shrine. When that fact came to light there were protests across Asia.

Nakasone's 'official' visit in 1985 brought even heavier invective and caused serious ripples in Japan's ties with China and other Asian countries. The *Peking People's Daily* criticised 'militaristic-minded people in Japan's government leadership'. Within Japan, Christian, Buddhist and other non-Shinto groups protested that Nakasone's action violated the constitutional separation of government and religion, and was a throwback to Japan's fascist wartime past, when it had been compulsory for all in the Japanese empire to worship the Japanese pantheon of gods – including the so-called 'living god', Hirohito – in Shinto shrines.

Nakasone had prepared for this piece of iconoclasm with thoroughness. In 1984 he commissioned a group of scholars and public figures to deliberate on whether government ministers should be permitted to worship at Yasukuni 'in their official capacities'. The chairman of the committee was a former officer of the military police, the *kenpeitai*, in China, an LDP Diet member called Seisuke Okuno. The committee, as expected, came up with the answer that Nakasone wanted to hear: that such ministerial visits would indeed be consistent with the Japanese constitution, in spite of its provision for the separation of state and religion. Newspapers objected that the Prime Minister was wrong to entrust such matters to an arbitrarily chosen panel, but public opposition was muffled.

The issue was not a clear one of 'hawks' against 'doves'. Some Japanese politicians of a strongly liberal and anti-war persuasion were among those who had themselves performed the customary act of worship at Yasukuni while in office: the first Prime Minister to do so in the post-war period had been Takeo Miki, a man with a clear record of opposing his country's military government before and during the Second World War. But Miki and other leaders had stopped short of describing their Yasukuni visits as 'official'.

Nakasone pressed on with his quiet revolution in favour of 'open patriotism'. He set up another council of experts to debate the large-scale reform of Japan's education system. The group produced a series of reports which, as well as recommending reforms on strictly academic topics such as the exam system, urged that schools should 'instil a spirit of patriotism' in the country's youth. This was to be done by stressing the proud aspects of Japanese history in classroom teaching, but in many respects the recommendations appeared unclear and even self-contradictory: the committee urged the 'fostering of creativity' in Japan's young people in order, it said, 'to prepare the country for the twenty-first century', while at the same time extolling the old virtues of respect for authority and for one's elders. The Ad Hoc Council on Educational Reform also favoured the reintroduction of 'ethics education' in schools – something which had been withdrawn during the Occupation because of its association with the ultranationalist brainwashing of the war years. The plans were attacked by the head of the Japan Teachers' Union, who objected that the government, in cahoots with powerful industrialists, was seeking to sweep aside the 'democratic' post-war education structure and to reinstate the pre-war system. Many parents and educators agreed that reforms were needed, but few had clear ideas about what exactly they should be.

The government's intentions were also attacked by some liberal and left-leaning sections of the Japanese press. Those suspicions hardened when the Education Ministry prepared to enforce the singing of Japan's national anthem, *Kimigayo*, and the hoisting of the Rising Sun flag in schools during entrance and graduation ceremonies; the left-wing Teachers' Union was set against those things because of their association with compulsory flag-waving and Emperor-worship in the past. The government also took steps to tighten state control on the vetting and issuing of history and other textbooks approved for use in schools.

The controversy was revived again in 1986, when the seventy-one-year-old Education Minister, Masayuki Fujio, spoke out of turn in a magazine interview: he appeared to seek to justify the colonisation of Korea in the first half of the twentieth century, saying that Japan had annexed Korea in 1910 'by agreement with Korea's rulers'. Following official South Korean, North Korean and Chinese protests, Fujio refused to retract his remarks, and Nakasone dismissed him from the government; it was the first time that a minister had been sacked for more than thirty years. The show of decisiveness helped to bolster Nakasone's image in the Asian region and to counteract the effect of the Yasukuni shrine row.

In the same year, the Prime Minister provoked a fresh storm with a series of controversial remarks on the issue of race. Japan's population after the war included some 700 000 Koreans – mostly workers shipped over in the colonial period to work in Japan's mines and factories – as well as smaller minorities of Chinese, and aboriginal Ainus, the original inhabitants of Hokkaido island. In August 1986, speaking at an informal gathering of LDP politicians in the summer resort of Karuizawa,

189

Nakasone remarked that the intelligence level of the Japanese was higher than that in the USA because 'the US has many immigrants, Puerto Ricans, blacks, who bring the average level down', whereas Japan was 'a mono-ethnic nation'. As a paraphrase of the way the Japanese are schooled to think of their own situation, the statement was not exceptional; indeed almost none of the Japanese journalists present thought it worth mentioning in their reports. When details did emerge, Nakasone was confronted with angry protests in the US Congress and by American minorities, and was obliged to make a series of public apologies – including one addressed to the American Congress and people.

Even then, the issue did not go away. A fresh row broke out over Nakasone's public endorsement of an official report to the United Nations that the country had no ethnic minorities who deserved special protection under the law. Representatives of Japan's Ainu minority lobbied in vain to have the official report amended; international civil rights groups objected that Japan's Korean and Chinese minorities also had serious outstanding claims against social and legal discrimination. The Korean minority stepped up its long-standing campaign for abolition of the law requiring non-Japanese nationals to have their fingerprints recorded on their Alien Registration Cards. They called the system humiliating, and argued that it encouraged discrimination at work and in marriage. Both the South and North Korean governments weighed in on the issue, but were unable to have the system scrapped. Instead, the Justice Ministry made minor changes, which included ordering the use of colourless ink instead of black ink for the fingerprinting process.

These episodes dented Nakasone's slogan about making Japan 'open to the world', but he maintained his touch concerning the day-to-day issue that mattered most between Japan and the West: trade. Ironically, during his five years in power, trade relations with the USA and the EC remained in a state of tension, yet Nakasone succeeded in presenting himself throughout as the one figure who could keep the country's links with the West from snapping. His weakness was that within the diffused system of authority in Japan's *keizai-kai*, the economic world, no real changes could take place without the active consent of all concerned parties – including ministries, industry associations and large corporations. A prime minister could prescribe, but had little power to enforce decisions about trade matters or even domestic business.

In any case, the trade surplus, as most Western as well as Japanese economists agreed, was 'structural': it was the outcome of long-term factors such as Japan's relatively high industrial productivity, and its high levels of savings and investment. As such it was likely to be only slightly affected by specific decisions, including Japanese export restraint, import promotion and increases in public-works spending.

The story of Japan's disagreements with the West on trade during the 1980s is a long catalogue of complaints, half-measures and mutual recrimination. The seven so-called 'comprehensive market-opening packages' announced in Tokyo between 1982 and 1985 brought limited increases in imports by lowering tariffs and easing complex import procedures. But they signally failed to remove the underlying cause of complaint: that in Japan, the public and private sectors regularly colluded to keep the domestic market controlled, with the effect of restricting outsiders to a small share. Western governments demanded much more drastic action. Several times they raised the idea of Japan's setting a specific target for increased imports: Japan always refused, pleading the need to avoid 'managed trade'.

The USA tried exerting powerful pressure for import liberalisation in specific areas, with puny results in the early years. Japanese farmers were confident in their hold on the governing party, the LDP, through the rural vote. They blocked all moves to allow the import of rice, and only grudgingly acquiesced in phased increases in the quotas of imported beef, citrus fruit and other foods. The Americans tried the tactic of narrowing the focus to specific industries – namely electronics, medical and pharmaceutical equipment, telecommunications, and forest products – and seeking to remove all Japanese trade barriers in those fields. These so-called 'MOSS talks' – MOSS standing for Market-Oriented Sector Selective – were long and at first yielded scant results, so much so that cynics laughingly interpreted MOSS as 'More of the Same Stuff'. But Japanese concessions on timber quotas, government policies and import procedures eventually satisfied the Americans; European and Asian firms also took advantage of the better market access.

On the trade problem, Nakasone employed his favourite method to try to whip up a mood for change: he created official groups of experts to plot long-range solutions. The first was headed by the former Foreign Minister and leading economist, Saburo Okita. In 1985 the Okita group produced a blueprint for opening the Japanese market called an 'Action Programme'. It comprised recommended changes in scores of laws and regulations, to be completed within three years, including fresh attempts to dismantle various non-tariff barriers at customs, and in the sales and distribution network, and a programme of Japanese government purchases from abroad.

Nakasone set out to dramatise the issue himself: he appeared on television, using charts and a ruler, lecturing the Japanese public on the facts of the trade problem. He pointed out that Japanese citizens were spending much less money on imported manufactured goods than their counterparts in Western Countries. 'Japan is like a mah-jong player who always wins,' he said. 'Sooner or later, the other players will decide that they do not want to play with him.' Nakasone made a surprise visit to a Tokyo department store, where he launched a 'Buy $100-worth of Foreign Goods' campaign. In a staged-managed piece of exhibitionism, he bought himself an American-made tennis racquet, French shirt and Italian tie. Government ministries ostentatiously went out and bought American-produced telephone sets; the government also invested in French-built helicopters. Despite everything, imports did not rise significantly.

Nakasone was not discouraged. In 1986 he commissioned another advisory report which he could show off to Japan's trading partners as evidence of serious intent. This was the 'Report on the Long-term Restructuring of the Japanese Economy'. The authors were a blue-ribbon collection of industrialists, economists and public figures, headed by a former Governor of the Bank of Japan, Haruo Maekawa. The 'Maekawa Report' prescribed long-term shifts in Macro-econ-omic policy and industrial policy necessary to make Japan's economic growth less dependent on exports, and more on a vigorous, deregulated home economy. The document called for the further phasing down of uncompetitive Japanese industries such as coal, and for a shift of priorities in favour of consumer interests and better housing standards, though it did not specify how to accomplish these things. The document included only one target figure: it called for Japan's trade surplus *as a percentage of Japan's GNP* to be brought down below the then current level of 3 per cent. It did not (as some foreign governments would have liked) set any target for Japan's level of manufactured imports.

The Maekawa Report was welcomed, as far as it went, by President Reagan and other Western leaders. But its terms of reference made it clear that this policy document would not by itself address the principal issue for the US Congress and Western governments: the trade imbalance. In any case, the report was less than official government policy. Nakasone, visiting Washington again, implied that it was; then, on his return to Tokyo, he met a barrage of criticism for giving away too much, whereupon he amended his stand, saying the report was only advisory. Nakasone certainly started a gradual change in public consciousness on trade issues, but the trade gap with the USA grew rapidly throughout his years in power and had reached $52 billion by 1987 when he resigned.

Some Americans believed that the root cause of the trade problem with Japan could be removed if Tokyo's financial and capital markets were made as open as New York's, and if the yen were to be revalued to make Japanese exports more expensive in terms of dollars and other currencies. Long months of talks resulted in 1984 in a 'yen–dollar agreement' for a phased lifting of Japan's interest-rate controls, encouragement for the gradual increase in the use of the yen as an international reserve currency, easier conditions for foreign banks and financial firms to operate in Tokyo's growing market, and the creation of an offshore market. The measures would in time eat into the traditional spheres of regulatory control of the Bank of Japan and Finance Ministry; and they would expose Japan's more vulnerable, smaller, banks to harsher competition for funds. Tomomitsu Ohba, a senior Finance Ministry official in the Japanese negotiating team, described the accord melodramatically as 'a jump from the Nikko falls' (a traditional Japanese place of suicide). In practice the measures were rather easily digested by Japan's financial world, and helped to strengthen Tokyo as a financial centre relative to New York and London.

Japan's persistent trade surpluses, supported by an undervalued yen currency, led to one of the most far-reaching decisions of the 1980s affecting the world economy. It was taken on 22 September 1985, when the central bank governors and finance ministers from the 'Group of Five' industrial nations – the USA, Japan, the UK, France and West Germany – gathered in the Plaza Hotel, New York. They decided that the US dollar was overvalued against other leading currencies, and resolved to intervene in the foreign-exchange markets to drive its value down. Over the following week the dollar experienced its steepest fall ever in trading against the yen; and in the course of the following two years the yen doubled in value against the dollar, from an exchange rate of 252 to one of 135. The impact was great, both on Japanese industry and on the buying power of the yen abroad.

At first it looked as though there could be many casualties among Japanese firms that relied heavily on exports. Suddenly, because of the currency rate, their products became twice as expensive when they were shipped abroad. But the government gave special loans to small businesses to tide them over. Nippon Steel, the world's largest steel-maker, was forced to put some of its workers on a time-sharing scheme. The great majority of blue-chip firms, making cars, electrical goods and cameras, suffered a period of lean profits, cut costs hard and came through the currency change stronger than before. No large firms went bankrupt because of the strong yen. Once they had learned to be competitive at the stronger yen exchange rate, they found their export profits higher than ever. In some cases, such as home VCRs, there was anyway no substitute for Japanese products.

The strong yen quickly made Japan the world's wealthiest country in terms both of foriegn exchange reserves and net overseas assets. In effect, the currency adjustment made Japan twice as rich outside its own shores as it had been before. Dollar-based assets of all kinds were cheap, and Japanese banks and large corporations found themselves, after the hard times were past, with more spare cash than ever before. Japanese firms, large and small, found it advantageous to move 'off-shore', away from Japan, because wage and other overhead costs were cheaper elsewhere. There was a new wave of Japanese manufacturing investment in the USA, and as the US federal budget deficit grew, the Japanese began to lend more and more to fund it. Japan, in effect, became America's banker, and then banker to the world.

The devaluation of the dollar against the yen failed, however, to have the effect the Americans had hoped for in reducing Japan's trade surplus quickly. The Japanese government reported that in 1987 Japan's global trade surplus peaked at a figure of $96 billion, more than half of it with the USA. The high figures were partly due to the so-called 'J-curve effect', whereby after a large appreciation of the yen the trade surplus measured in dollars goes up before it comes down; the reason is that for a period Japan's exports are worth much more in dollar terms, before the currency adjustment forces Japanese export prices up and gradually cuts into the volume of exports as well. Japan's critics in the USA were not impressed by such reasoning, and in 1987 Congress began to press for direct trade action against Japan. On 13 April 1987 the front cover of *Time* magazine showed an enraged Uncle Sam rolling up his sleeves to do battle with a Japanese *sumo* wrestler under the caption 'Trade Wars: the US gets tough with Japan'.

The crunch came over semiconductor trade. In 1987 the American industry lobbied the Reagan administration hard to declare Japan in breach of a bilateral agreement on semiconductors, signed the previous year. The complaints were that Japan had failed to honour a pledge to ensure US firms a 20 per cent share of the Japanese market in computer chips, and that Japanese firms were dumping memory chips in the USA and in Asian markets. In April of that year Ronald Reagan signed a presidential order imposing punitive tariffs of 100 per cent on a range of Japanese electronic products, including colour TV sets, sold in the USA as 'retaliation' for the alleged breach of faith. The Japanese government denied all the US accusations and issued a strong statement denying the specific charges made and 'deeply regretting' the American action as a blow against free trade.

The climate was further muddied by the revelation that a Japanese firm, Toshiba Machine Tools, had illegally exported to the Soviet Union computerised submarine-propeller milling equipment which had been used to improve the performance of Soviet submarines, making them harder for Western navies to detect. The parent firm, Toshiba Corporation, bore the brunt of American anger: it was barred for a year from selling its computers to US government agencies and it lost a lucrative contract to supply the Pentagon with laptop computers. As with the semiconductor issue, government and industry circles in Japan felt that such 'punishment' was unwarranted and unfair.

The glaring breakdown of the US–Japan dialogue over these things tarnished Yasuhiro Nakasone's image as a lodestone keeping the 'special relationship' special. Congressional reaction was predictably tough. The man dubbed 'the hammer of Japan', Senator John Danforth, thought Nakasone's approach was mere gimmickry, and he warned:

> The problem of Japanese trade barriers will not be solved by a single Nakasone speech, announcement or package of promises. The only thing that counts is results. Evidence of real market opening by Japan will have to be new sales of competitive American products.

Still, Nakasone stuck to his high profile and spoke out urging Japanese firms to increase their imports. Within days of the sanctions order he travelled to Camp David for a tête-à-tête with President Reagan, and was honoured with fulsome speeches praising his leadership. Nakasone excelled at these set-piece political occasions: he was entirely at ease as the host of the seven-nation economic summit meeting in Tokyo in 1986, at which the summit leaders called on the Soviet Union to publish the truth about the Chernobyl nuclear accident, and denounced Libya for 'sponsoring terrorism'.

American criticism was heard again on an old theme: that Japan was guilty of taking 'a free ride' from the USA on defence. The theme grew louder during 1986, after the Gulf War intensified and the US navy moved in to protect commercial shipping going through the Strait of Hormuz. After an American frigate, the USS *Stark*, was hit by Iranian missiles, with the death of thirty-seven men, there were calls in the US Congress for Japan as a major beneficiary of the American action to 'take its share of the dangerous task of protecting commercial shipping in the Gulf'. Japan was in the unique position, among the 'Group of Seven' industrialised countries, of maintaining close contacts, including an embassy, in both Tehran and Baghdad. Japanese diplomacy had been extremely active, pleading with both parties to stop attacking Japanese and other merchant ships, but ineffectual in bringing pressure to bear for an end to hostilities. Nakasone personally wanted to comply, and to send Japanese Maritime Self-Defence Force ships to assist; but the fear of protests from other Asian countries ruled out that possibility. The government resolved instead to give funds to friendly Gulf states to improve their maritime surveillance system.

Nakasone's role was important, too, in resolving one of the most sensitive of the trade skirmishes of the mid-1980s: the entry of foreign firms into Japan's fast-expanding international telecommunications business. Both the British and American governments strongly supported the bid of an international consortium to enter Japan's lucrative and fast-growing market. In 1986 the Japanese government decided to end the monopoly of the public telecommunications firm, Kokusai Denshin Denwa (KDD), and other bids were invited to form a rival organisation, a 'second KDD'. The Japanese government, in the form of the Ministry of Posts and Telecommunications, expected and apparently fully intended that the only competition to be admitted would be of a nominal sort. A group of Japanese corporations formed a consortium, International Telecom Japan (ITJ), which intended simply to lease KDD circuits as a parallel operation.

By contrast the British firm Cable and Wireless, together with Pacific Telesis of the USA, planned to lay a high-capacity optic fibre cable across the Pacific and to make Japan the hub of a competitive new international business. They argued that Japanese consumers, who paid among the highest rates in the world for telephone and telex services, would benefit. The Anglo-American interest allied themselves with chosen Japanese partners and formed a consortium called International Digital Communications (IDC).

The international plan was almost killed by restrictions imposed by the Japanese government in collaboration with various interested businesses. The Ministry of Posts and Telecommunications, seeing the IDC bid as a threat to its traditional preserve of authority, refused to discuss its business plan in detail; instead the government supported the formation of an *ad hoc* committee of Japanese business figures to thrash out the matter. The committee cheerfully proposed a 'compromise' solution under which IDC would abandon its business plan but play a minor part in a combined new service along the lines of the ITJ proposal. IDC's British and American specialists resisted, playing to the gallery of Western government opinion. The British House of Commons and the US Congress each passed resolutions urging the

Japanese government to abide by fair play. Mrs Thatcher called it 'a test case' of the openness of Japan's markets, and wrote personally to Mr Nakasone on the matter. He promised in return to give it his personal attention. After several months of laborious and fruitless discussion, the government did an about-face and allowed both IDC and ITJ to start up commercial businesses. Those Japanese vested interests that wanted to keep the market tightly controlled were forced to give in; and Japan's telecommunications charges came down from their astronomical levels to rates nearer to the international norm.

Nakasone was influenced in subtle ways by the climate of deregulation and the movement towards 'small government' elsewhere in the world: the principal exponents of which were Ronald Reagan and Margaret Thatcher, both of whom were in office when Nakasone came to power and were still there when he left. Japanese 'administrative reform' was much less wholehearted than the *laissez-faire* reforms in either the USA or the UK. Nevertheless, the changes that came over bureaucratic and corporate Japan in the Nakasone years were major ones within the domestic context.

Nakasone identified himself closely with the breaking up of long-standing government monopolies, including those in railways and telecommunications. Japan National Railways, the world's largest railway company, was split into six regional enterprises. JNR had become so overstaffed and poorly managed that its accumulated debt was even larger than those of Brazil and Mexico, the two biggest debtor nations, combined. The government also split up the tobacco and salt monopoly, and prepared for the 'privatisation' of the domestic telephone company, NTT. At first NTT was turned into a 100 per cent stock company, but all the stock was held by the government. Next the stock was gradually auctioned off, in a way calculated to profit the government to the maximum, to preferred clients and then to the general Japanese public (non-Japanese are still in 1990 legally banned from owning any of the stock). Later, after Nakasone left office, the government sale of NTT shares flopped disastrously, along with the company's performance, and angry shareholders demanded compensation for their investment losses.

By the summer of 1986 Nakasone was approaching the end of his second two-year term as President of the LDP, the maximum allowed to one individual under the party's rules. His rivals in the party were each manoeuvring for advantage to succeed him. But a Japanese Prime Minister, however beholden he is to the support of other faction leaders, has one card which he alone can play: he can decide the timing of a general election for the House of Representatives, the dominant house in the bicameral Diet. Despite strident opposition from his rivals within the party, Nakasone seized the chance to hold one at the most advantageous moment: in July, simultaneously with the scheduled election for half the seats in the Upper House, the House of Councillors. The higher turnout helped the LDP to a landslide victory: it won 300 seats. The result strengthened Nakasone's hand enormously. Tanaka's loyal followers leant on Noboru Takeshita not to challenge Nakasone's right to stay on longer in office. The Foreign Minister, Shintaro Abe, had declared he would 'fight like a tiger' for the premiership, but after the election he hastily backed off. The party bosses and elders agreed to bend the rules and give Nakasone an extra year in office.

Nakasone, as always fluent in the lingua franca of Japanese politics, appeared before the nation's TV cameras and with doubtful modesty described himself as 'wholly unworthy' of the great honour and responsibility newly bestowed upon him. He announced that he would see through a major overhaul of the nation's taxation system – the first since the economic disorder of the Occupation. The reform itself was widely seen as necessary to correct long-standing unfairnesses. In particular, a relatively heavy tax burden was borne by salaried workers, whose income tax was deducted at source, while self-employed groups, including farmers and doctors, were felt to be concealing much of their income and so avoiding payment of their due taxes. However, Nakasone and the LDP had made a firm campaign pledge not to introduce a large-scale indirect tax; now they accepted a plan devised by the Finance Ministry for a new sales tax, to be offset by income-tax cuts. The scheme was a violation of the election promise. Nakasone may have been guilty of hubris: he certainly wanted to win the credit for changing a taxation system that had become very unpopular. But his attempt failed, just as a similar plan proposed by Prime Minister Ohira had done in 1980.

Plans for the new tax were entrusted to an *ad hoc* LDP committee, which quickly compromised with a host of special-interest groups, including the farm lobby and the breweries. The government sought to introduce a 5 per cent sales tax on a range of items, while exempting scores of others (including food and some drinks). The plan alienated people on all sides, including many LDP supporters. The LDP's public support rate (regularly measured in opinion polls) slumped and the party lost a series of telling by-elections. The tax reform was abandoned.

Despite this débâcle, Nakasone had earned extraordinary statute for his diplomatic accomplishments, and his shadow hung over the process of selecting his successor. Each of the three so-called 'new leaders' –

Takeshita, Abe and Miyazawa – now made a bid for the premiership. The campaign for the party leadership was marked by a distinct absence of debate on real policy issues: the LDP had become so dominated by the *réal politique* of the factions that it was clear the factional numbers game would alone dictate the outcome. Noboru Takeshita controlled a much larger faction than either of his rivals; as the new boss of the old Tanaka faction, which had not held the premier's seat for the previous seventeen years, he was easily the frontrunner.

As part of their campaign, each of the three candidates appeared in turn at the Foreign Correspondents' Club of Japan and outlined their political ideas. Noboru Takeshita in his speech evaded any detailed discussion of defence, foreign or even economic policy. He declined, pleading ignorance of the subject, to answer a question about the situation in Tibet, where China had recently imposed martial law. The novelty of his campaign was the so-called *furusato* (home-town) plan, a loosely defined concept for reinvigorating the countryside and ending the over-concentration of wealth and population in Tokyo. One of its main planks was the idea that the central government should provide the round sum of 100 million yen (about $700 million) to each and every village and town council in the country, a ploy which other political parties described as the equivalent of bribes from the ruling party. Shintaro Abe rehearsed ideas of a general kind in favour of economic growth, welfare and 'creative diplomacy', but was short on specifics.

Kiichi Miyazawa's platform, entitled 'Under the Banner of Freedom and Fairness', stood out from the others for its detailed analysis of economic and foreign-policy problems and prescriptions for improvements. He argued, much as Japan's overseas critics were doing, that Japan's economy was still seriously distorted against consumers and in favour of over-powerful industrial and landlord interests. Miyazawa proposed a scheme similar in conception to that of his former mentor, Prime Minister Ikeda's 'income-doubling plan' of the early 1960s. Miyazawa's programme for the 1990s called for 'doubling Japan's assets'. The focus was to build up the country's poor stock of housing, roads and amenities, while shifting priorities from 'manufacturing and exports' to 'the quality of life and domestic consumption'. Miyazawa had the weakest political base of the three 'new leaders': his only real chance of becoming Prime Minister was as a compromise candidate in case of a deadlock between the other two.

In keeping with the LDP's traditional preference for deciding its leader by consensus rather than by an open contest, the three candidates agreed to leave the choice of the next LDP leader (and hence the next Prime Minister) to Nakasone. After a solemn show of consulting each of the contestants and other senior party figures, Nakasone announced his decision in favour of Noboru Takeshita – the man, he said, who could best unite the LDP and provide stability to the next government. Another piece of political theatre was thus accomplished, and on 6 November 1987 Yasuhiro Nakasone resigned and Noboru Takeshita was elected as the new Prime Minister in the Diet. Japan had installed a new head of government without serious discussion over the choice among the general public or even within the ranks of the ruling Liberal Democratic Party.

In the manner of choosing his own successor, Nakasone was conforming to an old and deep-rooted pattern in Japanese political life – the pattern of collective decision-making. At the moment of his departure from public office, he became a member of another body, the LDP's 'Council of Elders', a group of elder statesmen – including former prime ministers – who are consulted on all important party decisions as well as on grave matters of state. While in office, Nakasone had been a modern leader who sought to speed up the decision-making process; he had not been much constrained by the advice of these 'elders of the tribe', and was less of a consensus-builder than most of his predecessors. Yet, in a political culture that takes great account of personal debts and obligations, the act of choosing Naboru Takeshita was very important. Takeshita could be expected to 'protect' Nakasone in the same way as, for example, Nakasone had 'protected' Tanaka. Takeshita made his debt to his predecessor explicit, announcing that in matters of foreign policy in particular he would depend on the experience and advice of Mr Nakasone.

Yasuhiro Nakasone's achievements on his country's behalf during five years in power were considerable. He changed the tone of Japan's international relations for the better, and time and again gave reassurances to other countries that Japan would treat foreign interests without discrimination in trade and economic matters. He helped the process of decision-making in Japan to become slightly less opaque. Nakasone left a long-lasting legacy, which has strongly influenced the course of Japanese public life since his departure from office. The positive legacy was the concept and the practice of leadership; but he also left behind a cynicism towards the motives of those in public life. Many Japanese remember Nakasone as the leader who deceived them into voting for the Liberal Democratic Party under false pretences, since he tried to raise a sales tax after promising that his government would not introduce one. Under his administration very little was done to answer the public demand for electoral reform, or to end the widespread use of money for buying influence in politics and business.

200

The imbalance in the constituency system, favouring rural votes over urban, grew worse. The laws on political funds were quite inadequate to prevent the bribery of national politicians by those with vested interests, and members of the Diet were able to ignore their spirit and to collect almost unlimited funds from business without scrutiny of how they were spent.

As Nakasone left office to international applause for bringing Japan nearer to the centre of world affairs, his influence on future Japanese politics appeared assured. It looked as though he would dominate the foreign policy of the incoming government and perhaps even return to power at a later date – something unknown in Japan's post-Occupation political history. Instead, over the next two years the LDP experienced its most serious crisis since its foundation in 1955. Both Nakasone and his protégé Noboru Takeshita became political casualties of a financial scandal larger in scale even than the Lockheed affair. The 'Recruit scandal' showed beyond reasonable doubt that corruption was deeply ingrained in Japanese public life, and engendered a new climate of pessimism in Japan about the nation's political standards and towards its future, just as the country was becoming a major force in the affairs of the rest of the world.

7

The Mould

BEING JAPANESE

It had rained all morning in a cold, grey Tokyo. On 24 February 1989, the day of Emperor Hirohito's funeral, the crowds were slow to gather and, at about half a million strong, smaller than expected. The relationship between Emperor and citizens was never one of easy affection, but was laden with a sense of duty, and in the case of Hirohito with conflicting memories of the past. Many of those who lined the roads came from outside Tokyo. Many were also sixty or older: they had memories of the years before 1945 when they or their relatives had gone to war in the Emperor's name. They remained impassive as the motorcade with the bier containing Hirohito's remains drove past, making its way to the Shinjuku Imperial Gardens, four miles from the palace. This was their last salute to the man who had reigned for two decades as a 'living god', and for four more as a modern constitutional monarch, a symbol of Japan's own transformation from ugly militarism to mercantile prosperity. The funeral day, a Friday, was a national day of mourning. Banks, the stock exchanges, department stores and schools remained closed.

The death of the Emperor after an agony of waiting had been a release for the whole nation. Since he collapsed and was taken to hospital inside the palace grounds in September 1988, the nation had been in an almost constant state of alert, waiting for the end of the Showa age. Detailed medical bulletins broadcast live on television three times or more each day forced the nation to share the grim statistics of Hirohito's erratic pulse rate, blood pressure and temperature, as well as the indelicate details of his bowel movements, intake of liquid food and transfusions of blood (during his 111-day illness he received more than twice his own body-weight in blood transfusions).

A sombre mood of *jishuku*, 'self-restraint', took hold of the whole society. Business receptions and private parties were cancelled by the thousand. Companies toned down their advertising to cut out anything exuberant or sensational, and advertising income for newspapers and TV stations plummeted. At least two editors of news organisations lost their jobs because they allowed premature reports of 'X-day' – the day of the Emperor's death – to find their way into print. Even Japanese communities abroad joined in the mournful mood, cancelling parties, reunions and festivities of all kinds during the Emperor's illness. On the Tokyo Stock Exchange the Nikkei stock average remained on a plateau, as investors conspired to avoid any unseemly move either up or down which might distract from the reality that the Emperor was dying from cancer.

This fact itself could not, however, be reported by the Japanese media, even though the nature of the illness was transparently clear from the symptoms, including chronic internal bleeding. The court physicians said euphemistically that the Emperor was suffering from 'acute inflammation of the pancreas'. When the leading newspaper, the *Asahi Shimbun,* was bold enough to refer to the illness as cancer, its editors were severely reprimanded by the Imperial Household Agency officials. The *Asahi* never repeated this piece of *lèse-majesté* while the Emperor was alive. When 'X-day' finally came, the court doctors announced matter-of-factly that the cause of death had indeed been cancer, and palace officials claimed that the truth had been suppressed out of consideration for the feelings of the Emperor himself.

After several acute crises in his condition, Hirohito's death was widely expected, and the end appeared to many to be carefully stage-managed. After the week-long New Year holiday, on Saturday, 7 January, a day when the Japanese and worldwide financial markets were closed, a senior government official entered the special briefing room in the palace at 4 a.m. to announce that the Emperor's condition was 'critical'. The press assigned to cover the palace had been well briefed on the procedure: there would be only one 'critical' announcement; it would be followed within hours by an announcement of Hirohito's death. Sure enough, at 6.33 a.m. the chief Cabinet secretary, a senior Cabinet minister, appeared before the TV cameras to announce in solemn tones that 'His Majesty the Emperor has passed away'. The expression used, *hogyo saremashita,* is strange to most Japanese: it is used when speaking of the death of an Emperor and in no other context.

Hirohito was eighty-seven when he died, the longest-reigning, longest-lived Emperor in Japanese history. Hundreds of thousands of

203

people thronged the Imperial Plaza on that day, some pausing briefly to bow their heads towards the palace, others looking for all the world like tourists, simply wanting to share in this moment of historic meaning for Japan. The government called for two days of official mourning over that weekend. The neon signs were switched off in the Ginza, Roppongi, Shibuya and the other main entertainment centres in Tokyo, which were largely deserted. The nation was divided between those who wished to mourn Hirohito and those who preferred to avoid the subject of Japan's past or were simply indifferent.

The Japanese government eulogised the Emperor in an official statement, saying that he had 'ardently wished for world peace and the well-being of the people', that he had 'resolutely brought an end to the war that had broken out in spite of his wishes, out of a determination to prevent further suffering of the people, regardless of the consequences to his own person'. The same statement, in the name of the Prime Minister of the day, Noboru Takeshita, proudly recounted Japan's achievement during the Showa age:

> It has achieved remarkable progress by virtue of the untiring efforts of our people and has now become an important member of the international community. I feel keenly that these achievements have been made possible by the presence of His late Majesty as a symbol of the state and the unity of the people.

Left-wing extremist groups (*kageki-ha*) threatened to disrupt and halt the funeral ceremonies, and the police took every possible precaution against that: they even sealed the manhole covers on the route of the funeral procession. The only disruption was minor: a home-made bomb went off, partly blocking the road to the Imperial cemetery in Tama, western Tokyo; otherwise the day passed peacefully. The Japanese government was gratified by the numbers and the high rank of the delegations who flew to Tokyo for the state funeral. Hirohito – or to give him his posthumous title, Emperor Showa – was mourned by the representatives of 163 nations and 28 international organisations in the greatest assembly of world leaders and statesmen ever seen. The United States delegation was led by President George Bush, who as a young fighter pilot in the Pacific War had been shot down by the Japanese. France sent President Mitterrand; while the Duke of Edinburgh, amid protests from the popular press and former British prisoners-of-war, stood in for the Queen. After the ceremony in the Shinjuku Imperial Gardens the British party made a point of visiting the cropped lawns and flowerbeds of the British Commonwealth cemetery outside Yokohama to pay their respects to those on the Allied side who had died during the war against Japan.

The array of high-ranking mourners was an eloquent recognition of Japan's new international status. Japanese newspapers took the opportunity to reflect on the country's course, and in their comments pride in Japan's post-war economic successes was mingled with deep-seated doubts. The *Asahi Shimbun* raised the question of whether or not Japan had really changed from what the paper called 'its former infamous identity under the old Imperial system'. The *Asahi* was uncertain on this score, because, it said, 'Even the Japanese themselves are still in the process of defining exactly what they mean by saying that the Imperial system is "purely symbolic" '. The newspaper pointed up those aspects of Japanese society that are redolent of the feudal past, deploring the way that 'the Japanese public in general tends to bow to orders from above as a matter of course.' Somewhat defensively, the *Asahi Shimbun* concluded, though, that contemporary Japanese society allows the public to discuss the Imperial system and that 'over the last four post-war decades, we have built a democratic society where everyone is allowed to act on his or her personal belief'.

Since 1945 the freedom of belief and behaviour among the Japanese has in practice been circumscribed by powerful pressures within the society – pressures which can only be understood in the context of Japan's own history. The subject of the Emperor, like that of Japanese wartime militarism, remains largely taboo; only for a few days after his death did the normal rules seem to be waived and on television and in newspaper editorials public figures called for more openness in the 'Emperor system' and for a franker look at the wrongs committed during the militarist age in the first part of the Showa period.

That 'open house' was shortlived. To speak disrespectfully of the Emperor in public at any time is to risk physical assault from right-wing fanatics, as was evident when the Mayor of Nagasaki, Hitoshi Motoshima, suggested in December 1988 that the Emperor bore partial responsibility for the war: he received a written death threat, accompanied by a live bullet, from the All-Japan Patriots Federation, warning him not to go to Tokyo for the Emperor's funeral. As a public figure, Motoshima saw it as his duty to attend the funeral, and he did so. Almost a year later, in January 1990, a right-wing gunman shot him in the back at almost point-blank range as he left Nagasaki City Hall. Mayor Motoshima survived, and the attempt on his life was strongly condemned by all political parties; but it added to the climate of intimidation which colours the national debate on the Emperor's responsibility for the war and the wider question of Japan's behaviour in the militarist era.

The fierce controversy which attended Emperor Hirohito in life was present even on the day his remains were laid to rest. Its focus was the role played in the ceremonies by the native Japanese religion, Shinto. Although it ceased to have official government support in 1945, Shinto observances have remained the main focus of Japanese religious activity. While ordinary Japanese traditionally have Buddhist funerals, members of the Imperial family are customarily given Shinto rites. There was a strong Shinto flavour to Hirohito's funeral, which was conducted in front of the foreign dignitaries in a specially built shrine building beyond a freestanding Shinto shrine gate; yet the government maintained that the secular state ritual was separate from the 'private' Imperial funeral. This subtle distinction required a suspension of disbelief on the part of those present, but it was important to the government, as the post-war Japanese constitution insists on a clear separation of religion and state: Article 20 lays down that 'No religious organization shall receive any privileges from the State, nor exercise any political authority'.

Japanese Christian organisations, as well as some Buddhist and other religious groups, objected vehemently to the funeral arrangements, charging that the state sponsorship of the event would lead Japan back towards the dark days of state Shinto and wartime totalitarianism. Earlier, during Hirohito's prolonged illness, a group of Christian leaders had written to the Emperor's heir apparent, the then Crown Prince Akihito, urging him to make his father publicly repent the sins that had been committed in his name across Asia; the nature of Shinto, the petitioners argued, is to absolve men's sins without repentance, and unless Hirohito acknowledged before his death his responsibility for the whole nation's wrongdoings, the Japanese risked being caught up again in a spiral of greedy nationalism and repression. No reply from the palace was ever made public.

Japan moved with all the ritual characteristic of its ancient and highly self-conscious civilisation into a new era. A select group of scholars and high officials decided it would be called Heisei, 'Achieving Peace'; 1989 became the last year of Showa and the founding year of Heisei. It was a simple assertion of Japan's distinct cultural identity. The media scrambled to interview the parents of children born in the first few minutes of the first day of Heisei. Reporters asked people in the street what they thought of the new era's name. Most were non-committal: a common view was that 'Heisei' was a rather pedestrian choice. Some people wondered aloud whether it might signal that the era itself would be a disappointing one.

There were other, more solemn rites of passage. Within four hours of Hirohito's last breath the new Emperor, Akihito, ceremonially accepted the Imperial seals and the sword and jewel, two of the three 'sacred treasures' (the third, the mirror symbolising the Sun Goddess, is always kept at the Grand Shrine of Ise, the holiest of all Shinto shrines, on the Kii peninsula some 250 miles west of Tokyo), and for the first time the event was broadcast live on television. Akihito himself struck a mild blow for modernity by abandoning the stately and archaic court language reserved for the Imperial family and addressing the nation straightforwardly as *mina-san*, meaning 'all of you'. The heart of his first message from the throne was 'I pledge that I will always be at one with the people and uphold the constitution'. Akihito also performed other mystical rites of communion with the Imperial ancestral spirits, as ordained by his top advisers, in the secrecy of the Shinto shrines inside the palace grounds. The constitution and other laws say nothing about those rites. They are part of the ancient lore of the Imperial House, which considers itself the keeper of the essence of Japanese tradition.

Since 1945, as in Japan's colonialist days, the figure of the Emperor has represented an undefined focus of Japanese spiritual values. Apart from brief exceptional periods in Japan's history, Emperors did not wield real power. They were symbols of authority, spiritual and cultural leaders rather than temporal ones; many past Emperors have had an important influence as poets, scholars and literary figures. Under the strongly nationalistic Meiji Constitution of 1889 the Emperor was seen as the head of the Japanese 'nation–family'. The post-war constitution, describing the Emperor as the 'symbol of the state', does not directly contradict that idea, even though it upholds the ideals of democracy and justice under the law. A sitting member of parliament of the Liberal Democratic Party, Kiyoshi Mori, gave this interpretation of the Emperor's role within a week of Hirohito's death:

> All Japanese are subjects of the Emperor and we must cast ourselves at his feet. The essential concept of the Emperor has not changed, no matter how it is defined in law, since it is deeply rooted in the Japanese people's minds.

Even in modern Japan, a country of commercial frenzy, TV quiz shows and electronic wonders, superstitious appeals to national values can be a potent force. The particular man who is Emperor may be, as Akihito has shown himself to be, liberal-minded and modern in outlook. Still, an appeal in the name of the Emperor can act like moral blackmail, commanding from the individual unquestioning loyalty to the national ethos. In the words of a Japanese student in her early twenties, interviewed at an English-language school in Tokyo during the Emperor's illness, 'Talking about the Emperor is scarey ... there are extreme conservative people who think that the Emperor is god, and I'm afraid to talk about it.' She thought things would be different after Akihito took over: 'He will not be a real Emperor, he can't be; he'll just be a representative of the people, not a god like Hirohito.' Another young woman was sure that times had changed and a new generation did not care at all: 'There's no god, no Emperor, nothing: we just believe in ourselves, or money, or ambitions.'

The existence of a single, continuing imperial dynasty throughout the country's history sets the Japanese Emperors apart from either the Emperors of China, who were each overthrown in time, or the monarchs of Europe, who claimed a 'divine right' to rule but frequently fought for the right to wear the crown. Early in Japan's history, in the seventh century, the so-called Taika Reform declared the Emperor to be the direct descendant of the *kami*, the Japanese ancestral gods, and he was given the title of *tenno*, 'Heavenly Sovereign'. This was a way of guaranteeing the status and continuity of the country's socio-political system. It ensured, too, that in Japan political and religious power became intimately linked, rather than being in opposition to one another. The new constitution of that time laid down that harmony, *wa*, should be the first principle of society. That subjection of the individual interest to the communal will has characterised Japanese society ever since.

In order to bolster the dignity of antiquity for Japan's Imperial line, eighth-century scholars doctored the first historical records, inventing about 1000 years of recorded history up to the fifth century, as well as the names of the first fourteen Emperors, each of whom had a reign of Old Testament length, lasting up to 125 years. The aim was to put Japan on a par with China, which had a much longer history and threatened to dominate Japan as it did the East Asian continent.

The real origins of the Japanese Imperial family are still a matter of dispute among scholars. Some argue that the first historical Emperor in the fifth century AD was a recent descendant of immigrant warriors from the Asian continent; others point to the association in old myths of the Emperor with settled rice culture, and deduce that the Imperial family was the most powerful of the indigenous noble families in the Nara basin region in that period. The Imperial Household Agency has never permitted the excavation of the Imperial tombs, so ensuring the secrecy of archaeological evidence which would very likely settle the matter. The reason given is that it would be sacrilege to disturb the spirits of past Emperors which live on in the great tumuli. Thus the uniqueness and mystery of the Imperial institution are preserved, at the expense of an accurate picture of Japan's early history.

It was the special genius of Japanese political organisation that the Emperor was separated from actual political power. The Taika Reform was drawn up by Shotoku-taishi (Prince Shotoku), the son of an

Emperor, and thereafter real power was wielded by a succession of noble families, chancellors, regents and *shogun* – all in the name of the Emperor. The functions reserved exclusively to Emperors throughout history consist of a few highly symbolic fertility rituals, especially the annual planting of rice seedlings, and a mystical communion with the gods at harvest time. In the autumn of every year the Emperor explicitly plays out the part of a primitive agrarian god–king in a festival called *niinamesai* (Festival of Offering the First Rice Grains). He feasts with the spirits of his Imperial ancestors, asks for their continued protection in securing the nation's prosperity, and under-goes a spiritual union with the gods, so becoming the incarnation of the fertilising power of nature.

According to Shinto custom, in the year of a new Emperor's enthronement he must go through the most sacred of all Shinto rituals, called the *daijosai* or 'Great Thanksgiving Festival'. In this, the new Emperor awaits the coming of the gods in a specially built hall and feasts with them on consecrated rice. He is symbolically united with the Sun Goddess, Amaterasu, and is himself supposedly 'reborn' as an *arahitogami*, or 'manifest god'. The government decided to sponsor the *daijosai* with public funds as part of the enthronement ceremonies for Emperor Akihito in November 1990, on the grounds that it is an event of a public nature with a long history. That decision brought a fresh outcry from liberal and left-wing groups in Japan, who objected strongly to rites which traditionally signify the Emperor's divinity. In April 1990 a group of Christian university leaders in Japan issued a statement warning that the government sponsorship of the *daijosai* could 'only be feared as a movement toward a return to the Imperial divine sovereignty', and that it would endanger free thought and speech. A few days later a gunman fired two pistol shots into the home of one of the signatories, the dean of Ferris Women's College, narrowly missing him as he sat in his study. Notes entitled 'Punishment by Heaven' were found in the mailbox.

In fact the *daijosai* ceremony lapsed for much of the Tokugawa period (1603–1868), and was revived only in the mid-nineteenth century as part of the effort by nationalists in the new Meiji government to place the Emperor at the apex of the nation's affairs. Shinto under-went a strong revival from the eighteenth century, together with *kokugaku*, 'national learning'. *Kokugaku* was strongly nationalistic in character, as can be judged by this passage from *Shinkoku* (*The Land of the Gods*), a text written in 1811 by a leading scholar of the school, Atsutane Hirata:

> People all over the world refer to Japan as the Land of the Gods, and call us the descendants of the gods. Indeed, it is exactly as they say: our country, as a special mark of favour from the heavenly gods, was begotten by them, and there is thus so immense a difference between Japan and all the other countries of the world as to defy comparison. . . . Japanese differ completely from and are superior to the peoples of China, India, Russia, Holland, Siam, Cambodia, and all the other countries of the world.

In the first quarter of the twentieth century literature of that kind was accorded the status of orthodox truth and Shinto was made into the state religion, providing a pseudo-ideology justifying Japan's empire-building in Asia.

The Japanese religious sense has some features in common with that of other Asian peoples, but it has been moulded into a distinct entity by the experience of history. From earliest times, the Japanese worshipped many gods, recognising no all-seeing deity to whom the individual is responsible for his actions, and drawing no clear distinction between god and man, or between man and nature. Shinto holds that gods exist in all places of natural grandeur or mystery – in mountains, trees and streams; gods also live in the human spirit, and in the spirits of departed ancestors.

For centuries Shinto was not regarded as a full religion, but simply as a loose collection of seasonal observances and celebrations; its origins are in part simple animism, and it evolved as a means of preserving Japan's national spirit. It became more structured in the eighth century, in response to the spreading influence of Buddhism from China and Korea. Buddhism taught that everything in nature is connected in a 'chain of being' and that men should strive to eliminate desires, and it brought a wealth of knowledge and ideas from the Asian continent; but the sects that attracted the largest followings in Japan were those, like the Pure Land sect (Jodo-shu), which offered an easy path to salvation through the chanting of sutras and other simple observances. Zen Buddhism, an élite branch embraced by the *samurai* class, offers a path to enlightenment through meditation and 'the teaching of emptiness'. Zen, with its austere mental and physical discipline, served as a means to build up strong will-power and fatalism among Japan's warrior class. It was anti-intellectual, encouraging the belief that truth could be found in 'sincere actions' rather than in rational inquiry. Buddhist temples, however, served the important need for funerals and memorial services, and temple schools helped to spread basic education to the mass of the people.

Religion remained subservient to political power throughout Japan's history, even though for brief periods there was armed opposition to the government by militant Buddhist priests. The Buddhist sects were strictly watched by the *shoguns* to prevent their becoming a political threat. The Emperor was not only the high priest of the native religion: for the best part of 1000 years successive Emperors also took a leading role in advancing Buddhist learning and devotions.

The Buddhist sects proliferated during the Middle Ages, from the twelfth to the sixteenth centuries, and won the majority of the population as followers, but they co-existed with Shinto practices with little tension. Buddhist rites became a convenient vehicle for the Shinto tradition of venerating the ancestors. In many cases Shinto shrines and Buddhist temples were built close together in the same religious precinct; even though the buildings were similar they could easily be told apart because the shrine had a simple altar, with offerings of tangerines, rice cakes, sake and the like, while the temple had statues of the Buddha and his disciples, and an ornate altar as littered with candles and decorations as a Catholic cathedral. Today over 90 per cent of the population describe themselves as followers of Shinto and four out of five profess to be Buddhist at the same time. In practice Shinto is for the celebration of life – childbirth, festivals, marriage and other rites of passage; but Japanese people have Buddhist funerals and their ashes lie in Buddhist graveyards.

Shinto has three main strands, each of which is active today. Firstly it celebrates local clan spirits, originally called *ujigami*. These give expression to the idea of patriarchy: the clan (*uji*) and household are themselves seen as sacred institutions, and the ancestors – the departed heads of households – are venerated. The shrine complex at Nikko, Japan's most visited tourist spot, was built in honour of the *kami* enshrined there – none other than the first Tokugawa *shogun*, Ieyasu, who first unified the whole country at the turn of the seventeenth century.

Secondly, there is shrine Shinto, the folk aspect of the religion, which blesses local communities through their Shinto observances. Shrine festivals, *matsuri*, are usually held twice each year, at the transplanting of the rice in spring and at harvest time in autumn; they have always represented an important focus of Japanese community life. Festivals are often a mixture of Shinto and Buddhist traditions, but above all they celebrate the cycle of the seasons and the fertility of nature. The highlight of the main festivals in autumn is the parading of the *mikoshi* – portable shrine – through the streets of the local area: at the time of the *matsuri* the local guardian god is supposed to move from the shrine building itself into a small, portable shrine kept in the precincts. This is a finely carved and decorated wooden miniature house, designed for the god to inhabit temporarily, which is held aloft on a pair of fixed poles. Young and old people of the community boisterously parade the *mikoshi* around out of doors, symbolically allowing the local guardian god to greet and mingle with the people.

Thirdly, there is court Shinto, which ascribes to the Emperor the role of the supreme high priest. It also identifies Shinto unmistakably as an ethnic creed: the Emperor is seen as the head of the nation–family, and as the chief *kami* of the whole population. A host of Shinto court rituals continue throughout the year.

Whereas in Christianity man began in a state of innocence in the Garden of Eden and fell from grace, condemned to labour for his daily bread, in Japanese thought and literature there is no such Fall. Man is essentially innocent, and work has traditionally been seen not as a hardship but as a positive, life-asserting activity. The Christian concept of original sin is also absent from Japanese philosophical thought. On the contrary, the concept of 'original virtue', derived from Confucian thought, supports the Japanese assumption that men, and especially rulers or high-ranking people, are inherently virtuous. This idea was actively encouraged by the *shogun* in the Tokugawa period to bolster their own authority.

Rather than the concept of sin, the Japanese set important store by ritual purification. Thus at the approach to Shinto shrines worshippers customarily wash their hands in a stream, and at New Year households place small mounds of pure salt outside the threshold. Ground-breaking ceremonies held at the start of construction work, or before any organised endeavour, entail the exorcism of bad spirits by a priest waving a branch of the sakaki tree, which is deemed sacred, over the heads of the persons concerned.

Parallel in importance to the idea of ritual purification is the concept of pure intentions, or sincerity: *makoto,* which stems from both Shinto and Confucianist thinking, and is also consistent with the Buddhist idea of spiritual enlightenment. The stress on sincerity, in family and personal dealings and especially in relation to those in authority, has been reinforced and refined by centuries of Japanese living. In the Middle Ages, an age of shifting alliances and civil wars in Japan, this concept of inner purity of thought and action came to be upheld as a high ideal. It was closely connected to the concept of loyalty on the part of retainers to their feudal lords. Any allegiance to abstract or universal values not related to the social obligations of the present was strongly discouraged by the shogunate.

Confucianism, like Buddhism, was adopted by the Japanese in large measure from the Chinese and Korean models. It is a comprehensive code governing social relationships rather than a system of belief about man and god. It elevated conservative ideas of filial piety and the supremacy of the male over the female. It also reinforced the ideas of personal loyalty and obedience to authority as high virtues, and so was an important buttress to the fixed social hierarchy of the Tokugawa period. In those days there were four officially distinct classes – *samurai*, farmers (or peasants), artisans and merchants – with the outcaste class of *burakumin*, made up of those involved with the 'unclean' trades of slaughtering, leather-making and burying the dead, beneath them all. Confucianism was adopted as an official orthodoxy by the Tokugawa *shoguns*, and also underpinned the rise of nationalism from the late nineteenth century, when its emphasis on the 'correct' relationship between ruler and subject helped to justify the insistence on absolute loyalty to the Emperor.

As for Christianity, it was introduced into Japan by Portuguese and Spanish missionaries in the sixteenth century, but the Tokugawa *shoguns* banned it in the first half of the seventeenth century after the conversion of some noble families made them fear that the new faith might challenge their authority. Thereafter Christians suffered harsh persecution and have always remained small in number. Today there are about a million avowed Christians in Japan. They have only marginal influence on the values of society, although some leading schools and colleges were founded by missionaries, and eminent individuals, including the former Prime Minister Masayoshi Ohira, have been Christians. Japan's post-war leader Shigeru Yoshida was baptised on his deathbed.

After the war, religious freedom was guaranteed by the new constitution, but the major religions, all of which had been marshalled to support the war effort, were discredited among the Japanese public. To fill the vacuum, several so-called new religions sprang up, some of them claiming millions of adherents. The largest had been started in the 1930s but was suppressed in the war years for opposing state Shinto: the Soka Gakkai or 'Value-Creating Society'. It is based on the militant Buddhist teachings of the thirteenth-century priest Nichiren, and holds that the 'Buddha nature', present everywhere and in all people, can be harnessed by the initiated to bring peace and happiness in the world. The sect flourished after the war by offering spiritual solace to the underprivileged in the age of dizzyingly fast social change; at the end of the 1980s it had several million followers. Other new religions, including Tenrikyo ('Divine Wisdom Teaching'), grew out of Shinto and focused on the charismatic qualities of their leaders to make converts among the rootless first-generation city-dwellers. The new religions are distinguished by their large-scale fund-raising, and their success owes much to the strong need of their followers to share the sense of 'belonging' in the impersonal setting of the big cities.

Some characteristics of modern Japanese social behaviour can be traced to the nation's agrarian origins. The cultivation of rice, Japan's staple food, requires harmonious communal effort for irrigating the fields, planting, transplanting and harvesting. In Japanese ancient myth, the storm god, Susano no mikoto, symbolising the forces of savagery and destruction, ravaged the rice fields cultivated by his elder sister, the Sun Goddess Amaterasu, and desecrated the newly built palace at the time of the autumn rice festival by 'secretly voiding excrement' there. His punishment was to be sent to rule over the underworld. The myth symbolises the link between the divine, life-giving power of the sun and the authority of those who rule benignly over a fertile land.

In real life in agricultural Japan, communities enforced the codes of collective behaviour so strongly, with social sanctions against transgressors, that they came to behave in effect as a single personality. Each small community organised a variety of voluntary groups, known as *kumi*, which took care of communal services such as bridge-building, fire-fighting and dealing with crime. During local festivals the various *kumi* would (and in many areas still do) organise the ceremonial parade of the *mikoshi*. Members of these different groups developed a fierce sense of loyalty among themselves, matched by a strong sense of exclusiveness towards outsiders.

A similar sense of comradeship and homogeneity came to be shared among whole communities – *buraku* (communities) and *mura* (villages) – and was transferred to communities in towns and cities during the Tokugawa period. Then Japan was at peace, the merchant class thrived, and Edo (modern Tokyo) grew to be one of the world's largest cities, with a population that reached 1 million during the eighteenth century. The *kumi* units became the basis of a comprehensive system of mutual aid, developing into formal guilds and later into full-time occupations. The names of many present-day construction firms – such as Kumagai-gumi and Obhayashi-gumi – reveal their origins in the *kumi* (or *-gumi*), while the fire-fighting *kumi* contributed to the birth of professional fire brigades. This sense of group and local loyalty has become integral to the character of Japanese communities, both small and large: soft, secure and helpful to all on the inside, but hard and hostile to outsiders.

Alongside the agrarian tradition, with its stress on social harmony and collaborative effort, another distinctive feature of Japan's ideas about authority was the weight accorded to ceremonial activity, which

■ *25* Traditional funeral rites for the late Emperor Hirohito, February 1990.
■ *Overleaf 26* A tea farmer spreads fertiliser in preparation for the first picking in Shimizu, south-west of Tokyo.

■ *Opposite 27* Tokyo skyline, Shinjuku business district, 1989.
■ *28* Extreme over-crowding remains an uncomfortable reality for commuters in the Tokyo region.
■ *29* Schoolchildren and their mothers assemble for the opening ceremony on the first day of school.

■ *30* Housewives in
downtown Tokyo.

■ *31* Love hotel: a
conspicuous feature of
urban Japan.

■ *Opposite 32* Sunday
afternoon in the park: teenagers
dancing in the Harajuku
district, Tokyo.

■ *33* Sumo victory: grand champion Chiyonofuji uses his favourite arm throw to gain another win in January 1990.

■ *34* Swimmers enjoy the circular flowing pool at Toshimaen Amusement Park, Tokyo.

from the earliest days was associated with the right to govern. In the classical Heian period (794–1192) the life of the court nobility revolved around seasonal and religious ceremonies – an average of two per day to be observed throughout the year. In modern Japan at gatherings of all kinds – whether of legislators in the Diet, of families and guests at weddings, or of company colleagues at business meetings – those present are bound by a sense of formality and decorum which can astonish or perplex those unfamilar with Japanese practices.

As the twentieth century approaches its end, ceremonies of many kinds still have an extremely important place in the way Japan is governed and in Japanese social relations. Commencement ceremonies for schools, matriculation for university freshmen and company rites all take place in the month of April, coinciding with the appearance of the cherry blossoms in the capital. Mothers dress up in traditional kimono, complete with family crests on their sleeves. Parents and well-wishers overwhelm university auditoriums to witness the entry of new students. With good reason, the Japanese call their society *gakureki shakai,* a society organised by educational results.

From the beginning of the Meiji period, education was at the heart of Japan's attempt to catch up with the West in material ways. The closest foreign model was that of nineteenth-century France. The aim was that children throughout the country would receive approximately the same education at the same age, with the state closely determining its contents and values to suit its own purposes. The results were extremely impressive: by the end of the Meiji period in 1912 virtually the whole Japanese population was literate, and school attendance was close to 100 per cent. In that period education was explicitly made to serve the needs of the state. During the Occupation, Japanese education was overhauled at the direction of the Americans, who sought to 'democratise' the system of school administration and to encourage the spirit of enquiry in the classrooms. But old habits die hard: today, teachers for the most part still discourage open discussion in the classroom; and the American reform in favour of elected local education boards, which was designed to make them answerable to parents and the general public, lasted only until 1956, when the government reverted to the pre-war system of appointing board members directly from the centre.

MacArthur's changes to the broad framework of education have survived, however. Japan adopted the American model, the so-called 6–3–3–4 system: six years at elementary school between the ages of six and twelve, followed by three years of compulsory junior high school, up to the age of fifteen. The great majority of teenagers – the figure is currently around 94 per cent – then go on to three years at high school, and 36 per cent of all eighteen-year-olds proceed to a four-year university course or two-year junior college.

In the post-war years the measurable results have again been strikingly impressive. Academic standards in Japan's schools can hold their own with those anywhere. The US Department of Education produced a report in 1987 which gave Japan's education system credit for helping to bring about many of the most desirable features of Japanese life, saying

> it has been demonstrably successful in providing modern Japan with a powerfully competitive economy, a broadly literate population, a stable democratic government, a civilization in which there is relatively little crime or violence, and a functional society wherein the basic technological infrastructure is sound and reliable.

The American report stressed two distinctive features of the Japanese system: that education is used as a powerful instrument of national policy, and that schools inculcate into young Japanese the importance of harmony and co-operation with others. 'The Japanese believe that being a member of a well-organized and tightly knit group that works hard towards common goals is a natural and pleasurable human experience. Schools reflect this cultural priority.' The American educators disapproved of the Japanese emphasis on learning by rote, and on the still highly centralised government control of eduction; but they concluded that there is much that the USA could usefully emulate.

Keiko Takumi, like many Japanese girls in their mid-teens, asked her parents to let her go to a *juku* (cramming school) in the evenings after day school. Keiko lives in a suburb of Osaka city and attends Kozu Junior High School nearby. Her father, Kazuhiko, is a judge and spends very little time about the family home. Keiko's mother watches over her and encourages her actively. Keiko has not decided on her long-term career aim, but is doing well at school; she is determined first to get into a good senior high school and then into a good university. Her attitude is: 'If you don't study properly you are bound to have problems when you start work, so it's obvious that you have to study hard.'

In the months before she sat the exam for senior high school, Keiko went to the *juku* six days a week, and sat up studying every night until midnight or later. Kozu is a municipal school with more than 600 pupils of both sexes – a representative school in size, and slightly above average in academic standards. The curriculum is advanced by any country's standards: Keiko, at fourteen, is in the third year; she and her classmates are already studying integral calculus. In the science class Keiko and the other children learn to make a simple electric motor themselves. The teacher, Mr Kitano, says of this exercise:

> The strength of Japanese education is in the breadth of the knowledge which children acquire. Japan is an industrial society. Nobody knows what jobs each of them will do, but what they learn in primary and junior high school will be very useful in their work. We don't turn out geniuses, but there is a lot of brain power in Japan today, thanks to this system.

Japanese schoolchildren regularly come top of the list of those tested in comparative international tests of mathematics and science. They are relatively weak, however, in other skills, especially self-expression and the use of spoken foreign languages. At Kozu a British teachers' assistant sometimes takes Keiko's English conversation class; it is usually a trial for her to get the boys and girls to speak out and to react: they are firmly schooled for the rest of the time to be alert and well-disciplined, but passive, and among Japanese pupils and teachers alike there is a constricting lack of discussion about current public issues or the purposes of education.

At Kozu, as in many other Japanese schools, boys are dressed in Prussian-style military tunics, with brass buttons down the front; girls wear navy-blue 'sailor suits'. There are regular inspections to see that the children's hair is of the prescribed length: short back and sides for the boys, short and straight for the girls, no perms allowed. There is very little truancy. The emphasis of the teaching is on unremitting effort to improve the school performance of every student. Keiko's form teacher, Mr Matsumoto, admonishes the forty pupils seated upright at their desks: 'You must all remember, it is hard to get into a good senior high school. And your elder brothers and sisters may have told you that it's getting easier to find a job these days: don't pay any attention. The competition is tougher than ever.'

Most of the other fourteen-year-olds at Kozu go, like Keiko, to fee-paying cramming schools in the evening, followed by up to two hours of homework, which they do not finish until well after midnight; so for long periods they often catch only five or six hours' sleep a night. Each week the school clinic receives a few children who are physically and mentally exhausted. There is not much the nurse can do for them, and her advice is often contradictory: 'Try to rest more, but don't slacken in your studies,' she tells them. Some of the children are less enthusiastic than others in the race to succeed, but the atmosphere encourages most to believe that there is no alternative to trying one's best to reach goals set by others. The conviction that Japan is still a meritocracy is firmly held. Mr Yamazoe, principal of Kozu Junior High School, voices the commonly held Japanese view that 'in other countries there are class systems, so that even if you study hard your future is pretty well decided. In Japan it's different: if you try hard and study, you can become the boss of a company, or even the Prime Minister.'

To get ahead in Japan means starting very young. The pressures on young children and their teachers to achieve good results begin for the majority at the age of four. From that age more than nine children out of ten go to kindergartens, some of which have hotly competitive entrance tests. Keiko, like most of her friends, feels that she is missing out by not having much time to play, or to follow interests outside school. But she will not say that she thinks it wrong, only that 'I think it's a pity'. Her mother expresses the tangled feelings shared by a great many Japanese parents who want their children to succeed at almost any cost, but at the same time feel guilty over that cost:

> I feel that this is a heartless situation from a human point of view, but one has to put that aside. These days people are really impressed if you do well in your studies – they admire it. It's as though people who graduate from Tokyo University are somehow much better human beings. I only wish it could be the other way round: I'd like to have my children enjoy a wider range of experience and have more time playing with their friends; but they can't, because of studying.

The Japanese government itself has recognised the need for some sweeping changes in the way the education system is set up. Throughout the 1980s it wrestled with the question of what these changes should be, but with confusing results. The government's Council on Educational Reform produced a series of recommendations during the decade, aimed at easing the pressure of exams, ending the excessive uniformity of the educational system, and turning out more independent-minded and creative people to match the needs of the age. No practical changes have yet been agreed, however. In the early 1980s Japan's schools were the focus of several waves of violence and bullying, and although the problem is now declining and has never reached the scale it does in many Western countries, they have caused alarm as symptoms of a serious *malaise* within Japan's highly managed society.

State secondary schools, once the nation's pride, conspicuously lag behind the better private schools in academic standards, and wealthier Japanese parents are opting out of the public-school system in growing numbers. As of May 1986 three-quarters of all Japanese kindergarten children, three-quarters of students in further education, and 28 per cent of senior high school students were at private schools or colleges. The annual lists of successful entrants to Tokyo University, at the pinnacle of Japan's educational system, clearly show how much better the private schools are at producing good results. This means in effect that the equality that existed immediately after the post-war educational reforms is disappearing; increasingly, the opportunity to reach the heights of Japanese society depends on the ability of families to afford the high fees – over $8000 a year on average – of private schools.

The Japanese do not make the same claims of high standards for their universities as they do for their schools. After what is called the 'hell' or the 'war' of college entrance exams, the life of Japan's universities is generally undemanding and largely unsupervised. Students are awarded grades throughout their college career, and the final exam is neither very taxing nor especially important to the degree. Undergraduates in arts faculties do not begin to specialise in chosen subjects until their third year. Those studying engineering and medicine have a more rigorous course of studies to keep up with, but many others simply coast through the university experience, doing little more than the minimum required to graduate. Often university clubs and part-time jobs are given higher priority by students than lectures and study. Parents, academics and future employers tend to turn a blind eye: in practice, for many students in the arts and social sciences, campus life is widely regarded as a golden interlude between the strains of academic discipline at school and the embrace of the future company employer. Government schemes for making grants and loans to college students are undeveloped compared with the countries of North America and Europe. Most Japanese students rely on their parents for all or most of their fees and living costs, remaining financially dependent throughout their years at college.

For the great majority of Japanese, the broad lines of their future career expectations are decided by the time they are eighteen. It is then that they sit entrance exams for particular universities or colleges. As there is no standard common exam for the top universities, many young people take exams for several different target colleges. Their schoolteachers will already have decided, on the basis of internal performance ratings, which exams they may sit. Those who fail may become so-called *ronin,* or 'masterless *samurai'* students, for a year or more, then sit the exams again. Once a student has been accepted, three years stretch ahead before the next stage. Then they are expected to study the prospectuses of rival companies to decide which they want to make their own. In 1990 Japan's shortage of skilled labour was at a post-war peak, and each male college graduate had an average of three offers of employment.

□   □   □

In April 1990 the 300 new graduate recruits to Fuji Film, Japan's leading film-manufacturing company, stand outside the company's largest manufacturing plant, with the slopes of Mount Fuji rising majestically behind. They have been selected through a series of rigorous tests from among 20 000 interested university graduates, 2000 of whom were interviewed, and consider themselves among the élite of the country's workforce. The company has spared no expense to attract the best possible candidates and to bind them in the firm's lifelong embrace. Most of the new recruits expect to stay with the firm for the next thirty years.

The annual salary in large companies like Fuji Film begins at the relatively modest level of about 230 000 yen ($1350) per month, but after the first few years of service that figure rises quickly and is supplemented by between four and six months' salary (determined according to the company's performance) paid in mid-year and year-end bonuses. The annual income of a graduate entrant now aged in his late thirties is around 6 or 7 million yen (between $40 000 and $46 500), and that of employees who joined as high-school leavers is about 5 million yen ($33 000). For the first fifteen years or so there will be little distinction in rank or pay-scale among the 'intake of 1990'; thereafter, the most able will be promoted quickly, and some at least of the graduates entering Fuji Film in 1990 can expect to be among those who will be running the firm in thirty years' time.

The company has been able to choose from a strong field of applicants because it has good growth prospects. Today Fuji Film has over 10 000 employees and rivals Eastman Kodak in worldwide sales. Since the 1980s it has diversified into making video cameras, still cameras and magnetic tape. There are sixteen women among the new university-graduate recruits: Fuji Film, like the majority of large-scale employers, has for the past several years taken women into its career stream as 'general officers', not only as clerical and factory workers; but in practice very few women rise even to the level of general manager (*bucho*) in large Japanese firms, and women sitting on the boards of major companies are all but unheard of.

At the entrance ceremony all new *shain* (a term meaning literally 'company members' rather than 'employees') gather to hear a welcome address by the company president. Three graduates are selected to respond, publicly expressing their sense of good fortune and their 'vision' for their lifelong career with the firm. After joining some 300 high-school leavers, aged about eighteen, for a group photograph of the year's entire intake, they are sent on a three-week induction course into company life. They are told about the company structure, its business strategy, and the various departments which it comprises.

Each recruit writes a report containing his personal 'vision' of life with the company, and what kind of work he wants to do. At the end of the course they will all learn where the company intends to employ them – at headquarters, at the research centres based at the factory, in sales, accounts, personnel, public relations and so on. For many, the result will be a disappointment. The next day those who are to work at the headquarters beside Mount Fuji move to a company dormitory; those who have been selected to work in the Tokyo office will most likely return to their parents' home to prepare for their first day at work.

The relationship of the new recruits with their chosen company is based on a shared concept of mutual benefit. The uniformity is accepted as something inevitable. One of the 1990 intake, Hiroaki Shimosaka, puts it like this:

> In the West the word 'harmony' [wa] is considered to be the antithesis of individual freedom. But I don't agree. Perhaps it is partly thanks to the national character of the Japanese, who tend to be content with being average; but they don't prevent others from expressing their views. An old Japanese saying, 'The nail that sticks out will be hammered in,' certainly reflects the nature of a society which loves harmony. But the nail gets hammered in not just because it sticks out, but because it causes unnecessary damage.

Shimosaka's statement might well be taken as one principle of the Japanese post-war bible of human relations: avoid conflict, put your trust in others, do not abuse your authority when you are in a position to exercise it, and accept the consensus of the group.

Shimosaka does believe, however, that his chosen firm and others like it will have to adapt to the changing times:

> I think the so-called 'lifetime-employment' system certainly contributed to Japan's success up to now. The country's situation called for a kind of merging between companies and the people in them, between employers and employees. But from now on the key to Japan's success will be different: it will be to create a pool of talent which can contain various value systems and flexible attitudes, so the old, rigid system of life employment will prove out of date and may stand in the way of progress.

Another new entrant to Fuji Film, Hiroshi Tanaka, sees a definite difference in individual behaviour between Japan and the West:

> Foreigners seem to be much more high-spirited and outgoing than most Japanese. On a ski slope, for example, they exchange cheerful smiles and jokes, while Japanese people tend to look very serious and expressionless. It's the same in business. I am sure that people in other countries are far

more sociable than the Japanese. We must look to them as if we're wearing an inscrutable mask.

Tanaka expects to work hard during his years at Fuji Film, but emphatically rejects the thought that he could be classified as a 'company warrior'.

Kozo Noguchi is already well on the path of the successful *salarii-man*. At the age of forty-nine he is a section chief (*kacho*) in Fuji Film's research department. He and his wife Masuko live in a modest three-bedroomed company apartment on the first floor of the company block about two miles from the Ashigara plant beside Mount Fuji. When the weather is fine he can bicycle to work in ten minutes. The closeness is a significant boon, since millions of Japanese workers are forced to spend an hour or more each way commuting to work on crowded trains. Noguchi usually rises at 6.30 and eats the breakfast prepared for him by his wife before setting out. His cluttered desk is one of six arranged in order of seniority in the cine-film department.

Noguchi is the son of a university professor and in the 1970s he and his family spent a total of thirteen years in Fuji Film's branch in Düsseldorf, West Germany, an experience that left a strong impression. He does not subscribe to the idea that the Japanese way of life is unique, but he believes that there is a difference in attitudes to company and job:

> The basic fact in common between the East and the West is that the employer provides your livelihood. The difference is in the 'educational policy' of Japanese companies, which is aimed at making employees feel a genuine part of the organisation, that their day-to-day life exists within the company. ... I see my company as providing a sort of space where I can enjoy working with my colleagues.

Noguchi's marriage to Masuko was an arranged one. He had first planned to marry another girl, but the standard family-sponsored inquiry into his prospective bride turned up medical evidence that she was barren, so he gave her up. Carrying on the family name is still seen as the prime duty of the Japanese male in marriage.

Masuko Noguchi has sophisticated tastes and much enjoyed the time the family spent in Germany. After seeing her husband off to work and their fourteen-year-old son Tetsuro on his way to primary school, she often settles down to watch a snatch of the daytime TV programmes aimed at housewives. Sometimes she practises at home for her weekly calligraphy lesson in Tokyo. That is an occasion she looks forward to – a time to meet friends and sometimes join them for a meal or a visit to the cinema.

Masuko has had to bring up her two sons virtually single-handed, as her husband is often away on business trips, and even while he is in Tokyo he spends most evenings at the office or out with his work colleagues. She is dedicated to the task of being a good mother and upholding the high standards of the Noguchi family: 'He is the heir to the Noguchi family; so no matter where he chooses to live, whether in Japan or somewhere abroad, he must carry with him a basic knowledge and common sense about things Japanese.' She feels that the Japanese are not especially more hard-working than the Germans, the foreign nation she knows best; she reckons that both respect for superiors and formal worship for one's ancestors are also features of other cultures, not by any means unique to Japan.

> Perhaps the quality I would single out as being characteristic of the Japanese is steadiness [*jimichi*]. There is a Japanese proverb: 'To spend three years waiting on the same stone' [*Ishi no ue ni mo sannen*]. That shows the importance of endurance, consistency and patience. Japanese people never give up.

Blue-collar workers are expected to be equally diligent. Norio Kusukabe makes black caps for consumer film, and has given his life, in effect, to the firm. He used to live only five minutes away from work by bicycle, but in 1988 was suddenly given only one day's notice that he was being moved to a new job in a different factory further away. He made no murmur of complaint. Kusukabe's background is somewhat unusual: when he married his wife Toyoko in 1967 he agreed to her parents' proposal that, as they had no male heir, he would become their adopted son, take their name and carry on the family line. His parents-in-law live with him, his wife and their three children in a house built specially for them to accommodate all three generations. Ever since he joined Fuji Film, Kusukabe has made a habit of arriving at work forty minutes early; he uses the time to think up ideas for improving efficiency in the company, which he submits through the 'suggestion-box' system. His proposals have earned him several awards, of which he is very proud, from the plant director. Although Kusukabe is still in his forties and is looking forward to at least another ten years' work ahead of him, both he and his wife have already been sent on compulsory retirement courses in order to motivate them and help them prepare for the future. Corporate Japan looks after almost every imaginable need on behalf of its own.

About one-third of Japanese workers are in large organisations, with over 1000 employees and a lifelong employment system. Once admitted, the staff member of a company is bound to conform to its norms and practices. In most cases, he receives a small badge bearing the company's symbol to wear on his lapel. The company is a sanctuary, but it can also be a prison. A public opinion poll carried out in 1989 by the government found that as many as 25 per cent of Japanese working people said they wanted to change from their present job, but expected to continue in it. It is rare even for successful company men to gain an equivalent job with appropriate status in a rival enterprise, since poaching is still frowned upon. In smaller firms there is much more job mobility for the individual, but job security is also uncertain. In the new, fast-growing business areas of financial services and consultancy there has been since the mid-1980s a rash of defections and departures by high-flying individuals, and the head-hunting business has suddenly become important. Still, the vast majority of employees in Japan's larger firms stay on board until the firm asks them to take early retirement or to move to a job in an affiliated company.

A powerful factor in this decision is that the range of company benefits is unlikely to be duplicated elsewhere; many employees get company housing at a fraction of the market rate, and to sacrifice that benefit is foolhardy when the costs of land and rents in the big cities have already gone beyond the means of the ordinary salary-earner. Government figures show that the average cost of buying a small, 60-square-metre flat in Tokyo in 1990 was 86 million yen, or $575 000 – more than twelve times the average annual income of a middle-aged working person. A 100-square-metre plot of land costs on average 127 million yen ($850 000). Today, unless they inherit a home or great wealth, few newly-wed couples living in or near the capital can expect ever to live in their own home. Among the novelties which Japan has given to the world is the three-generation mortgage: some Japanese housing-loan companies now agree to grant mortgages on the understanding that the money borrowed will be paid back in a hundred years' time. The resulting glaring gap between haves and have-nots, like the decline in the standards of state schooling, undermined Japan's formerly proud claim to egalitarianism.

The Japanese are constantly on guard for signs that their work ethic is being eroded. In 1990 a survey of attitudes to work gave some support to that theory: asked which they regarded as more important, work or home life, almost half answered the latter. But there has been no corresponding fall-off in the number of schoolchildren applying for the prestige universities, or of students seeking to join the big firms. In Japan the average person works between 200 and 500 hours a year longer than his counterpart in North America or Western Europe. The government aims to narrow the gap, but the odds are against it: since the mid-1970s Japan has seen no overall reduction in working hours, as many firms have come to rely on overtime work rather than hiring more employees to meet demand. The Ministry of International Trade and Industry, a past master at social engineering, set up a think-tank called the Leisure Development Centre to study the 'problem' of Japanese overwork. It recommended that Japanese firms should move more quickly to a regular five-day week, and that the government should take steps to lower the cost of travel and recreation if the Japanese were to enjoy the fruits of the past decades of hard work.

When a round of golf – virtually the adopted national sport – can easily cost $200 and even a visit to an enclosed driving range in town may cost $10, it is not surprising that the most popular Japanese pastime outside work and home is the mindless one of *pachinko*, Japanese-style pinball. Overwhelmingly the most popular spectator sport is baseball, which was introduced from the USA in the nineteenth century. The progress of the professional league teams in the annual summer Japan Series championship becomes a national obsession. Each team is sponsored by a business firm – the *Yomiuri* newspaper has the Giants, the private Seibu Railway group has the Lions, the Mazda car firm sponsors the Hiroshima Carp. Baseball gives sometimes wild expression to the Japanese love of team spirit in action. Millions of Japanese are avid fans, and will turn out to watch their heroes in all weathers. Individualism is frowned on among the players, and membership of a team is strictly for life: there are no expensive transfers between clubs as there are, say, with European soccer stars.

The Japanese as a nation have less leisure time than people in any other industrialised country – a legacy of the relentless drive to 'catch up with the West'. The government lagged behind private businesses in moving to the five-day week, but lately central government ministries have adopted a system of giving civil servants two Saturdays off per month, although schools still open on Saturday mornings. One in three Japanese workers now expects to have a two-day weekend, but the national average number of working days taken off by Japanese company workers is rising only slowly: in 1987 it was a mere eight. Many companies do not in principle allow staff to choose when they will take their individual annual holidays; instead they close down the entire office or plant for several days at a stretch, usually at the time of the mid-August *bon* festival. The result is that at peak holiday periods the traffic jams on roads leading out of Tokyo stretch up to twenty miles in several directions.

Work exacts its toll on the factory hand and manager alike. The press has made much of the phenomenon of deaths from overwork – *karoshi* – in the offices and on the assembly lines of Japan. In some cases individuals who died in their thirties or forties from heart attacks

225

or strokes were found to have worked for 100 days without a day off, or as much as 100 hours of overtime in a week. When confidential *karoshi* hot lines were set up in the Labour Ministry to gauge the extent of the problem, they quickly became overloaded.

Although women make up about two-fifths of the Japanese workforce – 24 million out of 60 million people – and one in three university graduates is female, their representation in the large firms and government ministries is meagre. Only 1 per cent of managers in Japanese business firms are women, and one-third of large manufacturing firms still hire no women graduates at all as a matter of policy. Mitsui and Company, which claims to be the largest multi-functional trading and services company in the world, in 1990 had only one female member of staff among its management-stream career workers. The situation in other leading trading and manufacturing firms is little different. Teaching is the only profession in which women have traditionally been treated on an equal basis with men.

Very many Japanese families operate on a strict division of labour that hinges on the demands of the company. Women make most major decisions on family budgeting and attend unaided to the supervision of their children's education. They are often obliged to abandon their career ambitions at once after marrying, to become homemakers. Many fun-loving Japanese OLs ('office ladies') are dismayed when they learn these facts of life quickly after their honeymoon, finding themselves required to prepare their husband's *bento* (Japanese-style lunch-box) as well as washing his shirts and bearing his children. Social pressures are strong for newly-wed couples to produce children early in their marriage. Daughters are still generally taught to see their futures in terms of being 'dutiful wives and wise mothers': the ground is being prepared for another generation of like-minded women. For such families the home is often little more than a bed-and-breakfast unit for commuters and a space for the woman of the house to rear the children.

Over the past few decades the effect of this pattern on the Japanese family as an institution has been harsh. In 1986, fifty-nine people out of 10 000 got married compared with fourteen who got divorced; this is a much lower divorce rate than in the UK or America, but only just below that of France or Switzerland. In the mid-1980s, when many firms suffered sharp losses because of the climbing cost of raw materials in the wake of the realignment of the yen and dollar currencies, tens of thousands of company men were given early retirement at or before the age of fifty, instead of around sixty, as is the norm. In some cases the discarded company men were promptly divorced by their wives, who saw that their usefulness as wage-earners was at an end. They had, even if involuntarily, broken the unwritten marriage contract which says that the male will provide the family income, while the woman will take care of the home. Marital infidelity, once the preserve and privilege of Japanese men, is now as likely to be sought by wives, and the trend is lovingly illustrated in nightly television dramas. The divorce courts are, however, distrusted by many women as being 'in the world of men' and unsympathetic to them. Since the war, custody has been granted to the wife in 77 per cent of cases; but payment of child support is erratic: a government survey of single mothers in 1988 found that three out of four had never received it at all.

A growing number of educated Japanese women are dissatisfied with their virtual exclusion from the mainstream world of business and government, but in keeping with Japan's traditions against social activism there has been no 'women's liberation' movement of the kind that swept North America, Europe and Australia in the 1960s. In 1986 Japan's first Equal Opportunity Law came into effect, encouraging employers to give equal treatment to men and women in hiring and promotion. In theory it prohibits the long-established practice of forcing women to resign from jobs when they get married or give birth. The law contains no mandatory penalties for employers who break it, relying instead on moral pressure to make the companies change their ways.

Since then, employment prospects for women have improved some-what, especially in the service sector and in firms in fast-growing business areas, such as Suntory, the giant food and drink conglomerate, and NTT, the telecommunications company. But the large electronics firms and other businesses, such as banks, prefer all their career staff to be male. Women have excelled in specific areas not dominated by the big firms, such as fashion, interior design and interpreting. There are also some 12 000 all-female business corporations in Japan, mostly cottage industries – a statistic which itself bears witness to the dis-satisfaction of many would-be businesswomen with the conventional employers. Among the host of foreign loan-words entering Japanese in recent years was *sekuhara,* the new Japanised expression for 'sexual harassment'. At the start of the 1980s it was not publicly recognised as an issue at all. But Japanese culture is a force against sexual equality in employment: hundreds of thousands of women still owe their liveli-hood to the rich tradition of female service to, and entertainment of, the male, working in the 'water business' – bars, *karaoke* joints, cab-arets and the so-called 'soapland', Japanese-style turkish baths. For many women, owning or running a small business of that kind is the only realistic way to be financially independent.

Keiko Atsumi, who is married to an official in the prestigious Finance Ministry, runs her own small company producing a financial newsletter in Tokyo. She took an economics degree from a leading university in the 1960s but found that no major corporation wanted a woman with such qualifications. She judges that it is no exaggeration to say that most Japanese men are 'sexist' compared with men in the West: 'They expect women to be around them, to be subservient to them; they expect us always to be complementing their roles and functions at home and in their business lives.' She sees hopeful signs, though, that the long-standing male domination of Japanese society may be gradually crumbling and in particular took heart from the fact that the number of women in Japan's advisory Upper House of the Diet, the House of Councillors, increased in the 1989 elections from a mere 23 to 33 – mostly newcomers to politics who won with Socialist Party backing after a series of sex and money scandals had rocked the Liberal Democratic Party. 'Married women were fed up with their husbands, working women were fed up with their male bosses about the kind of treatment they had been receiving,' Mrs Atsumi says. 'The outburst of resentment was expressed in the latest election.'

However, in general elections for the main legislative chamber, the House of Representatives, in February 1990, only twelve women were elected out of 512 seats contested – not one of them from the ruling Liberal Democrats. For six months from the summer of 1989 there were two women among Japan's Cabinet ministers; but that was an exception which may not be repeated. There was no sign that the modest gains made by women in national politics would quickly be reflected in the world of business.

A solution for some graduate women is to find employment in foreign companies in Japan, a trend which is especially strong in banking, stockbroking and the like. When Hisako Sasaki graduated from university in the mid-1970s, leading companies did not employ women in skilled jobs. She took a simple clerical job in a large company but quickly lost interest. Now she is a marketing executive for a British company in Tokyo: 'If I work in a Japanese firm the job will be limited to supporting the male staff – like serving tea or cleaning the conference room – but working with a foreign company I have heavier responsibility on the job, and that's what I like.' Fumiyo Miyatake faced even more rigid barriers when she graduated some forty years ago. She now runs her own cross-cultural training company, and says she has found that unencumbered relations are possible in non-Japanese offices when English, not Japanese, is the everyday language:

In our company men and women work together without prejudice, and I think it's partly because our communication is in English, so the thinking is in English. [Therefore] 'myself' is always 'I'. But thinking in Japanese we have to pay attention to some different phrases, addressing superiors or clients or colleagues, or women, or men; with English communication I think the language itself helps to some extent with a horizontal equality in communication style.

The Japanese language is like a dictionary of the culture itself. When a person speaks, the language requires that his or her sex, age and status relative to the listener be made clear in the words used, and in the manner of their delivery. There cannot easily be equality between people in Japanese. Like the society, the language is thick with subtle barriers, and signposts of rank, to maintain the status quo. Different pronouns, prefixes, verbs and verb forms must be used to indicate the speaker's unflagging awareness of his or her standing. What Fumiyo Miyatake complained of is that women, by definition, are expected to use 'women's Japanese', involving polite and deferential pronouns and vocabulary. It is not considered becoming for women to speak plainly. So demanding is this cage of the language that to be rude to a person older or senior to yourself is technically a grammatical mistake.

It would be too bold to suggest that the lexicon of Japanese actually results in a society which is harmonious, respectful of authority and hierarchical. Japanese society is all those things, however, and it would be rash to dismiss the suggestion that the language positively helps to keep it that way. Many people from other cultures are baffled to find that the Japanese language has no distinction between singular and plural, just as they are surprised to learn that thousands of streets in Japanese cities have no names – they rely instead on an old postal address system based on separately numbered housing blocks in thousands of so-called *cho* ('towns'). It is little consolation when they learn that Japanese people can have almost as much difficulty just getting around as the rawest foreigner.

It is idle to ignore the factor of culture in Japan's social scheme. When one sees a society in which 90 per cent of the people categorise themselves as 'middle class'; in which schoolchildren do not buy beer from street-corner vending machines; or in which it is considered safe in some areas to put cash outside one's front door for tradesmen without fear that it will be stolen, it is obvious that powerful social conditioning is at work. When one sees, too, that in Japanese society millions of people work overtime without claiming any specific reward for it, and stockbroking firms buy into a falling market because they are advised to do so by senior government officials; when one sees the world's second largest economy being sustained by a nation where to speak the English language fluently is idiosyncratic and unusual, despite nine years of compulsory English classes at school, then one must recognise that cultural factors are at work in a serious way.

Japan's social habits cannot even be described in English alone, as the English language is missing the vocabulary to encompass much of what the Japanese hold most valuable in interpersonal relations. The cultural forces in Japan's business and government practices have lately become in themselves a hotly debated issue in Japan's relations with other countries. To write a whole 'grammar' of that culture would be a maddeningly complex task, but two key attributes stand out as factors in the way, often baffling to people elsewhere, in which the Japanese arrange their affairs.

The first is the national concept of respect. When the Japanese speak or interact with others in any way socially, as a rule they show respect in the most explicit manner possible: they bow frequently. In business, custom requires different depths of bowing for different circumstances: the general rule is 15 per cent for greeting, 30 per cent for leave-taking, and 45 per cent when making an apology. The Japanese are also schooled when conversing to make frequent sounds, designed to reassure the other party of one's continued attention, which have little or no semantic content: sounds such as *hai*, uttered sharply as though with a sudden realisation of something of unusually great importance, or *eee* (pronounced like 'air'), delivered with concern and a slightly falling tone. Both of these are affirmative, meaning anything from 'yes' to (in effect) 'I see – please go on.' A phrase much used in telephone conversations to ease the flow of talk is *A so desu ka?* – literally 'Really?' or 'Is that so?'

This kind of verbal exertion is expected on the whole only of those of junior rank; but people in positions of authority are absolutely expected to show their 'respect' in speech and behaviour as well. This they do by observing a rather complex code. They must not thrust themselves forward, but wait for the appropriate signals or introductions – which, happily, since almost everybody in the society knows the rules, can be awaited with confidence. Then they must speak without hurry, and in what they say must give due recognition to the hierarchy around them. This, too, comes naturally, as change occurs only slowly and is strongly resisted. This elaborate set of rules is impossible to avoid in business and public life. It operates instinctively when Japanese people gather on a golf course, or a railway station, or in an office at the start of a working day. It is the code which keeps the engine of human relations on track.

Respect is the outward show of *makoto*, sincerity. Sincerity means always being present when needed, well scrubbed and well turned out; it means unselfish behaviour, and acting in accordance with the loyalty one owes to others by virtue of birth, upbringing and social obligations. Sincerity requires frequent face-to-face meetings among Japanese people. Favours and business deals of all kinds are normally discussed as well as sealed by groups of people seated in the same room: the Japanese penchant for frequent and lengthy meetings surprises visitors and businessmen from other societies. But custom means that it is the only way to participate in the Japanese system. Gatherings are often called for purposes which outsiders might consider unnecessary: for *aisatsu*, 'greeting', and *uchiawase*, 'prearrangement of things', and *nemawashi*, 'preparation of the ground by an interested party'. These are the stuff of Japan's distinctive way of ordering affairs. They are backed up by frequent giving of gifts, often valuable ones, to persons in authority, including doctors and teachers. In business, not to give a present to a client at the prescribed seasons of midsummer and the year's end amounts to an affront. Many outsiders have come to grief by ignoring it.

Sometimes, not often, the code breaks down: when Japanese people are far from home, or during moments of licensed tomfoolery. The Japanese at play, in *karaoke* bars crooning in imitation of Frank Sinatra, or having their pictures taken at the top of Mount Fuji, often behave with abandon and a raucous disregard for everyone else around. But take those same Japanese people to the company assembly hall at the start of a day's work, or to any gathering where their duty has called them, and they will conform like gold. They will stand silently for hours, and stay as long as their presence is required, very likely without fidgeting or complaint – the outcome of the long years of training that begin at school.

The second and related pattern of behaviour, which is as distinctively Japanese as paper *shoji* screens or *sushi*, is the consciousness of belonging to groups or circles that carry onerous membership duties but also support the individual and help to form his identity. In practice most individuals 'belong' to a number of overlapping circles, each of them functioning like an exclusive members-only club. The circles which the average middle-aged Japanese male belongs to are his family, his company, the alumni (old boy) associations of the schools he has attended, and perhaps a sports club or similar. He will treat several of these entities with a close to religious devotion when called for. His family is only one part of this; the others may well be the more emotionally taxing and strenuous. For working people the company is the paramount place of belonging: hence when Japanese people greet one another they normally introduce themselves not by their given and family names, but by their company's name and their own surname only. An exchange of name-cards helps to fix the exact relationship between the two parties in the minds of both. Juniors refer to their bosses not by their names but by their ranks – *kacho* or *shacho*. Personal colour is downplayed even in the framework of the family: a wife, speaking to anyone who has a business connection with her husband, will often refer to him in the third person by the family name rather than as 'my husband', or still less by his personal name.

Individuals behave with strict decorum inside any one of their own circles, whether it be as an employee, a member of a local parents' and teachers' association, or something else. But they show little interest in, or sense of responsibility for, what lies outside that sphere. Towards wider social and public issues there flourishes an attitude of what a Japanese critic called 'educated unconcern'. The attitudes of the Japanese to public issues were apparent from government-commissioned opinion polls published in the 1980s. They found that Japanese people cared less about ethical standards among their public figures than people in other countries where the poll was carried out. Ordinary Japanese were less willing than people in any of the other countries to risk their own safety to prevent a crime or injustice being done to someone not personally known to them.

This portrait of an individual's world view has its parallel in society as a whole. In every area of human activity in Japan the status quo is made and defended by various overt interest groups which the Japanese identify as *batsu*. These can be described as clubs, guilds or hierarchies of people linked by a common and exclusive interest. They guard their territory, literally and figuratively, with jealousy, co-ordinating but also often slowing down or preventing real social change.

In politics, the main units of power are the *habatsu*, the factions. Junior politicians in the party of government, the LDP, have no other way of rising in the hierarchy than joining and following the rules of one or other of the factions. Other professions are similarly arranged; the military used to be described as the *gunbatsu*, military faction, but things military have been deeply out of fashion since the Pacific War. The *gakubatsu* or academic faction does exist, however. In universities and schools microcosms of it permeate common rooms: indeed every teacher or university lecturer of any standing will found his or her own following. Prominent families, whether of the old disbanded nobility or the new rich, are known as *keibatsu*: the term is used to imply a family dynasty.

In business, the pre-war *zaibatsu* have transformed themselves into new cliques, the *keiretsu*, and still ensure that business decisions by and about major public companies are taken in secret. In government the power of officials is called *kanbatsu*. Civil servants are normally hired by one particular ministry where they stay all their lives, fighting for its interests against all the other government departments. The system of *amakudari* reinforces the neo-feudal web of control by the ministry or regulating agency over that sector.

In journalism, each separate area of public affairs is covered by a *kisha* club, a reporters' club, which is exclusive to a certain number of companies and which formally organises press conferences. Altogether there are several thousand of these exclusive organisations around the country, attached to town halls, business federations and central government ministries. Other journalists, even from the same news organisation, are strictly unwelcome. The rule is: members only. They function like news cartels, sifting and setting the value of public information. They make Japan in effect an 'anti-news society' – since news is almost by definition concerned with conflicts of some kind, and in Japan those are ironed out or overlooked as much as possible. To ask the clubs to be neutral is unrealistic, as each feeds off a particular source of news with a direct interest in the contents of the reporting. Japanese journalists are close to the wheels of power and corrupted by the vapour they breathe there. The editorial line of the major news organisations is studiedly non-controversial: in a society where the ideal is to be the same as other people, the tutored news media hug the middle ground. Only the communist paper, *Akahata*, and the scandal sheets differ from the rule.

The upshot of Japan's two traditions, as outlined, operating side by side, is that Japan is peopled by a race of men and women who are bound by their culture to show respect, but who are at the same time bound by powerful bonds to give their loyalty to a number of restricted groups or circles, and not to betray that loyalty to outsiders. The concept of the public good in this scheme of thing is not well developed and often comes off a poor second to group interests.

The head-on clash of priorities – between public façade and private interest, which may be irreconcilable – gives Japanese everyday life a special timbre of solemnity mixed occasionally with the absurd. In a society where only sincerity will be tolerated, the inevitable result, as perceived from outside, is hypocrisy. Conflict is often not recognised as such: frequent critical outbursts against Japan by Western political and business leaders have met with an assiduous but serene attitude in Japan which has often perplexed those on the other side. When confrontation is obvious, as in the unions' annual *shunto* (spring wage offensive), it is made into a ritual with little real social disruption.

The Japanese language has two often-used terms to describe these

233

conflicting realities: the ideal or *tatemae,* and the actual state of things, *honne.* The constant interaction between these two makes up the major play of Japanese politics and public affairs. The *tatemae* is that Japan's political rulers are assiduously concerned with justice, wisdom and the rule of law: hence the regular policy speeches by prime ministers in the Diet are always filled with ringing phrases about the national welfare and achieving a rich cultural life. Yet the practice (*honne*) is that Japanese politics can move according to the crude inducements of money and the needs of entrenched power interests.

It is customary for Japanese politicians to act as the arbiters of conflicting interest groups within the society. They attach themselves to a sectoral interest group, such as the rice lobby or the tele-communications business lobby, becoming in the jargon a member of that particulat *zoku,* or 'tribe'. They will sit on the LDP committee handling that sector, and if possible the relevant parliamentary committees as well, building up the confidence of the lobby people as their influence over policy decisions grows. As a matter of course, the business firms and associations in that sector then sponsor the individual Dietman with financial contributions which may amount to tens of thousands of dollars. Often the *zoku* Diet members behave quite openly as advocates of that special-interest group during trade disputes.

Japanese national politicians in effect take the place of lawyers in the West, mediating to settle disputes and ending up the richer for it. They are expected to use their influence on ministries to get permission for local companies in their constituency to proceed with projects; they must appear frequently at weddings, funerals and the like as a great patron of the community. This is a costly business. The leading and very colourful LDP politician, Michio Watanabe, in a speech in 1988, estimated that Dietmen of his party are expected to attend hundreds of such events each year, or to send representatives in their place; and at each function they should contribute an average of 10 000 yen – making a yearly total of millions of yen. He added, only half in jest, that politicians like himself are so busy with such activities that they must travel around with 'a white tie in one pocket [for weddings] and a black tie in the other [for funerals]'.

The stress on respect towards existing authorities and against conflict leads to disagreeable and controversial subjects often being simply ignored: no mention is ever made in ministerial policy speeches, for instance, of the grievances of Japan's ethnic minorities – totalling about 3 million people – including Koreans and *burakumin,* former outcastes. Such problems are too embarrassing to raise publicly, so they are left unmentioned and unattended; but discrimination of

234

various kinds is deeply entrenched. When any Japanese gets married, his family as a matter of course will employ an agency to ascertain if the intended spouse has origins with any of the minorities: if so, the marriage is usually called off. In business, too, books listing *burakumin* and Korean family registers have often been circulated among employers to help them to intercept any applicant trying to 'pass' as an ordinary Japanese.

Lacking any agreed neutral figure to hold the ring, the nation's powerful politicians have been allowed to enrich themselves and effectively to create family dynasties: about one-third of all Diet members in the powerful Lower House, the House of Representatives, are sons or close relatives of Diet members. The government has failed to act to remove severe distortions in the electoral system, whereby for over a decade there has been an inequality of more than one to three in the number of voters per Diet seat in some country constituencies (which tend to support the LDP because of farm subsidies) and those in new suburban areas, where the opposition has a stronger following. Voters have challenged this inequality from time to time, but have been given no redress against the self-interested and supposedly self-regulating politicians.

Diet members stand or fall simply by the vigour and size of their numerous *koenkai*, support organisations, which receive favours from their Dietmen in exchange for large and often undeclared supplies of cash. Business in the national Diet is as a rule preordained, down to the amount of time to be given to every individual speaker from each party, and often even the questions to be asked. Privately, politicians and bureaucrats freely admit that this represents a charade. Free-ranging debates, in which any member can catch the Speaker's eye and speak his mind, simply do not take place. More fundamentally, dissimulation is built in to the fabric of Japan's foreign and defence relations, with a constitution that for historical reasons bans the maintenance of armed forces – the *tatemae* – while the *honne*, reality, is that Japan's conventional army and navy are the third most costly in the world. Such contradictions are allowed to remain because the Japanese have not developed the skill of resolving disputes through their parliamentary system, preferring the behind-the-scenes deal and public fudge.

Leading business firms enjoy a privileged place in the interlocking power balance. They have always been sheltered from any legal requirement to publish vital statistics on their business results; but they complain at having to pay a rate of corporate tax of 50 per cent, higher than that in other leading world economies. In stock dealing, the insider-trading laws were without any statutory penalty at all until

1989, when international pressure forced a tightening of Japanese procedures; even so, a common view among Western bankers and stockbrokers in Tokyo is that deals which would be classed as patently illegal in New York or London are not even investigated in Tokyo.

Japan is still recognisably a society in which obligations easily outweigh rights in the individual's life. Convention, rather than the letter of the law, commonly governs personal behaviour and the way that society's rules are upheld. Resort by citizens to the law is actively discouraged: the state-regulated supply of professional lawyers is quite inadequate to meet the demand, and with court hearings often spaced out at intervals of several months, cases frequently drag on for years without resolution. There are no juries, and under Japan's French-inspired legal system 99 per cent of criminal cases that come to trial result in guilty verdicts from the judges. The verdicts depend heavily on confessions by the accused which human-rights groups constantly challenge, charging that they are forced. Defendants are routinely denied access to a lawyer. In the penal system great stress is laid, as Confucian thinking dictates, on moral rehabilitation, and it is relatively successful in preventing second offences. Recorded levels of serious crime are low, with fewer murders, rapes and thefts per thousand people than a cross-section of other nations in the West and Asia.

It is a tribute to the strengths of Japan's indigenous heritage that in many respects it did not capitulate to the alternative model of society introduced after defeat in the Second World War. The American-dominated Occupation, although it challenged much of the existing society, could not invent a tradition of liberal values and transfer it to Japan like shiploads of grain. Japan's current leaders want to preserve the national heritage, but they also want the nation to have the benefits of the more open and consumer-oriented societies of the West. Former Prime Minister Nakasone preached the new gospel of 'internationalisation' and his successors have espoused the same goal, at least in public. Japan was forcibly opened to the West in the mid-nineteenth century after America sent its 'black ships'; today, as Nakasone said, is the moment for 'a second opening up of Japan'.

8

Japan's World

UTOPIANS AND REALISTS

Japan has the largest balance of payments surplus the world has ever known.... Today, Japan is the second largest donor of overseas aid. It is in the top ten in the world for defence spending. And it is competing with the UK to be the largest net creditor in the world.

The words were those of the British Foreign Secretary Sir Geoffrey Howe in a speech at the Japan National Press Club in Tokyo in January 1988. Within a very short time that assessment of Japanese influence and power was out of date: later that year Japan overtook the UK in terms of its cumulative outstanding assets worldwide, and in 1989 it outstripped the USA to become the largest giver of official development aid, with a budget of around $9 billion. Japan's spending on conventional arms also exceeded Britain's, to stand third in the world league table behind the two superpowers. Japan had taken over as 'banker to the world'. Well might Britain suggest to Japan that a 'partnership' was in the two nations' common interest. Already Ronald Reagan, a Californian well attuned to the idea of a 'Pacific century', had displayed a new set of priorities which included Japan. Each year Japanese investors have bought a large share of US Treasury bonds in successive auctions, taking up more than one-third of the US government debt. America has little choice but to get on with Japan.

At the historic superpower summit in Malta in November 1989, when President George Bush and President Mikhail Gorbachev declared the Cold War 'over', Japan was as passive as it had been when it began, but the end of the 'post-war era' signalled the start of a new age in which Japan is already playing a more independent and active role in world affairs. It is one of the countries that has reaped great

237

advantage from the post-war 'world order'. American scholar Chalmers Johnson put it like this:

> The Cold War is over and Japan has won – that is, the US and the USSR have been at war with each other ideologically, and in terms of all sorts of competition the Japanese have blind-sided both of us.... the USSR succumbed to 'imperial overstretch' – to use Paul Kennedy's term. In forcing them into imperial overstretch we became the world's largest debtor nation, and today Japan is financing that. And they may well turn out to be the financiers of Eastern Europe as well.

As the process of working out a new world order begins, Japan is shackled by neither the fear of colonisation nor the fear of nuclear destruction. Its stand at the Houston economic summit in July 1990 was a clear sign of its resolve to advance its national interests in a way that it never could while the superpower confrontation dominated talk at the summit table. The Prime Minister, Toshiki Kaifu, persuaded the other summit nations that the end of the Cold War must be carried into Asia too. As one element of that, he succeeded in getting the West's collective support for Japan over the disputed 'northern islands', occupied by the Soviet Union in 1945, included in the summit's final communiqué. Japan also stood out against giving development aid to Moscow until the islands are handed back. That alone, for Japan, would represent the undoing of what he called 'the legacy of Soviet Stalinist expansionism' and an end to the Cold War in Asia.

At the same time Kaifu was determined to consolidate his country's special relationship with China. He announced that Japan would end the economic sanctions that it, like the other summit nations, imposed after the bloody suppression of China's pro-democracy movement in the summer of 1989. Japan did not wait for a consensus among the whole summit group, but went ahead on its own initiative to unfreeze its package of official development loans, worth 810 billion yen – about $5.5 billion. Japan in effect broke ranks with the other summit nations on aid for China for powerful reasons of national interest, just as West Germany did over the question of giving aid to the Soviet Union.

Those moves were symbolic of the emerging new world order: in the words of the Japanese Foreign Ministry spokesman Taizo Watanabe, 'The summit members were under no external pressure to act; there was no ideological or military conflict with others, so they could focus on the adjustment of policies between themselves and on global issues.' Watanabe, with the reserve that still characterises Japanese foreign-policy pronouncements, described the inclusion of Japan's views on China and the Soviet Union in the final communiqué as 'not a victory, but a sign of the increasing understanding of the others about Japan's concerns'; and he added: 'We are going to have more of this in future.' The inference is clear: now that the superpowers are turning their nuclear missiles into scrap, the strategic reason for Japan's political subordination to the USA is fading.

Japan's economy is twice the size of that of even the new, unified Germany, and its economic dominance in Asia is correspondingly greater than that of Germany in Europe. The Nomura Research Institute – attached to Nomura Securities, Japan's leading stockbroking firm – reckons that by the year 2010 the country's GNP will be larger even than that of the USA. And Japan's geographical position, at the edge of the Asian landmass and far removed from the world's other leading economies, gives it a clear advantage in maintaining and developing its hold over the region of the world with the fastest-growing economy. Even excluding China, India and the Soviet Far East, the Asia–Pacific is a region of 600 million people with vast natural resources, and Japan has become the motor that drives it.

Japan, with its population of 123 million, is a superpower of a new kind, defined not by military strength but by its industrial, financial and technological leadership, and by its national self-confidence. It is a modern superpower, whose impact is being felt in every corner of the world. Like France's *mission civilisatrice* in its colonial age, Japan's present 'empire' is held together by language, culture and social mould.

By the late 1980s Japan had accumulated the greatest financial empire the world has ever seen. The nation's worldwide assets stood in 1989 at $350 billion. The USA, meanwhile, had built up the largest debt of any nation: $650 billion. The world's top ten banks were all Japanese. Between 1984 to 1989 the Nikkei Stock Index grew by almost four times in value, from 10 000 yen to over 38 000 yen, making the Tokyo market the most valuable in the world, bigger than Wall Street. The Nippon Telegraph and Telephone Corporation (NTT) was by a large margin the world's most valuable company: when its stock price was at its peak, the company alone was in theory worth as much as the whole of West Germany. Land values in central Tokyo went up over the same period by about two and a half times, and as a result it was calculated that on paper the 300 acres of the Imperial Palace were worth more than all the land in the American state of California. By the same token, the total land area of Japan was technically worth four times more than all the land in the USA. The figures are logically absurd, but the money power which they give to their Japanese owners is real enough.

In Japan foreign-exchange controls were lifted only in 1980, but in the latter half of the decade the outflow of capital from Japan was the biggest tide of investment in history. It surpassed even that of the USA to Europe in the years of the Marshall Plan. Japanese net purchases of foreign stocks and bonds in the five years from 1985 to 1989 totalled $433 billion, more than the annual economic output of Spain. Direct investment, including that in factories overseas, rose from a yearly total of $6 billion in 1985 to $45 billion in 1989 – more than the comparable figure for any other nation in that year. The rate of growth was still increasing as the 1990s began.

The acquisitions included more and more high-profile companies and properties: the Intercontinental Hotel Group, a quarter of all the banks in California, prestige golf courses such as Turnberry in Scotland, Bracken House (then headquarters of the *Financial Times*) in the City of London, as well as Bush House, containing the offices of the BBC World Service. A Japanese collector paid a new world record when he bought Van Gogh's *Portrait of Dr Gachet* for $82.5 million in a New York auction room in 1990. Two of the greatest prizes for corporate Japan were when Sony bought Columbia Pictures, and Mitsubishi Real Estate, which owns about a quarter of all the land in Tokyo's Marunouchi business district, acquired a controlling interest in the Rockefeller Center in New York. Pontiac car dealers in New York capitalised on the backlash against the Rockefeller Center deal by running commercials that said, 'It's December, and the whole family's going to see the big Christmas Tree at Hirohito Center,' adding, 'Go on: keep buying Japanese cars.'

The first wave of Japanese overseas direct investment was for straightforward manufacturing. But in the last few years there has been a surge in investments aimed at achieving the long-term goals of Japanese firms by moving into tie-ups with strategic purposes. The Mitsubishi group agreed with West Germany's Daimler-Benz to seek a partnership in making and selling cars and aircraft parts. The computer firm Fujitsu, having taken over Amdahl of the USA and built many semiconductor plants in its overseas markets, took over the British firm ICL, a leading force in software and computer architectures. Sony's purchase of Columbia Pictures was strategic: without the discs, tapes and films to show on its hardware – its CD players, video- and audio-tape players and high-definition systems – Sony might not be able to expand its market share in the audio and video business. By acquiring Columbia Pictures, Sony acquired a rich library of audio and video software of its own. There was hostility. 'Sony invades Hollywood' to gobble up 'a piece of America's soul', screamed *Newsweek* on 9 October 1989. Ironically, in that case as with every one of the high-profile Japanese takeovers, it was the Americans who courted Japanese money and management skill, not the other way around.

Behind the Japanese financial superpower is a formidable and well-oiled machine of human organisation and endeavour. The Japanese real economy was robust for most of the 1980s, growing by an average of 4 per cent a year throughout the decade, and roughly doubling in size between 1973 and 1989. Corporate investment was high at 16.1 per cent. In 1987 the Japanese trade surplus reached an all-time peak of $96.386 billion, and in 1988 stayed at $95 billion (a figure larger than the annual GNP of Thailand) before subsiding to $76.917 billion the next year. Japanese income per head had reached $23 190 by 1988, overtaking America and the wealthiest EC nation, West Germany. The surplus underpinned the long-term trend of the yen's strength against other major currencies, in spite of some backtracking in 1988 and 1989.

Japan's manufacturing empire is colossal, and as the 1990s begins it is growing still wider and more sophisticated. The Japanese make approximately one-third of all the world's cars, steel and ships; two-thirds of all the computer chips and consumer electronics products; and more than half the robots and machine tools installed in the world's factories. Japanese firms making facsimile machines turn out more than 100 new models every year. Car firms are preparing for the day, within the next decade, when the customer will be able to choose the exact specifications of the vehicle he wants to drive and it will be custom-made for him in the factory within days. Japanese firms are investing vigorously in the industries of the twenty-first century: biotechnology, new materials, nuclear power, aerospace and computers. Japan's obsession with making things, and with perfecting the systems that control their making, has not faded even with the ample achievement of the goals that government and business jointly set themselves in the early post-war years. The targets have expanded to include – among many others – computer software, very high-quality synthetic fibres, high-speed mag-lev trains (which float above the tracks propelled by superconducting magnets), lasers for micro-surgery, and organic forms of machine memory. Japan has long sought to be an independent force in space research. Its domestically developed HII heavy payload rocket is due to come into service in the mid-1990s, and Japan plans to have its own space shuttle commuting to its own space station by the year 2020.

Japan's industrial power, like its trade, is rapidly becoming global. Already 5 per cent of all its manufacturing is done in countries outside Japan, and the Nomura Research Institute estimates that by 2010 this will rise to 20 per cent. By then Japanese factories in the USA are likely to be making 2 million cars a year, one-fifth of America's whole output. Japan now controls 40 per cent of Thailand's manufactured exports. By contrast, total foreign investments in Japan account for only 1 per cent of the country's economy, 3 per cent of its retail banking and less than 10 per cent of all stock transactions. As of 1990, 5 million people of Japanese nationality or descent are living abroad, many of them helping to support Japan's business interests.

Japan has become the model for many developing countries. Since the early 1980s Malaysia has pursued a 'Look East' policy of copying Japanese methods of production and management. Each year delegations from up to eighty less-developed countries visit Japan asking for aid funds and loans for infrastructure and industrial projects, and for expertise to see them to fruition. President Alberto Fujimori of Peru, after his election in 1990, used the fact of his Japanese ancestry to attract fresh investment from Japan to his adopted country. Fujimori is the first person of Japanese descent to become the elected leader of another nation. Across the Pacific, Europe and the Americas, quality-control engineers from Japanese manufacturing firms and department-store chains are stationed or make regular tours of inspection to ensure that production standards are maintained. In the UK, as elsewhere, one impact of the arrival of the three largest Japanese car companies as local manufacturers has been to raise the quality of components in the industry as a whole. Nissan is now leading British component-makers to enter the more value-added area of designing as well as manufacturing.

Japan's fabulous wealth rests, therefore, on the foundation of a stable, productive, growing economy. There is, nevertheless, an element of make-believe about it. The valuations of Tokyo stock prices – the ratio of each share's face value to its actual earnings – had by 1989 reached around fifty. That was five times higher than those in London or New York. Such ratios were possible because of the expectation of a substantial rise in capital values, an expectation amply fulfilled every year during the 1980s. It was also encouraged by the stable monetary environment: with the Bank of Japan controlling interest rates, companies could borrow long with little fear of having to repay their debts in a hurry. The official discount rate – charged by the Bank of Japan to commercial banks – stayed at an all-time low of 2.5 per cent between 1987 and the spring of 1989. The stable system of cross-holding of stocks among friendly Japanese companies gave them a guarantee against hostile takeover attempts. The result was greatly inflated asset prices and a surfeit of 'hot money' with no obvious outlet. Investment in productive activity, such as construction and manufacturing, reached its limit in 1989. The exaggerated stock prices and excess capital led to two related shocks to Japan within a single year: one threatened the foundations of the financial system, the other Japan's corrupt political structure.

Although Japan took only four months to recover fully from the stock-market crises that affected the rest of the world in 1987 and 1989, in 1990 things were different. A particularly Japanese set of problems led to the equivalent of a nervous breakdown in Japan's stock and bond markets which lasted for months and left the patient wary and chastened. In late 1989 stock prices had spiralled beyond reasonable limits to a record of 38 915, 30.9 per cent up in a single year. Price-earnings ratios had reached dizzying new levels, in some cases as high as one hundred. Shares in the colossus, NTT, slumped to half of their peak value, and the government was forced to delay the planned sell-off of its remaining stake in the company. The biggest worry of all was the thought that Japan's wildly inflated land prices, the foundation of many companies' overall asset values, might go through the floor. The money supply had climbed well above 10 per cent, bringing the certainty of higher inflation.

The yen was depressed, largely because Japanese interest rates were much lower than those in the USA and Europe. Ironically, that was owing partly to Japan's fulfilment of its agreed role in co-ordinating exchange rates among the Group of Seven nations in order to support the dollar and the USA's economic recovery. At a time of increasing competition for credit, as Eastern Europe broke free from its socialist past and the newer economies of South-east Asia continued to expand, the Japanese authorities had been too slow in recognising the necessity of raising rates. Japan was exposed. In the first two months of 1990 bond prices tumbled and long-term yields rose from 5.72 to 7 per cent.

For days the news was black. In a few weeks in February and March 1990 the Nikkei stock average fell by 25 per cent of its value. Trading was extremely thin, but the slide went on as very few investors were prepared to step in and buy. The resulting book losses represented more than the entire value of the London Stock Exchange. The familiar soothing sounds from the Finance Ministry and the Big Four brokerage firms, which together control the bulk of the trades on the market, all failed to halt the descent. Only during April, with company profits and the whole economy still showing healthy growth, did investors begin gently to dip their toes back in again; but the 'triple merits' which had buoyed up the market – a strong yen, cheap oil, low inflation – were now conspicuously absent.

□   □   □

On 5 September 1988 millions of Japanese people watching the evening television news saw a scene that stood out as an allegory of Japan's money-soaked society: a national politician and a businessman were discussing the appropriate size of a bribe which one of them was offering to buy the other's silence. The setting was the office of an opposition Dietman, Yanosuke Narazaki, a member of the United Social Democratic Federation, a small splinter group. The meeting had taken place three days earlier. Unbeknown to his visitor, Narazaki had invited a TV company, the commercial Nippon Television Network, to record the scene with a concealed camera.

The video recording showed Hiroshi Matsubara, an executive of the rising real-estate firm Recruit Cosmos, calling at the politician's office. His aim was to persuade Narazaki to stop asking awkward questions in the Diet, as they were proving deeply embarrassing to both the company and the government. At a meeting the previous month, Matsubara had offered Narazaki 5 million yen ($30 000) in cash. Now after the preliminary courtesies, the visitor said, 'About the envelope I brought you the other day: I did not mean to offer you money. It is just a token souvenir.' 'How much am I worth?' Narazaki demanded. 'I understand that politicians cost a lot of money,' came the reply. 'I'd like to offer you a suitable amount, but it would be rude of me to mention the figure in front of you. I just ask for your help.'

Narazaki refused all the offers of cash, and after his visitor had gone he resolved to bring a charge of attempted bribery against Matsubara and his company. Nippon Television Network got a scoop. The 'Recruit scandal' had begun in earnest.

The outlines of the affair could already be dimly made out from press coverage and allegations in the Diet. The Recruit group, a leading force in publishing, telecommunications and land development, was trying to join the ranks of the top *keiretsu*. Its founder and chairman, Hiromasa Ezoe, sought to build up a network of friends in high places in order to get ahead in the company's various business fields. In Japan important administrative decisions – such as granting building permission on prime urban sites – are often taken at the discretion of politicians and bureaucrats. The company had donated hundreds of millions of yen directly to politicians in lawful ways, by bank transfers and by depositing money at lavish political fund-raising parties. But Ezoe had decided to go much further, using the stock market as a means to launder vast sums of cash into the hands of influential people.

Before his subsidiary property company, Recruit Cosmos, was officially listed on the Tokyo Stock Exchange, Ezoe's staff had distributed shares with a low face value to at least seventy-six chosen individuals. After the official listing in October 1986, the shares' value soared by four times and the stockholders each stood to reap profits of tens, or in some cases hundreds, of thousands of dollars. Such methods are common in Japan among firms launching themselves as public companies, and the law does not forbid them; but the ambitious scale of Recruit's apparent attempt to buy influence beggared all previous cases. Many of the privileged Recruit Cosmos stockholders had been offered interest-free loans from another Recruit affiliate so they did not even have to put up their own money for the deal. In the Diet Narazaki demanded that the government reveal the full list of Recruit Cosmos stockholders; his call was adamantly refused. Recruit had overstepped the legal limit of fifty individual stockholders – in itself not an offence serious enough to lead to criminal charges. Some public figures were alleging, however, that the share deals represented the most systematic attempt ever made by a business group in Japan to bribe Cabinet ministers, legislators and others.

The seeds of the Recruit scandal were in the behind-the-scenes political money-gathering which reached a crescendo during 1986. In that year all the political parties were gearing up for an election, and the LDP faction leaders were trying to expand their power bases in anticipation of an expensive intra-party race when Yasuhiro Nakasone left office. Politicians were collecting funds both directly from businesses and indirectly through their many supporters' organisations.

Recruit was the country's leading publisher of job-placement magazines – a business made possible by a gentleman's agreement among Japanese firms not to begin contacting prospective recruits from the universities until August each year. Recruit's publications, which gave details of the leading companies, were essential reading for many of the 1.5 million graduates and the more than 2 million school-leavers looking for employment.

Recruit also earned large profits from its flourishing tele-communications business. This lucrative field was in the process of being deregulated, but little could be done without powerful government friends. It was also at the centre of the US–Japan disputes over trade. A decisive moment for the firm's fortunes came in 1986 when Japan came under pressure from the Reagan administration to redress the trade imbalance quickly. Prime Minister Nakasone responded by announcing that the government would buy two Cray supercomputers, helping to trim Japan's surplus at a stroke. The supercomputers, it was later disclosed, were re-sold to Recruit and installed by the publicly owned NTT in its own switching centre. Recruit was awarded the right to sublease NTT data circuits to business clients.

The Narazaki video tape prompted a formal inquiry by the public prosecutors. In October they raided Recruit's offices and those of

NTT. Cabinet members were faced with public pressure to declare their Recruit Cosmos share dealings, as well as donations received from the Recruit company. It quickly became apparent that most of the members of the Nakasone Cabinet had directly or indirectly profited from the share dealings, while most of the members of the current Cabinet, including the Prime Minister Noboru Takeshita himself, had received significant money contributions from the company, while its property, communications and magazine empires each grew rapidly.

Press articles openly speculated that Nakasone would be the main target of the eventual prosecution indictments. The first major political casualty, though, was Kiichi Miyazawa, who as Finance Minister was responsible for plans then being drawn up to tighten the rules on insider trading. In November 1988 it came to light that his name was on the list of those who had dealt in Recruit Cosmos shares in their own name, and he promptly resigned from the Cabinet. A socialist Dietman linked to the scandal also resigned his seat, and the chairmen of two other opposition parties, the Komei and the Democratic Socialist Parties, in turn resigned their titles.

In February 1989 the indictments began. The first to be arrested were Hiromasa Ezoe himself and three other members of the Recruit management, followed by Nakasone's former right-hand man in government, Takao Fujinami. Also charged were Katsuya Ikeda, a Diet member of the opposition Komei Party, and the bureaucrats in overall charge of policy in the Ministries of Education and Labour. One of Japan's foremost captains of industry, Hisashi Shinto, formerly president of IHI Shipbuilding and since 1985 the chairman of NTT, was accused of accepting Recruit Cosmos shares as a bribe for selling Recruit its privileged data lines. All but one of the defendants, a section chief in the Labour Ministry, denied the charges.

By April 1989 the Takeshita Cabinet's public support rate was down to a mere 4 per cent – the lowest figure recorded since such polls began after the war. The final straw came when Takeshita himself, after declaring categorically that his office had received no valuables from Recruit other than the unlisted shares his secretaries had between them, was forced to acknowledge that he had in fact received 151 million yen ($1.2 million) in political donations as well. On 25 April he announced that he would resign as soon as a successor could be chosen and the annual government budget bill passed through the Diet. He apologised to the Japanese public for allowing the country's parliamentary politics to fall into disrepute through the revelations of the Recruit affair, but sought to shuffle the substantial blame off on to his associates: 'I would like to express my profound apologies for the increasing public distrust in politics which arose from problems concerning my assistants. To restore the public's trust in the government, I have decided to step down.' The next day one of his secretaries, who had taken receipt of a $300 000 loan from Recruit, hanged himself.

There followed a delicate tug-of-war between the prosecutors' office and the political barons who are accustomed to running Japan without disagreeable questions being asked. The formal end of the investigation came on 29 May 1989. The only Diet members who were charged were Takao Fujinami and Katsuya Ikeda. Eleven other national politicians known to have profited from dealing in recruit shares escaped action in the courts. The sense of national anti-climax was palpable. An editorial in the *Asahi Shimbun* commented: 'The outcome of the investigation was far from what the people had expected, which was the exposure of the most influential and corrupt elements of the political world.'

The public had waited with keen interest to see whether or not former Prime Minister Nakasone would be indicted. He was not. But he was obliged to appear in the Diet to answer questions about his own role in the Recruit affair. The focus of the suspicion was that Nakasone had himelf master-minded the plan to favour Recruit with government licences and supercomputers at knockdown prices. Nakasone testified before his peers, and he got the better of the ill-prepared opposition questioners, insisting that he had done 'nothing wrong'. However, he did forfeit much of his political reputation. In a customary act of atonement for disturbing the harmony of his group, Nakasone resigned first from his own faction and then from the Liberal Democratic Party.

The LDP as a whole was also now required to put on a show of atonement: public opinion demanded it. But all the traditions of the party were against an open election in which a genuinely reform-minded leader might come forward and cleanse its now sullied name. Instead, the power-brokers of the LDP began a search with this contradictory aim: to find 'one honest man' in their midst who could convince the electorate that the party meant to reform itself, yet who would not disturb its power structure. Above all, he must not launch into sudden reforms which could undermine the party's ability to win elections by superior wealth and patronage.

A reform-minded party elder, Masayoshi Ito, aged 64, was pressed to take over as leader. He let it be known that his preconditions were that the party must adopt a sweeping set of reforms. However, in line with the LDP's habit of keeping the most important political decisions completely secret, Ito did not spell out his views in public. Instead they were widely reported through the traditional, ambiguous *kisha* club system of news-gathering. Japan's political journalists spoke with the cabal of top politicians in private and in print hinted at Ito's requirements. They included the resignation from the Diet of all LDP members who had profited from Recruit share dealing, the dissolution of the party factions and the appointment of a younger generation of party members to the top jobs. This medicine was too strong for the LDP bosses to swallow, and Ito formally announced that he was no longer in the running. To save everyone's face, it was suggested that poor health was his reason. Throughout this process, Japan's influential media hedged their bets: they almost uniformly kept up a homily in favour of 'reform' without daring to insist that Ito's presumed reforms must actually be carried out.

The LDP's compromise was to let Ito announce a one-year ban on Recruit-tainted politicians holding Cabinet or senior party posts; then the search for a new leader was resumed. The man eventually chosen was Sosuke Uno, a former MITI and Foreign Minister, who happened to be a member of the Nakasone faction. He was regarded as a competent minister, but he was no one's first choice, and the appointment aroused some dissent within the ranks of the party.

In May 1989 a salacious sex scandal engulfed the new Prime Minister. A former *geisha* (female entertainer) appeared in a television interview saying that twenty years earlier Sousuke Uno had kept her as his mistress. The woman added spice to the story by describing him as arrogant and – to the Japanese public even more damaging – meanminded: she claimed to have been paid a low rate. Uno made no public reply, but he had his wife appear on stage at a meeting and declare her total support for her husband. It was rumoured that the scandal had been leaked by a faction within the LDP which had opposed the choice of Uno and wanted to discredit him.

It was a period of near-paralysis for the government both at home and abroad. Uno expressed his wish to resign before the economic summit meeting in Venice in June, but that was not practical. The mood of public disillusionment found an outlet in elections for the Upper House, the mainly advisory chamber of the Diet, in July. A populist woman politician, Takako Doi, had been elected leader of the Socialist Party in 1987. Before entering politics she had been a lecturer in constitutional law, and she reflected the growing public view that the ruling party had become incorrigibly complacent and corrupt. The strong feelings of many Japanese women over the Uno scandal were fuelled once again when the Minister of Agriculture made a speech deriding Takako Doi's leadership and saying that 'women are useless in the world of politics'. The Socialists chose more than thirty women as election candidates and made a meal of Uno's embarrassment. The LDP's campaign organisers, fearing a public humiliation, carefully ensured that Uno went through the whole fifteen-day campaign without once appearing in the street to give his election speeches.

The LDP's unpopularity was fuelled by its handling of the matter of tax reform: in December 1988 the Liberal Democrats used their crushing majority to ram through a new version of Nakasone's tax-revision plan – this time for a 3 per cent 'consumption tax'. The new tax had the support of the main business organisations, but opinion polls showed that the majority of the public was against it. Takako Doi used it to wound the government, and her party also stole the LDP's clothes over the key issue in the countryside: farm price support. The Socialists, judging rightly that they could upset the LDP's long-standing domination of the farm vote, took a strongly protectionist stand and attacked the government for selling out the farmers' interests under foreign pressure. They were rewarded with victory in twenty-three farming constituencies where the Liberal Democrats had been secure for a generation.

In the election the Socialists doubled their strength in the House of Councillors, winning 46 seats out of 126 being contested, compared to only 36 for the LDP. It was the first national election in which the Socialists had ever beaten the Liberal Democrats into second place. In the vote for candidates on the parties' proportional representation list, the so-called 'national constituency', the Socialists won 35 per cent of the popular vote compared to only 28 per cent for the LDP and 37 per cent for the various other parties. The LDP lost its overall majority in the House of Councillors for the first time, and was unable to find any opposition party willing to join a working coalition. The ruling party still controlled the Lower House, which has sole authority to pass important budget-related bills, but its loss of control in the Upper House meant that for the first time the opposition would play a formative part in the process of legislation.

The Upper House election defeat gave Uno the opportunity to resign, and he took it gratefully. Once again, the Liberal Democrats needed to find a politician untainted by Recruit who could lead the party out of danger. It appeared entirely possible that the opposition might win the next general election, due in 1990, unseating the LDP from government altogether. Frantic and jealous deliberations were resumed in closed-door sessions among the faction bosses and party elders. Shortly after they agreed on an outsider as their candidate: Toshiki Kaifu.

Kaifu, then aged fifty-eight, was from the minor faction headed by Toshio Komoto (formerly the Miki faction). He had served twice in the Cabinet, both times as Education Minister, and was relatively free of Recruit connections, having acknowledged receiving from the company only a relatively modest sum in contributions. Kaifu's lack of an independent power base was not a problem but a merit as far as the bosses were concerned: it would make it easier to displace him whenever they might judge the time was ripe.

Some of the more modern figures in the LDP demanded a vote, rather than simple acclamation of the new leader. Two rivals to Kaifu appeared from the party ranks: Yoshiro Hayashi, a former Health Minister, and Shintaro Ishihara, the former bestselling novelist, now a spokesman for the LDP's nationalist wing. For the first time in seventeen years the LDP decided the leadership with an open vote. At a stormy party caucus meeting several younger Diet members took the floor to berate the old-style bosses for 'ignoring democracy' and treating the LDP as their own private fiefdom. But Kaifu won with 279 votes against 120 for Hayashi and 48 for Ishihara. He pledged (as Uno had done before him) to make 'political reform' the top priority of his administration.

Toshiki Kaifu quickly established himself as a representative of a 'new generation' of politicans, struggling against reactionary forces in his party for more modern policies and methods. Two ambitious faction leaders who had been obliged to stand down from the leadership race, Shintaro Abe and Michio Watanabe, waited for their chance to supplant him. The new Prime Minister at once earned some public esteem, though, for his early decision to keep all those who had received Recruit shares out of his Cabinet. Almost immediately, another sex scandal dating back thirty years forced the resignation of Tokuo Yamashita, the sixty-nine-year-old Chief Cabinet Secretary. But Kaifu astutely replaced him with Mayumi Moriyama, a woman member of the Upper House who had worked in an official capacity on Japan's adoption of Equal Opportunities legislation some years earlier. She was a popular choice, and the appointment turned out to be the first in a series of shifts of fortune which robbed the opposition of their first real chance to gain power for more than forty years.

With general elections looming, the LDP, along with its allies in the business community and the press, encouraged the formation of a consensus that Japan should turn its back on the obsession with political scandals. In November 1989 the trials opened of fifteen people accused of giving or receiving bribes in the Recuit affair. The courts judged that bribery involving thousands of dollars was not serious enough to warrant imprisonment. Hiroshi Matsubara of Recruit, whose attempted bribery had been played back on TV, was the first to be found guilty; but he received only a suspended jail sentence. With so little follow-up either in the courts or in the Diet, public attention towards corruption in politics started to wane. A year after the Recruit case charges were brought, no one has had to serve a single day of a jail sentence over the affair. (The same was true of the Lockheed scandal more than a decade earlier.)

A Japanese proverb says that 'a nasty rumour lasts seventy-five days'. The public's attention span is not much longer and, except when forced by outside events, the pace of reforms is generally glacial. So it was with 'political reform'. During 1989 the only change in that area was a law forbidding politicans to send their representatives to weddings, funerals or other events to pass cash gifts to voters. First-hand contributions remained legal, and in the run-up to the general elections in February 1990 the LDP took full advantage of the lax laws on political funds which they themselves had failed to tighten in time to affect those elections.

The LDP owned to spending 30 billion yen ($200 million) in election funds; the Socialists spent less than a quarter of that. All the opposition parties suffered, as always, from a shortage of good candidates. Even so, they had a chance to upset the ruling party and they spoiled it. Takako Doi attracted the largest crowds, but she did not have the power to neutralise the Marxist-oriented mainstream group inside her own party. Despite a year of contacts with the other non-communist opposition parties, the Socialists failed to come up with a combined policy platform on which to fight the election. The other opposition groups were concerned that the Socialists had not clearly renounced their old ideas – especially that American troops should leave Japan and that the Self-Defence Forces should be scrapped. At a news conference in the last week before the poll a key figure in the opposition revealed his distaste for working with the Socialists and threw away any chance there might have been of bringing about an LDP defeat. Takashi Yonezawa, Secretary-General of the Democratic Socialist Party, said that if the combined opposition were to win the election and then try to form a coalition, the ensuing Cabinet 'would not last more than three days'.

The LDP won a landslide victory, with 290 seats out of 512, a majority of thirty-three (and seven other victorious candidates who ran as independents also took the party whip when the Diet reconvened). In the words of American political scientist Chalmers Johnson: 'The election of 1990 was won by old, vested interests – by the agricultural co-operatives, by the construction industry, by small retailers and by second-generation politicians.' Despite the months of upheaveal, the politics of patronage were still intact and the outlook for the promised 'political reform' was not bright.

The national fiasco of the Recruit affair has suggested to some Japanese that the country now needs a set of reforms as sweeping as the Great Reform Acts which ended the 'rotten boroughs' and widespread electoral abuses in England during the nineteenth century. The centenary of the Japanese parliament, in November 1990, became a target date for enacting a package of reforming laws; but partisan considerations by all the major parties stand in the way of agreement.

The opposition parties argue that the first reform must be to attack the root causes of corruption in politics: the power of patronage linking administrators and LDP politicians in a web of common benefits, and the lack of real limits on the flow of funds from business to politicians. The government wants to tackle all the major issues together, and has favoured replacing the present multi-member constituencies with single-member ones, perhaps in combination with a proportional-representation system. This proposal would end one recognised reason for abuses: the intense competition among candidates of the same party for seats within the same constituency. It should thus reduce the influence of the factions (each of which currently sponsors its own roster of candidates) and make elections less expensive. But among the opposition parties strong doubts exist. Some believe that such a system might easily lead to several more decades of dominance by the Liberal Democratic Party.

Public opinion polls in early 1990 showed that 27 per cent of Americans believe Japan is already 'the strongest economic power in the world today'; more than half think Japan's economic might is a greater threat to US security than Soviet military power; and nearly 45 per cent consider Japan the USA's least trustworthy ally. The statistics suggest that America's gradual loss of world economic leadership to Japan is a painful process. They are also evidence of Japan's failure to clarify the political dimension of its economic power. The Japanese have not made clear to the rest of the world *why they are doing it*.

Until the 1980s Japan's diplomacy was directed overwhelmingly at achieving narrow national goals. In particular, it wanted to create economic security for itself. In pursuit of that end it sometimes behaved like a blind man, stumbling into uncharted territory and offending against local conventions. Stories of the 'ugly Japanese' spread throughout Asia, as high-handed factory managers from Tokyo bossed whole communities in remote regions of Indonesia or Papua New Guinea. Japan was berated by Americans over oil deals with Iran, castigated for selling submarine-engine soundproofing equipment to the Soviet Union in violation of Cocom rules, described as 'a dangerous threat' by the French Trade Minister, and scolded by Margaret Thatcher for beating Britain to a plum contract to build a second Bosporus bridge with the help of a well-judged mixture of government aid and money from big business.

The race for the commanding heights in technology and industry has brought bruising collisions with the West, and there are sure to be more in future. Japan and the USA confronted one another over the question of Japan's choice of a new mainstay fighter aircraft for the Japanese Air Self-Defence Forces in the early twenty-first century. Hawks in the Pentagon were determined that Japan would buy in an American model, so allowing the USA to hold on to its technological lead in that branch of aerospace, and redressing the trade imbalance. Japan's heavy-industry chiefs, especially the leading military contractor, Mitsubishi Heavy Industries, were equally determined to design and build the new plane domestically. After three years of tense negotiations a compromise was reached in 1988 whereby the Japanese would incorporate the basic design of the General Dynamics' F16 but develop the engine and avionics themselves.

The contest is especially fierce in the field of advanced electronics and computing. In the 1980s Japanese manufacturers and NHK, the publicly funded Japan Broadcasting Corporation, sped ahead in developing their own system for high-definition television transmission. European firms, coming late to the area, applied political leverage on their governments to delay the setting of a universal technical standard, in order to protect their home markets. The Americans also resisted Japanese domination in this area: some American experts predicted that if Japan were able to set the standard for high-definition TV the result would be the loss of millions of American jobs and some $30 billion in revenue to US industry. It is one of several areas where the contest has reached bedrock, with Western nations determined that Japan must not be allowed to displace local high-technology industries as it did the West's motorcycle, camera and consumer electronics industries.

Still, technology waits for no one, and Japan's lead in computer hardware is propelling it to an ever more commanding position in world markets. Well over half of all the computers in use in the world have Japanese-made memory chips and central processors. In the summer of 1990 Hitachi unveiled its prototype of a single computer chip that holds 64 million 'bits' of memory, four times more than the products of its nearest rivals. In supercomputers, which are essential in scientific research and also have a host of industrial applications, four Japanese firms are each pressing hard to overtake the one remaining American manufacturer, Cray Research. In the past Japan has been dependent on other countries for much of the software in these machines, but MITI is supporting an intensive effort by leading national firms to make software superior to all others available, eliminating the need for imports in this area.

MITI's role in directing Japanese industry is less formative now than it was after the oil crisis or at the time of the VLSI programme in the late 1970s. But the single-minded pursuit of expanding market share in a wide range of high-technology products is as much in evidence as ever.

A small minority of influential Japanese have lately asserted that Japan should reject America's 'superior' attitudes and humiliate the USA with a display of superior technological and financial muscle. They include Shintaro Ishihara, the LDP politician, who in 1989 teamed up with the chairman of Sony, Akio Morita, to publish a collection of essays entitled *'No' to ieru Nihon* (*The Japan That Can Say No*). Ishihara openly accused Japan's American critics of racism, and claimed that the USA only resolved to drop the A-bombs on Hiroshima and Nagasaki in 1945 'because the Japanese belong to the yellow races'. But the majority of Japanese political and business leaders disagree with him. The senior politician Kiichi Miyazawa believes that 'The US and Japan have been sharing the same value system for a long time. In spite of all the international changes, no matter what changes take place, we should hold on to this very basic thing: sharing a common system of values with the USA.'

In many obvious ways, however, Japan does not share the common values of the West. It is a society which often places expedience over conscience, and social stability over the active exercise of individual rights. Japan denies most foreign workers the right to employment in Japan because of the disruption they may cause to its own carefully preserved social order. The number of Vietnamese refugees accepted into the country is limited to 5000 in total, while the USA alone takes hundreds of thousands. Japanese women are denied the chance to compete directly with men in most areas, and the whim of male officials denies them the choice of whether to use the contraceptive pill. Japanese men still normally expect to spend their evenings with male colleagues, not with their wives.

Yet Japan is today much better integrated into the value systems of other countries than it was a generation ago. This is a triumph for the post-war world. The government is sponsoring large-scale programmes to invite Asian students to Japan. Through regular meetings of a host of international organisations – from the Group of Seven on exchange rates to the World Health Organisation on eradicating cholera – Japan is closely involved in solving the world's problems of poverty, disease and debt. It has its share of fanatical nationalists and racketeers, but they do not threaten the welfare of other nations. Japan is working within the framework of the world's treaties and conventions, not seeking to break them down.

The country's ruling élite of politicians, administrators and businessmen has come to accept its special responsibility in trade matters. In 1990 Japanese and American officials sat down in Tokyo at the end of a year of talks (in the Strategic Impediments Initiative, on 'structural trade barriers') and Japan made a number of concessions. It agreed to strengthen the powers of its own Fair Trade Commission, which has been moribund for forty years. Already the government has undertaken to stop the custom of bid-rigging among its own firms for public-sector construction contracts, heeding the Americans' complaints. MITI has been investigating how collusion among Japan's big firms leads to higher prices in Japan for some Japanese products than for the same products in North America and Europe. Slowly, the helter-skelter pursuit of corporate wealth is giving way to other concerns. The Construction Ministry has adopted a plan for increasing the amount of park space per head in Tokyo from 6 to 10 square metres – more in line with the lifestyle in Western cities. The longstanding ban on all imports of rice for the dinner table is giving way.

Japan is slowly abandoning the pretence of uniqueness. Its new rules on insider trading began to be applied for the first time in 1988. Japanese banks are slowly shifting away from their voracious pursuit of larger 'market share' in favour of Western-style profits, as the rules on 'capital adequacy' devised by the Bank for International Settlements take effect. There is a long way to go. Sir Leon Brittan, the EC Commissioner for External Economic Affairs, listed three common Japanese business practices that would be illegal inside the EC: the forming of cartels among competing manufacturers to fix prices or share out markets; retail-price maintenance by producers; and 'captive' distribution networks, which discourage price competition. But a former MITI official, Taichi Sakaiya, is leading a campaign for the Japanese to understand that such talk, from Europeans or Americans, is not 'Japan-bashing': 'The US is not bothered to intervene in Japanese domestic policies,' he says, 'but simply demonstrates to Japan "the rules of their game".' If Japan does not accept, the former mandarin concludes, it will be the loser. 'Whether Japan changes itself to remain as an equal partner to Europe and America or not is entirely a choice by the Japanese.'

Japan, like Germany, has been released from its political shackles by the end of the Cold War. Like Germany, which opted to remain within NATO, Japan prefers to stay in the comfortable embrace of its alliance with America. The thirtieth anniversary of the present Mutual

Security Treaty, in June 1990, was marked by a statement from President George Bush and Prime Minister Toshiki Kaifu declaring that the treaty would be a basis for the two countries' relations 'in the decades ahead'. Four months earlier, the US Marine Commander in Okinawa had spoken out of turn in a newspaper interview with the *Washington Post*, saying that US troops should remain in Japan for at least a decade more for the main purpose of ensuring that Japan did not rearm too quickly; the Americans, he said would be 'the cap in the bottle'. Even this remark was allowed to pass without a fuss.

Will Japan build a new military empire? This seems improbable, since at present it has neither the motive nor the means to do so. How many divisions has Japan? The answer is 13. Japan now possesses 63 destroyers and frigates, about the same number as Britain, but far fewer than the Soviet Union nearby. It supports almost 250000 military personnel, 1 200 tanks, 15 submarines and over 360 combat aircraft. Japan has remade its wartime dream of an East Asia Co-Prosperity Sphere, but it is not poised to threaten the use of force against the rest of Asia. The Self-Defence Forces have trouble finding enough recruits. Japan, like the rest of Asia, is content to have the USA as the major military power in the area; Singapore's Prime Minister, Lee Kuan Yew, says, 'If America were to pull out suddenly there just isn't the balance that could take over and a big arms race would take place. And I think that's known in the region and known to America.' The Pentagon wishes now to see Japan play a more substantial 'burden-sharing' military role in conjunction with American units in the region. Influential Japanese policymakers agree: Takakazu Kuriyama, the Vice-Minister for Foreign Affairs, announced his country's foreign-policy goals for the 1990s: they are for Japan to erase the 'unfair' image spawned by its past behaviour, to achieve 'the foreign policy of a major power' and to support the international framework of peace and free trade. Japan, he says, accepts a position in the world which corresponds to its relative economic strength: that is, the formula of 5–5–3, where the USA and the EC are each five and Japan three. It is the same ratio as that devised in the Washington naval conferences of 1921–2, which many hawks in Imperial Japan resented as humiliating.

This manifesto is based firmly on the idea that, as weapons of destruction lose their power to frighten and cajole, economic power is taking over as the decisive force in world affairs. Within that framework Japan is by far the dominant force in the eastern hemisphere. Its financial reserves give its views as much weight as those of any of the Group of Seven industrialised countries and in 1990 its voting rights in the International Monetary Fund increased to match its contributions. Yet Japanese values are recognisably different from those established by the West in international affairs: Japan above all values harmonious relationships, order and prosperity. It represents a different model of conduct and society.

The Japanese are Utopians. Japan's social engineers are busy trying to turn their dream of a perfect society into reality. To a remarkable degree, in their own terms, they have succeeded, thanks to the legacy of the repressive Tokugawa age. Today, the Japanese can claim the best health care, and the longest life expectancy of any nation – 74 years for men, 80 for women. The 1980s saw the final demise of the left-wing trade union structure: all the main labour federations merged together and renounced their socialist ideas. Consumer associations rarely challenge the methods of Japanese big business. Like other mainstream organisations, they shun conflict. Standards of public safety are high. The Shinkansen bullet train has carried 2.9 billion passengers between Tokyo and Osaka or points west over the past twenty years without a single accident.

The Ministry of International Trade and Industry has published a new 'Vision' of its policy in the 1990s, in conjunction with business and academic representatives in the advisory Industrial Structure Council. Instead of charting a wholesale push into specific industrial sectors as in past 'Visions' – steel and ships in the 1960s, electronics in the 1970s, computers and robotics in the 1980s – this policy guideline calls for consolidating Japan's all-round economic and industrial power, improving the quality of life of the Japanese, and the exercise of 'extraordinary care' to minimise the expected confrontations with the rest of the world as Japan's economic impact grows. The Economic Planning Agency, whose authority covers the whole sweep of socio-economic affairs, has a more humane vision of what the next century ought to be like. In its sketch of the idealised (if implausible) lifestyle for the average Japanese forty years hence there are no more crowded commuter-train journeys; instead there is affluence, leisure and rewarding work. Japan is a triumph of cultural conditioning over other commonplace motives, including individual profit.

Japan still has to overcome the legacy of mistrust from other nations which do not share its easy vision of the ideal. Singapore's Lee Kuan Yew says of the current prosperity of the Japanese: 'They deserve it, through their hard work, their ingenuity, through their intelligence. . . . They are doing a service to the world. But they shouldn't go capturing people's lives in the process.' South Korea's relations with Japan have been embittered for many years by the perception that the Japanese have never had to come to terms with the enormity of the injury their country inflicted on the Korean peninsula before 1945. Some of the damage was repaired when Prime Minister Toshiki Kaifu declared, during South Korean President Roh Tae Woo's visit to Tokyo in early 1990, that Japan had inflicted 'unbearable agony' on the Koreans, and expressed his 'sincere remorse and honest apologies'. Still, the Utopians are at work to beautify the past: most approved Japanese school textbooks still omit any description of the employment of Korean forced labour for Japan's Pacific War effort. The textbooks approved in 1990 came more up to date: in several, the mandarins of the Education Ministry forced out references to the political corruption that was exposed in the Recruit affair.

In the 1980s other Asian nations rose up against injustice and oppression: South Korea, the Philippines, Burma and China. The West has no monopoly on the human spirit. Japan, though, was almost completely left out of the party; despite the provocation of Recruit and the financial shenanigans of the big companies, there was no tide of rebellion among Japan's docile, middle-class masses. In embracing China a year after the democracy movement there, Japan sealed its 'friendship' by sending back dozens of dissident Chinese students against their will to their own country. Yet in many ways Japan is seeking to use its influence to help others: it has pledged substantial aid to Poland and Hungary. Japanese money will be an important factor in the eventual reconstruction of war-torn Cambodia, when it comes. It is already a lifeline for the Philippines, as for many struggling economies in Asia and South America. The crisis over Iraq's invasion of Kuwait has shown Japan to be still hesitant over getting involved in a 'shooting war'; yet the Kaifu cabinet has been quick to renew its loyalty both to the United Nations and to the political leadership of the USA. Unless international order breaks down again as it did in the 1930s, Japan can be relied upon to remain a law-abiding citizen of the world community, prepared to employ all measures short of military intervention to support the West.

Is Japan slowing down? Only on the surface. In thirty years' time it will have the highest proportion of old people to breadwinners of any industrial nation. Yet its income per capita will continue to grow, thanks to the power of money, and thanks to the success of the formula which its leaders devised once in the Meiji era and again in the post-surrender decades: effort, learning and respect. Today, what Japan needs is more intellectual honesty: to put more realism into Japan's dreams, and more humanity into its hard-headed quest for profits. The determined bid for national greatness, born a century ago, is still driving Japan forward.

Appendix 1

Post-war Japanese Prime Ministers

22 May 1946*	Shigeru Yoshida
22 May 1947	Tetsu Katayama
10 Mar. 1948	Hitoshi Ashida
15 Oct. 1948	Shigeru Yoshida
10 Dec. 1954	Ichiro Hatoyama
28 Dec. 1956	Tanzan Ishibashi
25 Feb. 1957	Nobusuke Kishi
19 July 1960	Hayato Ikeda
9 Nov. 1964	Eisaku Sato
7 July 1972	Kakuei Tanaka
9 Dec. 1974	Takeo Miki
24 Dec. 1976	Takeo Fukuda
7 Dec. 1978	Masayoshi Ohira
17 June 1980	Zenko Suzuki
27 Nov. 1982	Yasuhiro Nakasone
6 Nov. 1987	Noboru Takeshita
2 June 1989	Sousuke Uno
9 August 1989	Toshiki Kaifu

* Date of initial cabinet formation

Appendix 2

Glossary of Japanese Terms

aisatsu greeting
amakudari 'descent from heaven' (recruitment of retired bureaucrats into private firms)
Anpo US–Japan Security Treaty
apaato apartment store
arahitogami manifest god
arubaito second job
avekku go on a date

batsu club, guild, hierarchy
Beheiren Citizens' Committee for Peace in Vietnam
bon Festival of the Dead
bucho general manager
burakamin outcaste class
buraku community
bushi samurai warrior
bushido the way of the warrior

cho town
Chukaku-ha Central Core Faction

Daijosai Great Thanksgiving Festival
danchi apartment block
demokurashii democracy
depaato department store

furoshiki wrapping-scarf
furusato home town ('old village')
futon mattress

gakubatsu academic faction
gaman endurance

geisha female entertainer
gohan rice
gunbatsu military faction
gyosei shido administrative guidance

habatsu political faction
honne real state of things

jimichi steadiness
jishuku self-restraint
Jodo-shu Pure Land sect
juku cramming school

kabuki classic play
kacho section chief
kageki-ha left-wing extremist group
kami ancestral god
kamikaze 'divine wind'
kanban 'ticket number', or 'just-in-time' factory-supply system
kanbatsu bureaucratic faction
kanryoha ex-bureaucrat politician
karoshi death from overwork
keibatsu family dynasty
Keidanren Federation of Economic Organisations
keiretsu business grouping
Keiseikai Foundation of Policy Society
keizai-kai economic world
kenpeitai military police
kinken seiji money-power politics
kisha kurabu reporters' club

koenkai support group
kokugaku national learning
kokutai 'national structure'
Komeito Clean Government Party
kumi voluntary group

makoto pure intentions, sincerity
mama-san woman bar-owner or manager
matsuri shrine festival
mikoshi portable shrine
misogi purification
mura village

Naimusho Home Affairs Ministry
nemawashi preparation of the ground, consultation
niinamesai Festival of Offering the First Rice Grains
Nikkeiren employers' organisation
Nokyo Union of Agricultural Co-operatives
nomiya drinking house

ojo-san well-bred young lady

pachinko Japanese pinball
pan bread

raisu rice
Rengo Sekigun United Red Army

salariiman white-collar worker
samurai warrior class
san Mr, Mrs, Ms
Seiranjuku Blue Storm School
sekuhara sexual harassment
sensei teacher
seppuku ritual self-disembowelment
shain company member
shogun military commander

Showa Enlightened Peace
shunto annual wage offensive
sogo shosha general trading company
Sohyo Japan General Council of Trade Unions
Soka Gakkai neo-Buddhist organisation
sokaiya gangster specialising in intimidation at shareholders' meetings
sumo wrestling
sushi raw fish

tatami straw floor mat
tatemae surface motive
Tatenokai 'Shield Society' (Mishima's private army)
Tekko Roren Steelworkers' Union Federation
tenno Heavenly Sovereign
tennosei Emperor system
toha career politician
Tokaido eastern sea-route
tokkotai secret or 'thought' police
torii shrine gate

uchiawase prearrangement of things
uji clan
ujigami clan spirits
ura nihon 'the back of Japan', or Japan Sea coast

wa harmony

yakuza gangster

zaibatsu big business grouping
Zengakuren militant student federation
Zenji-roren car-workers' union
zoku tribe

Bibliography

Abegglen, James C., and Stalk, George, Jr, Kaisha – The Japanese Corporation, Harper & Row, 1985.

Adams, T. F. M., and Hoshii, Iwao, A Financial History of the New Japan, Kodansha International, 1972.

Beasley, W. G., The Modern History of Japan, Charles E. Tuttle, 1990.

Buckley, Roger, Japan Today, Cambridge University Press, 1990.

Burstein, Daniel, Yen! – Japan's New Financial Empire and Its Threat to America, Simon & Schuster, 1988.

Buruma, Ian, A Japanese Mirror – Heroes and Villains of Japanese Culture, Jonathan Cape, 1984.

Cortazzi, Hugh, The Japanese Achievement, Sidgwick & Jackson, 1990.

Curtis, Gerald L., The Japanese Way of Politics, Columbia University Press, 1988.

Cusumano, Michael A., The Japanese Automobile Industry, Harvard University Press, 1985.

de Bary, W. H. Theodore, Tsunoda, Ryusaku, and Keene, Donald (eds.), Sources of Japanese Tradition Vols I & II, Vol. II, Columbia University Press, 1964.

Doi, Takeo, The Anatomy of Dependence, Kodansha International, 1973.

Dore, Ronald, British Factory–Japanese Factory, University of California Press, 1973.

Dore, Ronald, Flexible Rigidities: Industrial Policy and Structural Adjustment in the Japanese Economy, 1970–80, Stanford University Press, 1986.

Dower, John, Empire and Aftermath: Yoshida Shigeru and the Japanese Experience, 1878–1954, Harvard University Press, 1979.

Duke, Benjamin, The Japanese School, Praeger, 1986.

Dunn, Frederick S., Peace-Making and the Settlement with Japan, Princeton University Press, 1963.

Gayn, Mark, Japan Diary, William Sloane Associates, 1948.

Halberstam, David, The Reckoning, Avon Books/Yohan, 1987.

Halloran, Richard, Japan – Images and Realities, Charles E. Tuttle, 1970.

Hibbert, Howard (ed.), Contemporary Japanese Literature, Charles E. Tuttle, 1978.

Inoguchi, Takashi, and Okimoto, Daniel (eds.), The Political Economy of Japan, Vol. 2: The Changing International Context, Stanford University Press, 1988.

Johnson, Chalmers, *MITI and the Japanese Miracle*, Stanford University Press 1982; Charles E. Tuttle, 1986.

Kamata, Satoshi, *Japan in the Passing Lane*, Unwin Paperbacks, 1984.

Keizai Koho Center, *Japan 1990 – An International Comparison*, Japan Institute for Social and Economic Affairs, 1990.

Kosaka, Masataka, *A History of Postwar Japan*, Kodansha International, 1972.

Kuriyama, Takakazu, *New Directions for Japanese Policy in the Changing World of the 1990s*, Ministry of Foreign Affairs, Tokyo, 1990.

Lincoln, Edward J., *Japan – Facing Economic Maturity*, The Brookings Institution, 1988.

Livingston, Jon, Moore, Joe, and Oldfather, Felicia, *Imperial Japan*, Random House, 1973.

Livingston, Jon, Moore, Joe, and Oldfather, Felicia, *Postwar Japan*, Random House, 1973.

Mainichi Daily News, *Fifty Years of Light and Dark – The Hirohito Era*, Mainichi Newspapers, 1975.

Maruyama, Masao, *Thought and Behaviour in Modern Japanese Politics*, Oxford University Press, 1969.

Minear, Richard H., *Victors' Justice – The Tokyo War Crimes Trial*, Charles E. Tuttle, 1972.

Mishima, Yukio, *The Sea of Fertility* (tetralogy), Charles E. Tuttle, 1972–4.

Morishima, Michio, *Why Has Japan Succeeded?*, Cambridge University Press, 1982.

Nakane, Chie, *Japanese Society*, University of California Press, 1970.

Nomura Research Institute, *Nomura Medium-Term Economic Outlook in Japan and the World*, Nomura Research Institute, 1989.

Okimoto, Daniel L., *Between MITI and the Market*, Stanford University Press, 1989.

Pacific War Research Society, *Japan's Longest Day*, Kodansha International, 1968.

Patrick, Hugh, and Rosovsky, Henry, *Asia's New Giant*, The Brookings Institution, 1976.

Prestowitz, Clyde, V., Jr., *Trading Places: How America Allowed Japan to Take the Lead*, Charles E. Tuttle, 1988.

Reischauer, Edwin O., *The Japanese Today*, Charles E. Tuttle, 1988.

Richie, Donald, *Japanese Movies*, Kodansha International, 1961.

Seidensticker, Edward, *Low City, High City*, Alfred A. Knopf, 1983.

Seidensticker, Edward, *Tokyo Rising*, Alfred A. Knopf, 1990.

Stokes, Henry Scott, *The Life and Death of Yukio Mishima*, Charles E. Tuttle, 1975.

Storry Richard, *The Double Patriots*, Greenwood Press, 1973.

Tanaka, Kakuei, *Building a New Japan*, Simul Press, 1973.

Thayer, Nathaniel B., *How the Conservatives Rule Japan*, Princeton University Press, 1969.

Van Wolferen, Karel, *The Enigma of Japanese Power*, Macmillan, 1989.

Vogel, Ezra F., *Japan as Number One*, Charles E. Tuttle, 1980.

Weinstein, Martin E., *Japan's Postwar Defence Policy, 1947–1968*, Columbia University Press, 1971.

Yoshida, Shigeru, *The Yoshida Memoirs*, Houghton Mifflin, 1962; reprinted Greenwood Press, 1973.

Zengage, Thomas R., and Ratcliffe, C. Tait, *The Japanese Century – Challenge and Response*, Longman, 1988.

Index